Prairie Cathedral

These tall cathedrals,
Towering o'er the plains,
Have no stained glass windows,
Gothic arch nor buttress;
No leering gargoyle,
No needle-pointed spire;
No penitents
Kneeling on the stone.

These elevators house our crops,
The corn and the soy—
Food for man and beast.
This from the black land
Where it giveth birth.
When starving people all around the earth
Turn their hearts this way as they pray,
Pray for food,
These elevators answer in God's mercy.

Marguerite Threlfall, 1964
(Wife of W. S. Threlfall, Staley employee)

THE KERNEL AND THE BEAN

The 75-Year Story
of the Staley Company
by Dan J. Forrestal

SIMON AND SCHUSTER
NEW YORK, NEW YORK

Copyright © 1982 by A.E. Staley Manufacturing Company
Published by Simon and Schuster
A Division of Gulf & Western Corporation
Simon & Schuster Building
Rockefeller Center
1230 Avenue of the Americas
New York, New York 10020
SIMON AND SCHUSTER and colophon are trademarks of
Simon & Schuster
Designed by Edward Carenza
Manufactured in the United States of America
Composed, Printed and Bound by Haddon Craftsmen, Inc.
1 3 5 7 9 10 8 6 4 2
Library of Congress Cataloging in Publication Data
Forrestal, Dan J.
The kernel and the bean.

Includes index.
1. A. E. Staley Manufacturing Company—History—
20th century. 2. Corn products industry—United
States—History—20th century. 3. Soybean industry
—United States—History—20th century. I. Title.
HD9049.C8U52   1982   338.7'664725   82–10669
ISBN 0-671-45825-6

CONTENTS

FOREWORD

A sports editor, perched in the press box, would use football and baseball scorecards in appraising the history of the A. E. Staley Manufacturing Company. The sports editor would stress touchdowns, fumbles, home runs, and strikeouts.

A business editor, positioned on Wall Street, would bring a different perspective to the company's 75-year ball game, citing the ups and downs of corporate activities in a business stemming largely from the processing of corn and soybeans. The business editor would stress financial and operational performance, share-of-market, technology, and various telltale trials and triumphs during the 1906–1981 period.

The sports editor's sum-up would say, "*No other company* can list the legendary George Halas, perennial owner of the Chicago Bears professional football team, as a former employee who coached a semipro team under corporate colors and led it to a national championship in the dawning days of professional football. In 1920, while serving as a clerk in the Staley company's scale house, responsible for weighing deliveries of corn, Halas helped set in motion the formation of the organization that became the National Football League. And in 1921, Halas and his intrepid Decatur Staleys were virtually bribed by their Decatur employer to pack up their uniforms, footballs, and liniment and head for the big city of Chicago where they'd rather promptly become the famous Chicago Bears."

The sports editor would also point out that, additionally, Staley had a razzle-dazzle semipro baseball team in the "good old days" and that its star was no less than Joe "Iron Man" McGinnity, who had pitched 29 major league victories for Brooklyn in 1900 and 26 triumphs for Baltimore in 1901 before moving to the payroll at Decatur, Illinois.

Indeed, the baseball Hall of Fame at Cooperstown, New York, and the pro football Hall of Fame at Canton, Ohio, are sanctuaries where five former Staley stars, in total, are permanently enshrined—an unusual footnote in corporate annals, to be sure.

The sports editor would conclude by saying, "*No other company* has had such involvement in sports."

A business editor would note, "*No other company* can say it became the first commercial processor of soybeans in the United States—as far back as 1922 when soybeans were a major crop in the Orient and a novelty on the American scene. As a consequence of this Staley pioneering, Decatur, Illinois, became known as 'The Soybean Capital of the World.'"

In addition, the business editor would want to update his or her assessment by adding, "*No other company* in the early eighties can claim world leadership in producing high fructose corn syrup as a replacement for sugar in soft drinks and foods."

But the distinctions don't end there.

Staley has left a special imprint on its hometown and has helped mold the personality of the community. Staley is ubiquitous in Decatur. Because of Staley, there is a recreational point-of-pride called Lake Decatur. Because of Staley, an east-city viaduct helped the community expand to the north. There's a Staley Library at Millikin University and a Staley Pavilion at Decatur Memorial Hospital. But most noticeable of all, there's a 14-story-high landmark, once called "The Castle in the Cornfields," at the east end of town, that serves as an architectural milestone, as administrative headquarters, and as a towering exclamation point in the rich flatlands of central Illinois.

Remarkably, there have been only three chief executive officers at the corporate helm over 75 years—A. E. Staley, Sr., the resourceful and risk-taking founder; A. E. Staley, Jr., his conservative and deliberate son; and Donald E. Nordlund, a new breed, non-family-related executive whose influence has been sharply and beneficially felt since the early seventies.

The founder—known as Gene—emerges as the picturesque, swashbuckling entrepreneur of this narrative. Artfully dodging or dueling with creditors during his frequent early-day flirtations with bankruptcy, Gene Staley was not only a pioneer in sports and soybeans but was equally a pioneer in what has since been referred to as creative and imaginative financing, putting up his boldest front when he had his back to the wall. Packing his own Cream cornstarch, peddling his own stock, pleading persuasively with bankers, engaging in eleventh-hour desperation efforts to meet his own payroll, scrambling to find funds for purchasing incoming grain, sweet-talking new customers, and occasionally calling on Lady Luck to guide him through the perils of the futures market at the Chicago Board of Trade, Gene Staley was the nonstop dynamo who gave the company its early breath and breadth.

This, then, is the story of a company that was incorporated in 1906, destined to face innumerable internal and external tests over the span of its first 75 years. It is the story of tapping the ceaseless wonders that nature has entrapped in corn and soybeans. It is the story of three distinct management styles—ranging from picturesque to punctilious to progressively professional. Caught up in the shifting currents of the various eras, employees at all levels have been remarkably responsive to the challenges of the times and have often provided the will and the way to win, particularly when the company's valleys seemed more prodigious than its peaks.

Anecdotes from employees at all echelons—some on the payroll and some in alumni ranks—are freely interspersed on the following pages. The adventures of Staley men and women—in plants, in offices, in the field—along with their frequent triumphs, are among the many poignant human experiences presented in this 75-year profile. In many cases, their experiences are set forth in their own words. As the saying goes, they were there.

Realizing that credibility in a sponsored history is achievable only through a sorting out of a company's ups and downs, chairman Don Nordlund summoned the author in 1980 and set the tone of the project, from the start, by outlining his insistence on a straightforward recapitulation. Nordlund had come across a quote from the Spanish philosopher and poet George Santayana, who wrote: "Those who cannot remember the past are condemned to repeat it." Nordlund added, "Perhaps our company's history holds lessons for future guidance."

The author wound up having free and unfettered rein in reaching out for new and old information. Thus, he takes total responsibility for that imprecise thing called editorial judgment—the decision to "include this and exclude that." No two authors would have used the same judgment in such a subjective exercise. In the case of the Staley book, only two questions were used as yardsticks in determining the author's acceptance or rejection of material: (1) Is such information interesting? and (2) is such information significant? Some items seemed both interesting and significant. Others seemed one but not the other. When information seemed to strike out on both counts, it was ignored. Ultimately, the reader has been kept in mind at every turn.

The Staley story is, in many ways, the story of the risks and rewards in America's profit-or-loss system of business venture. Too often observers who hail the capitalistic "profit system" forget that potential losses inevitably lurk at the other side of the ledger. They forget—or, at least, seem to forget—that management is charged with the responsibility of achieving a return on investment and further charged with accountability in allocating the rewards equitably to stockholders, employees, communities, customers, suppliers—not to mention the layers of taxes enabling the private sector to underwrite the staggering costs of the public sector at the federal, state, and local level. The Staley story is a resounding Exhibit A in Economics One.

If a list were to be assembled containing the names of the people who contributed to this narrative, it would be formidable. As a group, retired employees were particularly helpful contributors. Some old-timers were on the scene as far back as World War I. Current employees were also, and obviously, important. Among other resources were civic and professional people living in Decatur; industry spokesmen; financial analysts on Wall Street; several generations of the Staley family; journalists; librarians; and old-time friends who were on the sidelines as the company flowered from nothing to something.

In particular, G. David Satterfield, John P. Clifford, and Thomas C. Garren were the trusty in-house allies who helped keep the author's research and writing on track. Having juggled this regimen among their many continuing responsibilities, they merit substantial credit for the fidelity and earnestness of this comprehensive historical experience. If inadvertent oversights or shortfalls are noticeable on any of the following pages, the author takes a large share of the blame. In any event, a conscientious effort was made to play the game objectively—"down the middle."

Granted, 75 years is a long time. The Staley company grew from poverty to $2 billion in sales during the interval. Yet it is important to note that 75 years is only a prologue. One wonders what adventures lie ahead during the next 75 years. If there is a single element worth identifying and isolating, based on past experience, that element is best expressed in one word—spirit. This narrative, hopefully, captures the spirit and flavor of an unusual, cohesive, and adventuresome group of participants.

DJF

Precede One

THE KERNEL

Consider a kernel.

On an average ear of hybrid corn, a kernel is almost half an inch long, a quarter of an inch wide, and less than a quarter of an inch thick. It weighs about one-hundredth of an ounce.

But it packs a mighty wallop.

That little kernel is an unrivaled storehouse for energy and nutriment. It represents the Number One grain crop of America in value and in acreage planted. Each year, people find new wonders in its derivatives.

When used as seed for tomorrow's crop, rather than for consumption, a single kernel will launch a plant about 7 feet tall, approximating the legendary altitude of "an elephant's eye" as celebrated in the lyrics of the musical *Oklahoma!*

The resultant plant will produce an ear of corn containing up to 1,000 kernels, each similar to the one that gave birth to the plant in the first place. In a well-developed crop, there will be 16 or 18 rows of kernels per ear with about 50 kernels per row.

Standing proud as a renewable resource, corn is a literal wonder of the world, serving almost every industry with a fraction of its magic. Particularly in the United States corn is an agricultural bounty, if for no other reason than that America is the world's principal corn producer and is an exporter—to a hungry world—of a fourth of its annual crop. (China, whose statistics are elusive, is almost certainly Number Two. Brazil is Number Three.)

Most of corn's history—ancient and modern—involves the western hemisphere. Mayan civilization and, later, the cultures of the Incas and Aztecs were centered around corn. When Columbus returned to Spain from his journey to the New World, he brought with him some golden grains of the wondrous plant. In his letters to King Ferdinand and Queen Isabella, he described abundant fields of corn.

It remained for the American Indians to merit the reputation of being the real pioneers in developing corn and its uses—in South America, Central America, and North America. Early U.S. settlers called it "Indian corn." Indians used the kernels for food, the cobs for fuel, and the husks for weaving into scratchy mats or for shredding into scratchy beds. Even when Indians found their corn yield insufficient for their current requirements, they were usually farsighted enough to save a small supply of seeds for a subsequent crop.

In the current era, the populous world of the 1980s is more conscious than ever of those many bounties from nature that are, on the one hand, crucial and that are, on the other hand, finite. Similarly, the world is increasingly appreciative of those other gifts from nature that are replenishable and, importantly, related to the fundamental source of life called food. Peter Drucker, the economist and business analyst, has said "the dramatic depletion of petroleum supplies has helped us differentiate between resources which are finite and those which are infinite. Before we had lumped them all together as long as the supply lines were full."

In such a context, corn ranks alongside replenishable wheat and nonreplenishable petroleum as one of the world's most valued resources. Yet, even as corn's uses multiply, its role remains as a ho hum commodity to most of its ultimate beneficiaries who, understandably, are not familiar with its unseen role. Corn makes few headlines in the general press despite its contributions to the world food supply and to the manufacturing industries relying on starch and its derivatives. Yet, when corn production is crippled by the heat and dryness of a brutal summer, such as that of 1980, it does become a front-page item in the *Wall Street Journal* and the *New York Times*. Extremes are news. Normalcy is not.

Examples of general nonrecognition of corn abound:

> Good old grits and eggs for breakfast?
> A ham and cheese sandwich for lunch, along with a glass of milk?
> Beef, pork, or chicken for dinner, with ice cream for dessert?

Item: Cattle and hogs and poultry thrive on corn feed. Dairy products stem from the initial nutriment of corn.

About three-fourths of the U.S. corn crop goes into animal feed or into export. The remaining corn, not so used, has interesting processing outlets. Distillers, in their considerable wisdom, use it for making whiskey and other blithe spirits. They also make industrial alcohol. "Dry millers" use corn for crunchy cereals and for bakery supplies. "Wet millers" (thus christened because they use about 12 gallons of water for every bushel of processed corn) make starches, syrups and oils for many industries.

Soft drinks have recently become a beneficiary, using a sweetening agent, high fructose corn syrup, which is derived from the starch locked in every kernel.

Most Americans meet corn face-to-face in the produce, frozen foods, and canned vegetable sections of supermarkets. But that's sweet corn, a special strain which accounts for less than 1 percent of the total U.S. crop. Sweet corn—delicious though it may be—is not what this book is all about. Nor is that even smaller specialty called "roasting ears," which are in the minority of minorities. This book deals mainly with refining field corn, a crop that reached 8.1 billion bushels in 1981. This supply comes mostly from farms in the midwestern Corn Belt states.

Starch is king in the world of corn. Removing starch from corn involves a relatively simple process, but derivatives from starch represent an unending challenge. Sophisticated research programs, rivaling those that are intrinsic in the aerospace and electronics industries, are the pulse and promise of the starch industry (though largely uncelebrated in general journals). Such research is a manifestation of man's investigative spirit and ingenuity. Starch is an intriguing raw material that will always invite fresh research.

In perspective, the adventures in corn have only just begun —adventures in growing corn, harvesting corn, shipping corn, refining corn, and in capitalizing on the chemical wonders of corn's proliferating derivatives.

It was no less than a former vice president of the United States (1941–1945), also serving as Secretary of Agriculture (1933–1940), who was a major influence in the development of hybrid corn. Henry A. Wallace, Iowa farmer and son of the publisher of the periodical known as *Wallace's Farmer,* was a persuasive evangelist who encouraged the agriculture community to capitalize on emerging and revolutionary technology.

As far back as World War I, theoretical geneticists had published the results of experimental work in the development of hybrid strains which would, they postulated, increase yields and compensate, to some degree, for less than ideal growing conditions. Yet it was Henry Wallace who took the cause directly to the farmers and who popularized the concept of "better hybrid seed means better crops." His crusade started in 1920 and culminated in a 1925 book he coauthored with E. N. Bressman, a book entitled simply *Corn and Corn-Growing.* It was printed on his father's presses in Des Moines. It was a beacon, showing the way to genetic advances in the development of hybrid superseeds.

Today, in the eighties, there are hundreds of hybrid brands available to farmers. Each new one has its own built-in trade-offs—advantages (many) versus disadvantages (few). To quote Robert P. Bear, a longtime hybrid expert in Decatur, Illinois: "The only purpose of cross-breeding two different strains is to wind up with a new plant which contains the most desirable features of both. The search is endless. Our industry has come a long way since the days of Henry Wallace but there is no limitation on what is possible in what we call the science of chemurgenetics. Our challenge is to develop a product, better and better all the time—a product which does not exist per se in nature."

What do the leading scholarly experts in the field look for in their research and development? What are their objectives? They are concerned, first and foremost, with yield. Farmers' fortunes are won and lost on yield. Yield means quantity and it also means quality. From yield comes starch and starch is a fundamental component of corn.

A stalk's standability is important. A corn plant has to stand erect, like a soldier in formation, until harvest—windstorms and other forces of nature notwithstanding. Moisture during the growing season and moisture content of the kernels at harvest time are important. Some hybrids are designed to endure dry weather; others are for wet weather; some are designed to mature rapidly; others, to mature slowly; some, to resist disease and pests. The checklist is long. And, of course, the individual farmer's judgment and skills are immensely important. The farmer sits at a "Las Vegas of variables." He places the bets. It's his farm, his money, his harvest. It is his fortune or misfortune.

Now to the subject of developing new strains . . .

How, one might wonder, do different corn crops in nearby fields "get together" and send forth new progeny into a waiting world? How is a new hybrid conceived? To quote Bear: "We're in the business of sex control. Each stalk of corn has a male part, the tassel; each has a female part, called the shoot, which develops into the ear. It's a matter of carefully planned and controlled cross-fertilization between various strains. It's a mating game. Controlled pollination is our specialty."

Bear is a hybrid seed breeder. He sells seeds to corn farmers. The seeds come in 80,000-kernel bags, ranging from 35 to 60 pounds depending on the variety. Bear's medium-sized investigative company has plenty of competition—from larger as well as smaller developers of hybrid seed. Big names such as DeKalb and Pioneer are dominant. Farmers will purchase those seeds which, in their judgment, are most likely to assure a bountiful harvest in keeping with the peculiar circumstances of their locations. There is no such thing as an all-purpose strain. Hybrids of normal Yellow Dent (dent meaning a small dimple in the kernel) are the most popular in Corn Belt states.

So much for the generalities of a grain crop called corn (or in Europe and other overseas areas more often called maize).

When a motorist drives along highway 48 in central Illinois, corn is visible everywhere during the summer months. After it is harvested in the fall, it is stored in bins and elevators. Much of it is shipped to A. E. Staley Manufacturing Company or to other "wet millers" for processing.

The motorist on highway 48 may also notice shorter, squatter patches along the roadside—soybeans. Quite often, in rotation planting, the crops replace each other in regular cycles. Yet soybeans are a separate story, equally adventurous.

The Staley company uses both corn and soybeans as raw materials for 99 percent of its manufacturing requirements. Most of the crops used by Staley's headquarters-based manufacturing operations at Decatur, Illinois, are grown within 75 miles of the plant.

Precede Two

THE BEAN

Consider a soybean.

On the average soybean plant are pods containing almost-round beans, each bean being approximately one-quarter of an inch in diameter. The bean is light tan in color and about two-hundredths of an ounce in weight.

But it's a heavyweight on the world scene.

Despite its humble appearance, the soybean is called "the pill for life" and the "wonder food nutritional bonanza" for many among the world's 4½ billion—and growing—population. That tiny bean has a staggering potential, mainly because it's packed with more protein per gram than meat and almost as much protein as eggs.

The simple soybean represents the Number One "cash crop" of the United States, "cash crop" referring to off-the-farm volume (as compared with the tremendous on-farm volume of corn fed directly to livestock).

When a soybean is used as a seed for tomorrow's crop, rather than as a raw material for processing, a single seed will create a bushy plant averaging 3 feet in height. If a plant has ample space to stretch out and bask in the air and sunshine and to absorb bountiful nutrients and moisture from the soil, it will reward the farmer with several hundred pods. But if a plant is crowded into a position immediately adjacent to its neighboring plants—which is customarily the case—it will produce fewer than 100 pods. The trade-off for crowding is a higher total yield, of course. And yield is the "bottom line" in soybeans as it is in corn. Any other measurement is distantly secondary.

A pod is in the range of 2 to 2½ inches long. Each pod contains a maximum of four beans. In experiments aimed at increasing productivity, as many as 1,000 beans have been propagated on one plant, each being similar to the one minuscule progenitor bean that gave birth to the new plant in the first place. Not unlike renewable crops of corn, renewable crops of soybeans are a demonstration of nature's never-ending gift to humanity.

From a bushel of soybeans (59 pounds) processors extract more than 11 pounds of oil, for a hundred uses, and more than 47 pounds of meal, mostly for protein-packed supplements in livestock feed mixtures but increasingly for human edibles. Broken down into its basic components, each little soybean contains about 40 percent protein, 25 percent carbohydrates, and 20 percent oil, the remainder being minerals, fiber, and moisture.

The United States is the world's principal producer of soybeans, accounting for about 65 percent of the global crop. Brazil is Number Two at 15 percent and China is Number Three at 11 percent. More than 50 percent of U.S.-grown soybeans are exported, thus aiding Uncle Sam's constant balance-of-payments problem.

That part of the crop which remains at home goes directly to companies—such as Staley—turning out meal and flour and oil for food and nonfood manufacturers where new uses have proliferated for the centuries-old bean.

The soybean is a rather recent U.S. immigrant, its roots having long been deep elsewhere, especially in the Far East. Some historians trace knowledge and utilization of the leguminous plant as far back as 2838 B.C.; others reach back only to

200 B.C.; others cite a more recent dawn of knowledge—the third century A.D.

Disagreeing as they may on the dates, soybean scholars seem to agree that China, Manchuria, and Korea were the early locations for discovery and use of the magic bean. Employing crude methods for crushing, ancient peoples used the bean's meal for food and fertilizer and the bean's oil for lamps. Missionaries have been credited with bringing soybeans to the western world during the nineteenth century, but the principal credit for creating awareness in America inevitably has gone to a man named W. J. Morse of the U.S. Department of Agriculture who distributed samples after World War I, mainly in two of the then 48 states: North Carolina, where the founder of the Staley company was born, and Illinois, where the Staley company has long had its principal proprietary interest. (Illinois was the leading producer from 1924 until 1980 when Iowa moved out in front due to a more favorable growing season, retaining that position in 1981.)

Despite their many attractive features, soybeans do not lend themselves to hybridization, as does corn. The many strains of soybeans—and there are many—were originally developed from so-called wild original strains, in China and elsewhere. More recently, different strains were created through a complicated process in which geneticists have used tweezers to select and transfer pollen from the flower of one plant to that of another—and the geneticists have thus achieved cross-fertilization.

Much as in the case of hybrid corn, the geneticists constantly seek improved varieties in their breeding programs, aiming for strains that will best combat disease, insects, marginal climate, low moisture, and other poxes.

Soybeans are actually self-pollinating. Both male and female reproductive systems are built within a single flower. No pollinating substance is carried by a friendly breeze from one plant to the other. Birds and bees occasionally serve as genetic transports, but the principal task of developing new super-strains is left to the devices of humans.

Despite such a challenge, yields have increased dramatically in recent years, averaging nearly 2 billion bushels annually on almost 70 million acres.

Except in the soy sauce sprinkled on chop suey and in a few other obvious soy-related items, the little legume is a hidden ingredient unrecognized by the general public.

The big markets for soybean meal involve livestock and poultry feeds. Yet human uses of meal and flour (made from meal) are growing dramatically—beyond such current uses in bakery goods, sausages, cereals, prepared mixes, and baby foods. "The food uses for soy protein hold a great potential," says Dr. Keith J. Smith, director of research for the American Soybean Association, St. Louis.

Nonfood uses of soybean derivatives include adhesives, detergents, building materials, paper, textiles, and even the foam for fire extinguishers.

On the oil side, examples include margarine, shortening, salad dressing, frozen desserts, bread, crackers, and canned soup. Soybean oil also has multiple uses in nonfood products, including paints and cosmetics.

But the heroic role of the soybean will always be in food products, either directly in food for humans or indirectly in livestock mixes. No other farm-grown crop is so packed with protein. And protein is essential for human survival.

Consider the comment of Dr. Jean Mayer, former professor of nutrition at Harvard University and current president of Tufts University. A world-renowned authority on food and persuasive proponent of nutritious diets, Dr. Mayer has pointed out that the life expectancy of Seventh-Day Adventists—who have long been consuming soy protein products instead of meats, as well as engaging in other healthful habits—is well above the national average. Dr. Mayer specifically has endorsed the use of soy-enriched, vegetable-based protein products in the government's school lunch programs. In countries with rampant malnutrition, the need for food protein is obviously even more urgent. (Soybean-based textured vegetable protein is used as an extender in ground meat as well as in chili, tamales, pizza, and other meat-containing prepared foods. The extender costs less than meat, and it also helps to reduce shrinkage during cooking.)

Research moves onward. Some of the newer soybean-containing food products—such as textured soy protein in the form and flavor of bacon bits and of other natural foods—are innovations standing on their own merit.

At the Staley company, soybean processing has been part of the product mix since 1922. From that time on, soybeans have had a roller-coaster ride at Staley—sometimes up, sometimes down. But in recent years they've reemerged in high prominence. The various adventures into soybeans are chronicled in the later pages of this book, starting with Chapter Four.

THE KERNEL
AND THE BEAN

CHAPTER ONE

HOW IT ALL BEGAN

The tall, straight poplar trees fell upon the gentle slope. As they thumped onto the ground, one by one, they sent up puffs of dust from the dry, red earth of the Piedmont region of North Carolina (Piedmont meaning the fertile, rolling region between the broad coastal plain and the towering Blue Ridge Mountains).

In the peaceful era of the 1830s, Zebedee Hinshaw, Randolph County farmer, was in an expansionist mood. He wanted more tillable land and fewer trees. He needed a new clearing for new crops. With the help of several workers he sawed through the poplar trunks at ground level. Down they came.

Surveying the scene, Zebedee Hinshaw put the second phase of his plan into action. This part of his well-planned strategy involved getting more than 100 trees hauled away without his personal botheration and expense. His scheme was as simple as it was successful. He sold the trees for 15 cents apiece, cash-and-carry.

On an adjacent farm a neighbor named William Ledbetter had all the open space he needed for his crops—265 acres of land that were largely verdant and tillable. Ledbetter needed logs for a new cabin which would provide a better hearth and home. He was Zebedee Hinshaw's first cash-and-carry customer.

Shortly after a new 20-foot by 20-foot log cabin was erected, Ledbetter sold his property to a lanky stranger from Maryland named William Staley—for $2 an acre.

In sum, the various transactions for logs and land were favorable to all concerned—Hinshaw, Ledbetter, and Staley.

William Staley was a bachelor when he began working his newly purchased farm, just before the Civil War. Undaunted by the prospect of sunup to sundown labor, he had no illusions about the regimen of farm life. He and two brothers had lived on their parents' farm at Harper's Ferry, Maryland, prior to the time when all three young men decided to head out on their own, separately, for the sun and soil and opportunity of North Carolina. Harvesting nature's bounty was in their blood. Their parents' ancestors had known the good earth of England before sailing to the United States earlier in the century.

On October 28, 1865, William Staley married into the Ledbetter family, taking unto himself a quiet and personable girl named Mary Jane whose ancestors also traced back to British roots. Early in 1867, when William Staley was 27 years old and his wife 25, their first child was born in that cabin made of poplar logs.

They named the newcomer Augustus Eugene Staley, an infant who was destined for fame far beyond the graceful hills of Randolph County and who would grow up to be the founder of one of the nation's foremost agriculture-based corporations— the A. E. Staley Manufacturing Company of Decatur, Illinois. The lad's emergence from nowhere to somewhere can best be understood by a brief backward glance into the trying times of the nineteenth century in North Carolina.

During the Civil War (1861–1865) North Carolina had been one of the eleven states in the Confederacy. Sitting squarely between anti-Yankee Virginia on the north and anti-Yankee South Carolina on the south, North Carolina felt entrapped. So it mustered in on the side of the Confederacy—but with some foot-dragging. In Randolph County a pro-North attitude was dominant, but local residents were nonetheless required to abide by their state's overall decision to march to the spirited songs of the Confederacy.

William Staley, industrious farmer in a remote area later to be called the Julian region, was an adamant conscientious objector. He leaned strongly to the side of the North. Determined not to fight for a Southern cause he didn't believe in, he hid out successfully in caves and barn lofts; meanwhile, Confederate hunters encountered frustration but never the master on the Staley farm.

One Randolph County farmer was so intent in his pacifist conviction that he wore a dress, apron, and bonnet while working in the fields and was never bothered by Confederate recruiters. He—or she—had a tenth of the farm's crops delivered to a Confederate storehouse (as all farmers were required to do), but was never summoned to go to war.

In the postwar period of painful adjustment, North Carolina and its Confederate sister states had their morale boosted by a beneficent President Abraham Lincoln who welcomed the defeated rebels back into the federal fold by saying, "Finding yourselves safely at home, it is immaterial whether you had ever been abroad."

North Carolina–born Andrew Johnson, who moved into the presidency following the assassination of Lincoln in 1865, called the grief-stricken and economically disastrous late sixties a period of renewal and reconstruction. It was that and more.

In the Randolph County area where the village of Julian would be founded almost 20 years after war's end, the William Staley farm was, in perspective, a prosaic rural outpost when measured in terms of national, state, or county importance. Julian itself would become invisible on all the maps—ignored at a time when even small hamlets were duly noted by mapmakers. Yet, to the farm's owner, William Staley, the area was a land of opportunity and a takeoff point for a fulfilling career in agriculture.

The farm was almost a half day by horseback from High Point (20 miles) and a bit closer to Greensboro (14 miles). To assure maximum utility of his acreage, William Staley had decided to add tobacco as a crop and to expand the farm's output of vegetables. The earlier owner had concentrated on wheat, corn, and cotton and the new owner was intent on developing a broader and more productive spread.

Trading paths—and that's what they were called—originally established by Indian tribes gave access to those who later inhabited and developed the region. The paths were subsequently widened to accommodate a horse-drawn cart or wagon. Many such paths ultimately became the routes for state-built and county-built roads and highways.

Tobacco was still not a major crop in the northwest part of the state in the 1860s and 1870s, but William Staley wanted to grow it anyway. Tobacco had a ready market for the manufacture of chunks, called plugs, which were sold at retail for chewing—or chawing—and for twists to be shredded into fragments for use in pipes, including the pipes of women who habitually enjoyed a few relaxing puffs every evening after supper when day was almost done.

The beneficial environment based on the soil and climate of Randolph County was the call to this hidden outland. The promise of abundant crops was the siren's song. Those pioneers who rallied to the call faced the prospect of back-breaking and sometimes heartbreaking work in fields warmed by a ceaseless sun. Ox-pulled, horse-pulled, or mule-pulled plows were the only supplement to farmers' energy.

In the early 1880s, when the Cape Fear and Yadkin Valley Railroad announced plans to come into Randolph County and Guilford County, local residents caucused and decided to charter a village. They also decided to christen the village Julian in honor of a family of early settlers from Virginia who had been among the largest landowners and slave-owners in northwest North Carolina.

Thus, the village of Julian was founded in May, 1884. The railroad whistled in two years later, followed by such early

Company founder A. E. Staley, Sr., poses proudly with his Masonic emblem in his lapel. Born in 1867, he died in 1940.

This is the grave of William Staley, father of the company's founder. The cemetery is located adjacent to the farm where Augustus Eugene Staley was born, near Julian, North Carolina.

Mr. and Mrs. William Staley are shown in this early photo, made near Julian, North Carolina. Their first child, born in 1867, Augustus Eugene—who would become the founder of the Staley company—is at the left. The other children are Georgiana, Arthur and Wilhelmina. The photo was made circa 1880.

Starting in 1898 with $1,500 capital, Mr. Staley set the groundwork for the A. E. Staley Manufacturing Company by selling Cream Corn Starch to housewives and small grocers in the East.

Below, one of the earliest subscriptions for shares of preferred stock in the Staley company. Note the 1907 date. The company was incorporated the year before.

SUBSCRIPTION FOR STOCK
OF

A. E. Staley Manufacturing Company

Royersford, Pa. March 4th, 1907

I hereby subscribe, and agree to pay, for *Ten* shares of the Preferred Stock of the A. E. STALEY MANUFACTURING COMPANY (incorporated), bearing a 7% cumulative annual dividend, at the par value of One Hundred Dollars ($100) per share, total $ *1000.00*; payable *July 1st 1907*, each at time of subscription, and twenty per cent. in cash each thirty days thereafter until paid in full. It is understood that said total amount when paid fully pays for said stock, and that same is non-assessable. It is further understood that with each TWO shares of Preferred Stock purchased as above, there is to be given as a bonus ONE share of the Common Stock of said company of the par value of One Hundred dollars, which shall be full paid and non-assessable. I instruct that the certificates for the above stock be issued in the name of

Arthur E. Richards

WITNESS *E. Staley.*   Name *Arthur E. Richards* (Seal.)

Address *Royersford Pa.*

Draw all checks and remittances to the order of A. E. STALEY MANUFACTURING COMPANY.
Credit to Missimer & Bahr, Pottstown, Pa.

Incorporated in 1906, the Company purchased this defunct corn processing plant in Decatur in 1909 and began operations three years later.

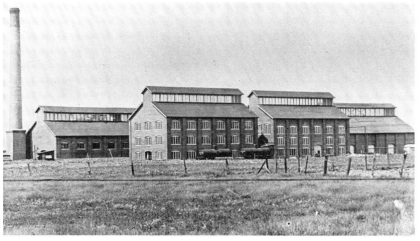

Pictured above in a *Decatur Review* of 1912 were "structures on which $150,000 is to be expended in remodeling by the A. E. Staley Manufacturing Company, which will employ 200 men when in operation."

ABOVE:
George E. Chamberlain was hired as general superintendent in 1912 with the assignment to "run the plant." He held the same position until his death in 1926.

ABOVE, RIGHT:
W. S. "Billy" Pritchard, originally hired by Staley to pack Cream Corn Starch, was the oldest employee in point of service. More than once, when the new business was performing poorly, Pritchard nearly resigned, only to be induced to stay. Originally hired as a salesman, at a salary of $3.25 per week, Pritchard ultimately was elected to membership on the board of directors.

Charles J. Schuster was hired as secretary-treasurer in 1903 at the Staley company's Baltimore office, remaining there until the office was closed during the Great Depression 30 years later.

A five-room frame building, with a brick vault added as an afterthought, provided ample office space for the company in 1910. Later growth could be marked by the way additions were built on to the structure. By the time it was demolished in 1930, the frame structure was a large two-story building.

Providing hot meals for employees in a plant was an innovation in 1911. Staley people of that day remember eating heartily of "home cooked" meals served at a counter.

The tall, slender gentleman disguised by the distinguished-looking beard and Panama hat is a much younger George Chamberlain.

marks of progress as a railroad agent and a telegraph operator; and then by such milestones as a post office, barber shop (haircut, 10 cents), and a general store with a "loafer's bench" out front for men who sat, chatted, whittled, and spat. And, ultimately, the first black family was welcomed in Julian, headed by a man with the appropriate and joyous name of Lazelle Free. Julian, still small in size, had grown up and had joined the surge and spirit of the outside world.

Up until February 25, 1867, William and Mary Jane Staley had been the only occupants of the log cabin on the highest point of the 265-acre farm. Then the twosome became a threesome when Augustus Eugene came aboard.

A lad endowed with such a full and flowing name deserved full and flowing finery, his parents believed. During his mother's final weeks of pregnancy and during the first weeks after the boy's birth, Mrs. Staley busied herself by carding and spinning yarn and weaving cloth from the small supply of cotton that grew alongside the cabin. Augustus Eugene's christening dress—destined to be preserved and handled with care deep into the twentieth century—was brilliant in hue, the browns and reds resulting from dyes the mother made from roots and berries.

Once the baby became a toddler his parents decided that summoning "Augustus!" or "Eugene!" to supper was a bit too formal for the circumstances. So they began to call him Gene. The boy's period of nonproductive childhood was brief. Growing up fast was a necessity on a farm. Particularly on the long days of summertime when humdrum work piled atop humdrum work, Gene Staley was introduced to the chores of daily life.

By the time he was old enough to go to school the boy was an active participant in workaday routine around the farm. He was especially needed among the rows of tobacco plants where, under his father's tutelage, he crawled on hands and knees for the purpose of inspecting tobacco leaves. His job was to search for 4-inch-long hookworms—to be removed worm by worm.

Obviously, languishing in a schoolhouse would have seemed

a time-wasting luxury considering the unrelenting demands on the farm. Gene Staley later said, "The North Carolina school system was badly disorganized, anyway." At best, young Staley was an infrequent drop-in at school, mainly during the winter months when the farm's workload had subsided and when the hookworms had gone to wherever hookworms go during ice and snow.

School, advantageous as it may have been, was accordingly not a major influence in the character development of the Staley youth. In total, he achieved an attendance record short of the equivalent of third grade—in a one-room schoolhouse where a single teacher scheduled classes to accommodate the requirements of a wide variety of boys and girls ranging from 6 to 16 years of age.

Staley later added: "I walked three miles to the schoolhouse, sometimes in mud and sometimes in snow. The pupils were not divided into grades so I don't know how far I actually had advanced when I decided to quit. I never studied arithmetic or English grammar, but I remember well the old blue-backed Webster spelling book. I was the best speller in the class!"

Prior to reaching his teens, Staley had learned all he wanted to know about plows and rakes and hoes and worms. His attitude about farming could be summed up in four words: He didn't like it. But he knew the old maxim: When there's work to be done, there's work to be done. When a brother (Arthur) and two sisters (Georgiana and Wilhelmina, called Willie) joined the family, the log cabin became a bit crowded, but the trade-off was favorable because a larger family meant more boypower and girlpower to share the daily chores.

Young Staley's favorite escape was an event called a camp meeting at a grove near Shiloh Methodist Church which was not far in miles but was a world apart in terms of enjoyment. The camp meeting had a strong religious purpose but to Gene Staley it was a release, a picnic. With leisure, good food, and hymns on the agenda, it was the highlight of the young man's life. He encountered no problem in praising God under such a praiseworthy circumstance involving no work and no hookworms.

8

A camp meeting lasted for several days. Some attendees brought cows to assure a proper supply of milk. Everyone brought meats, bread, and cakes. Attendees slept on straw in rustic cabins or in farm wagons.

At one camp meeting, in 1880, Gene Staley's father met a Methodist missionary who had recently returned from China and who had brought back a basket of strange beads called soybeans. Gene Staley later recalled, "The missionary gave my father a handful of the beans. My father turned them over to me to play with. I planted two rows of the beans in the family vegetable garden. I was proud of them. I weeded them and picked them. Then I planted some more. The missionary said they would be good for the soil. I believed it—even if no one else did."

(In the 1930s, when Gene Staley recalled the youthful experience of seeing soybeans for the first time at that camp meeting, he added, "There are still some soybeans in North Carolina parented by that original handful from China which I planted when I was a boy.")

In 1880, Gene Staley observed that becoming a teenager was essentially the same as becoming an adult—on a farm, that is. Feeling like a captive, he fantasized about the fruits of freedom and wondered what would happen if he'd get the chance to try out his dreams in the harsh reality of unfamiliar territory populated by strangers.

In the following year, when he was 14, he was courageous enough to inform his parents of his conviction that there must be something better on the other side of the hill. He was a salesman even then. He persuaded his parents to entrust him with a responsibility heretofore undertaken only by his father, namely: selling some of the farm's produce in Randleman, a town of almost 300 people—9 miles away. An expedition!

The big day for the adventure had been planned well in advance. The young boy took particular pains to watch over the potatoes and cabbage he would later take to town. The produce, he felt, would not only be the pride of the farm, but it would also be his passport to the outside world.

Dawn couldn't come too soon on that important day of 1881 when the journey was scheduled. The prior evening he loaded a wagon with potatoes which would fetch 30 cents a bushel plus plump heads of cabbage which would bring 3 cents each.

His parents were also eager for the start of the new day. His father helped harness horse to wagon. There was a sense of excitement in it all, especially for the barefoot boy.

Barefoot? Yes. Without proper apparel? No. His mother, who shared in the take-off checklist, had made the trousers, shirt, and undergarments for her son's debut as a businessman.

Soon, all was ready. As the lad pulled away, he turned back and waved. Then, suddenly, he was gone—beyond the crown of the southwest hill. It was a breath of Brigadoon. It was a boy crossing from the past into the future.

Randleman was a good market for the Staley farm's wares. Situated on both sides of a shallow stream called the Deep River and serving as the site for one of the region's busiest cotton mills, Randleman was a moderately prosperous place where many men were so busy at the mill that they didn't have sufficient time to grow vegetables for the family table.

Gene Staley peddled his produce up and down every street, knocking on almost every door. By midafternoon his wagon was empty. It was time to head home in triumph. On arrival he summed up his exuberance in a single sentence: "I'm going to be a businessman." A fair forecast.

Subsequent trips into Randleman provided the kind of successful encores that fortified the youngster's career aspirations. During a two-year period he became more and more of a salesman. Despite the pressing workload on the farm, the boy's mother nurtured her son's ambitions and became his greatest source of encouragement. She knew he belonged somewhere beyond Randleman, maybe even as far away as the city of Greensboro, up north.

And Greensboro it was, starting in September, 1883. When Gene Staley learned that the Odell Hardware Company's retail store on South Elm Street had hung out a "Boy Wanted—$15 a Month" sign, he hightailed it to Greensboro and got the job.

He believed it would be fun to stand behind the store's counters and sell to retail customers.

Yet, alas, he never got as far as the front of the store. He was a back room employee, hired to load storage racks with plowshares, harnesses, bars of iron and steel, boxes of nails and bolts, and other heavy items. Instead of learning selling, he learned lifting. He also learned how to stretch $15 a month, considering that $10 went for room and board.

The experience at Odell's was less than exhilarating, but young Staley was intent on sticking it out. The day before Christmas, however, the store manager, Charles H. Ireland, called him into his office and told him he was fired. Being dismissed at Christmastime was sad enough, but the manager added such Scrooge-like comments as: "You'll never make a businessman, Staley. You better go to Sargent's Foundry and get a job where you can use your brute strength."

The frustrated apprentice promptly headed for home. He didn't know it at the time (but learned later) that another young man, in a nearby Greensboro store, also was a frustrated apprentice that holiday season of 1883. The other boy, William S. Porter, was clerking at Clark's Pharmacy even though he was impatient for a career as a creative writer.

In retrospect it is known that Staley grew up to be a towering businessman and that Porter grew up to be a towering figure in the world of literature, writing under the pseudonym of O. Henry.

It can be said, perhaps a bit cynically, that Charles Ireland of Odell's Hardware had an imprecise view of Gene Staley's potential as a businessman and that Ireland's discouraging comments in 1883 were less of a hex than they may have seemed at the time.

Charity prompts no investigation on whether Charles Ireland got into anyone's "Who's Who," but his scolded serf wound up making the major honor rolls in the various business halls of fame. Odell's Hardware nonetheless grew into a prodigious establishment in Greensboro, abandoning the retail end of the business in favor of becoming a successful wholesaler. Which is another way of saying that both Staley and Odell's survived the 1883 confrontation.

For the ensuing 14 years—1883 until 1897—Staley became the quintessence of that slice of Americana known somewhat affectionately as the traveling salesman. He became an itinerant gypsy visiting faraway locations—such as Seattle, Washington, which the North Carolina family folks regarded as being on the other side of the earth.

But he was more than an itinerant vendor. He was a successful itinerant vendor. He wound up with an annual net profit of $5,000 in 1896, which was a literal treasure at the time. Gene Staley's own words on this period were, "Up until I was thirty years old I was selling and roving and I had no fixed location to call a home of my own."

All his business affiliations in the 1883–1897 period involved salesmanship. The jobs included experiences with consumer products companies needing on-the-road representatives to convince far-flung retail outlets that the companies' products belonged prominently on the shelves. Compared with product distribution to retailers almost 100 years later, the old system was "the hard way." And in terms of Staley's experience, "the hard way" involved travel by train, stagecoach, horseback and, quite often, on foot. Overnight accommodations involved "living out" (a euphemism for not having protection overhead), "living in" (at a home with a spare bedroom, at a fee or free, preferably the latter), and occasionally sleeping at stagecoach stops or railroad division headquarters where a cot or bunk could be rented for 10 cents a night. Yet later as his career blossomed he was able to afford hotels, including some fancy ones.

Staley's employers were many during the period. Each in its own way offered an opportunity for him to upgrade his skills in salesmanship. The employers included the Southern Manufacturing Company of Richmond, Virginia—tea, coffee, spices, and baking powder; Bloch Brothers of Wheeling, West Virginia—Mail Pouch tobacco; Price Baking and Flavoring Company of

Chicago—baking powder and food flavors; and the Royal Baking Powder Company of Chicago—baking powder exclusively. In all instances, these were manufacturers whose fate hung on acceptance by retail merchants.

Staley learned the ins and outs of salesmanship, to be sure. His compensation depended in whole or in part on his sales performance. But he learned more than salesmanship. Day by day he was able to observe those elements of business that seemed to succeed. He noted the importance of such matters as courtesy, service, and merchandising. He learned the importance of the listening process, and in so doing he became an habitual listener, realizing that the experience of others would be a valuable education for him.

He even learned about training other salesmen. During an episode with one company experiencing a heavy turnover of sales troops, Staley said, "I even had to train the rookies not to blow out a gas stove; I had to show them how to order a meal from a menu card, and I had to show them how to pull the chain in a hotel lavatory." Once the rookies got squared away on such surprising niceties of life, they were ready to start successful careers, assuming their willingness to work 10 to 12 hours a day.

Late in 1897, Staley spent several days in Decatur, Illinois, developing new business for Royal Baking Powder, not knowing he'd ever wind up living in Decatur and establishing a major company there. But his ultimate path led to bustling Baltimore, Maryland, where he had an immediate business purpose in mind, namely: to start his own company and run his own show.

He not only decided on Baltimore but he also decided to go into the starch business.

Starch business?

Why starch?

There are several answers.

1. In his role as a salesman for other products, he had observed that most general stores and grocery stores were doing a steady, if not brisk, business in starch. It was a powdery

substance used by consumers for adding body to puddings, pie fillings, gravies, and other kitchen delights. To a lesser degree it was used in a lump form for laundry purposes.

2. It was a noncyclical staple, in demand 12 months a year.

3. But most of it was sold in bulk form and was not merchandised properly, Staley believed. It needed an imaginative thrust. It needed "wings" enabling it to fly higher in public recognition and acceptance. Above all, it needed attractive and convenient packaging.

The major starch manufacturers had been selling their retail products in a routine manner, Staley believed. The whole approach was dull, in Staley's view.

He knew he could purchase starch in bulk from any one of several major manufacturers—in barrels and in bags—at 2 cents a pound. He knew he could sell 1-pound packages to retailers for 7 cents each and make a nice little profit. And he knew retailers would have no trouble getting 10 cents a unit from consumers.

Selling was his specialty. Over the years Staley had developed contacts with more than 2,000 retailers who, he felt, would be willing to give his "Staley all the way" product a try.

Such was the 1897 plan.

The implementation went as follows:

1. He took over a loft room in a small Baltimore warehouse for an office and for packing his product into 1-pound containers. Rent for the loft space: $200 a year.

2. He purchased what he regarded as an ideal trademark— Cream starch. Owner of the asset was the estate of Thomas Cumpson, Buffalo, New York. Price for the trademark: $200. (It is pertinent to note that Cream starch stayed in the Staley catalogue until 1981, when it was sold to Purex along with many other consumer products.)

3. And, hallelujah, on March 3, 1898, Staley made his first sale. The jubilation was based on the fact that the packaged starch had his own label containing his own name and his own newly acquired trademark. Now, for the first time in his life,

he was flying solo as proprietor of his own company, even making a sale!

Despite the fatigue involved in running a one-man show, he was exhilarated. Granted he needed help up in the loft. He needed additional arms and legs to assist in packaging, in selling, and in keeping records. Yet on the day of that first landmark sale his only reaction was celebration. When his customer wrote out a check and handed it over, in the store, Staley told the shop-owner, "After I cash this and after the bank sends the canceled check to you, please let me have it because I'd like to keep it forever."

"I hadn't saved any money," he later explained. "A considerable share of my earlier earnings had gone back to the folks on the farm. [His father had died at age 45 in 1885.] Yet somehow I managed to get together $1,500. That was the entire capital on which this business was founded.

"But the $1,500 dwindled rapidly and finally disappeared. There was many a day when I didn't have a nickel in my pocket. I'd work nights packing starch and attending to correspondence and books. Then I'd go out in the daytime and sell enough to get money to tide me over.

"The work proved to be too heavy for me to carry alone. One day in Oster's grocery store in Baltimore, where I had gone to make a sale, I noticed a boy in the meat department who seemed industrious, cheerful, and courteous. His name was Billy Pritchard. I asked him how much he made. He said $3.00 a week. I asked him if he'd object to making more, and he said no. I invited him to visit me in my boarding house room that night. And I hired him, my first employee, for $3.25 a week. After that, things moved a little faster. I was able to spend more time selling while Billy Pritchard did the packing.

"But my financial burden increased because I had

to scare up the money for Billy's wages. And the burden continued to increase when I hired a girl, too, plus another girl. Fortunately, I had a gold watch. Saturday was payday and when I was short of cash, as often happened, I'd take the watch to a pawnbroker and get enough money to pay my help. By the following Monday or Tuesday some money would usually come in from my customers and I'd redeem the watch. Billy Pritchard could see what a hard time I was having, and even though he was loyal to the core he became pretty nervous." (Pritchard—a Baltimore native whose correct name was Thomas G. Pritchard—became an almost omnipresent fixture at the Staley office, abandoning starch occasionally in order to perform in public concerts on the flute and oboe. Yet he was determined not to be neglectful of Staley starch and he wound up, by the way, as a vice president of Staley's corporation.)

And oh, yes . . .
Romance came into the life of 31-year-old Gene Staley—romance sparked by a bit of effective salesmanship. On December 14, 1898, Staley was married. The 23-year-old bride was Emma Tressler, daughter of Andrew J. and Emeline Richardson Tressler of Bryan, Ohio.

Staley had seen the young lady for the first time late in 1897 under rather unusual circumstances in Chicago. He had accompanied a Royal Baking Powder friend to a piano concert where the featured soloist was Miss Tressler, an exemplary student at the Chicago Conservatory of Music. Even though Staley was only mildly interested in classical music, he wound up being captivated by the artistry, demeanor, and attractiveness of the pianist.

At intermission he turned on the salesmanship. He hastened across the street to a florist's shop and ordered several dozen red roses to be delivered promptly to the young lady's dressing room. When the concert was concluded, Miss Tressler encountered (in this order): (1) roses from an admirer and (2) the admirer, knocking on the dressing room door.

The lady was obviously impressed, as evidenced by her subsequent capitulation to his invitations for a rendezvous here and a rendezvous there, for luncheons and dinners. When she told him she'd have to return to her home in Bryan, Ohio, he arranged his sales schedule to concentrate on retail stores there.

One evening he proposed marriage. Emma Tressler responded with a conditional affirmative. "Settle down in Baltimore and have a home I can share with you" was the condition she set forth. Gene Staley agreed to the requirement and began to plan toward trimming back his career as a roving ambassador for packaged starch.

The wedding late in 1898 was a somewhat newsworthy event in Bryan, Ohio. Even the Toledo papers took note. Granted no one in the area had ever heard of the wandering salesman from North Carolina and Baltimore, but the bride's father was the influential president of Bryan's largest bank.

By the end of 1898, Staley had sold $1,700 worth of his own packaged starch, largely to Baltimore merchants. Yet, alas, the bottom line showed a net loss. The second year sales were $5,000 and the net loss was very small. In the third year, 1900, sales of $9,000 brought a modest profit. Then came real earnings on sales of $17,000 in 1901, $33,000 in 1902, and $49,000 in 1903. The net profit was almost $10,000 in 1903 and the proprietor felt he could hire two salesmen to sell Staley starch on the road, keeping in mind the proprietor had promised his wife to restrict the roaming.

Mr. and Mrs. A. E. Staley lived in a rented house at 1721 St. Paul Street. She continued her piano studies at a Baltimore conservatory.

In 1903, Staley employed a man named Charles J. Schuster, a sound businessman with a flair for figures, who ultimately would become the most needed and appreciated secretary-treasurer the founder ever had.

By 1904 things were moving in an upbeat way. Staley had the semblance of an organization plus the important dimension of

17

what he called a "home life at home." Then came a tragedy to go down in history—a disaster known as the Great Baltimore Fire. Thousands of businesses were wiped out. Staley's warehouse loft wound up in ashes. He was insured, but his policy was worthless, considering that his insurance company was obliterated. Triumph had turned to tragedy.

Again Staley found himself in that familiar position of needing funds. In order to get a new and larger space for an office, he borrowed $2,000 from his wife, promising to pay back the debt (which he did). In order to afford new supplies, he established a line of credit with a "shrewd, old Quaker banker who had taken an interest in me and who commented 'we can't afford a growing business like yours to be ruined by an accident not likely to occur more than once in a lifetime. Order whatever materials you need. We'll let you have whatever money you want.' "

So Staley was off and running once more. Despite the fire, he turned a profit in 1904 and during the following year was doing so well that he could hardly keep up with the orders. Three more salesmen were promptly added to the staff.

But there was one little problem . . .

"As my business grew and as starch manufacturing got into the hands of a few big companies, the various manufacturers weren't so eager to sell bulk quantities," Staley observed. Their reluctance was understandable. Staley's Baltimore operation was too small for the big companies to worry about back in 1898, but by 1905 it loomed as a serious competitor, outselling all other brands at many retail outlets in the northeastern states. Also, the little company was introducing a second product called Staley's Cameo laundry starch. The big manufacturers knew there was one sure way to slow Staley's march in starch, namely, cut off his supply of raw material.

Backed into a corner, Staley's options were: (1) to fold his tent or (2) to find a way to become his own manufacturer. Giving no real thought to the former and lured by the challenge of the latter, Staley summed up his plight in a single question: Where would he get the money to start up a factory?

18

The answer was clear. He would file papers of incorporation and find stockholders who would provide capital and would share with him those future rewards that he was dead sure would materialize.

On November 12, 1906, the A. E. Staley Manufacturing Company of Baltimore, Maryland, was incorporated under the favorable auspices of Delaware law, with Gene Staley as president and Charlie Schuster as secretary-treasurer.

Now proprietor Staley had two jobs immediately ahead of him: (1) to continue selling Cream starch for food use and Cameo laundry starch as long as he could get barrels and bags of bulk material from one of the big suppliers, and (2) to sell stock in his newly incorporated enterprise. He felt his starch customers would be the best prospects for the sale of stock— approximately 2,600 retailers who knew Gene Staley directly or indirectly and trusted him. What neither he nor they knew was this: If they'd buy in, as owners, and if they'd have the good sense to hold on to their shares, they'd achieve a return on their investment beyond anyone's expectations.

A new era had arrived.

Financial panic of 1907 (as it was called) notwithstanding, Staley was too busy hustling to be discouraged. "Come on in on a good thing" was his invitation. The response was salubrious. Staley was on the road to glory. He had built up an inventory of almost 900,000 pounds of raw starch and seemed to be approaching a period of temporary independence. He had a happy home. He had a gleam in his eye. He was determined not to be outfoxed by the foxy folks in the hierarchy of the starchmakers' gentlemen's club. His new high road to fulfillment was a corporation that would invite others to join up for the adventurous years ahead.

CHAPTER TWO

THE HIGH ROAD TO DEBT
AND DECATUR

For those young wizards in the year 1906 who were studying hard at the University of Chicago Business School (founded in 1898), 180 miles northeast of Decatur, the following case history would have been an appropriate classroom teaser:

"Assume a businessman named John Smith, for example, wants to get into the specialty of refining corn.

"Assume further that Smith has recently incorporated his company and has capitalized it at $3,800,000, issuing 18,000 shares of 7 percent preferred and 20,000 shares of common stock, each of the 38,000 shares carrying a $100 par value.

"Assume, further, that Smith's personal wealth is rather limited and that he has no alternative other than to acquire funds by selling his company's shares to several thousand small store-owners, most of whom have never owned a share of stock in their lives.

"Also assume that Smith has quite deliberately christened his newly incorporated organization the 'Smith Manufacturing Company' even though he has, in fact, zero manufacturing facilities. But it should be added that he does intend to get into manufacturing as soon as circumstances permit.

"Should he use his stock proceeds to buy a rickety old plant and tidy it up and let it chug along into gradual stages of improvement?

"Or should he try to achieve financing to build a sparkling new plant?

"And how should he plan his sales strategy in a highly competitive industry?

"What nostrums, earnest students, would you recommend?"

So much for the generic case history.

During Gene Staley's (not John Smith's) actual, true-life corporate emergence, things were not really all that simple. The full scenario contained a few extra complications beyond those recited in the case history.

Much as Staley would have enjoyed devoting all his time to selling stock and thus acquiring funds for the purchase of a manufacturing site, he had other obligations. In Baltimore he had, by 1906, a total of 16 people on his payroll and he very much needed to stay in business by selling packages of starch to retailers. Yet his suppliers, the nation's big manufacturers of raw starch, were threatening to try the old squeeze play mainly because they were beginning to regard his Cream starch as a pestiferous intruder in the marketplace.

Rather than sit idly by, worrying, Staley bought big supplies of raw material wherever he could get them, scrambling from month to month in order to keep his own packaged product moving. In order to build up raw material inventories for the seemingly inevitable day of cutoff, and in order to keep his employees employed, he even went so far as to achieve an alternate source of supply—from William Alexander & Co. in Glasgow, Scotland. Considering that oceanic freight rates were reasonably low, the Scottish starch helped sustain both his business and his morale.

He found the big U.S. manufacturing companies were inclined to shed few sympathetic tears in his behalf. It was a hard-boiled world, he knew. Late in the nineteenth century and early in the twentieth, many small and medium-sized starch-making organizations had been purchased by larger companies and had been consolidated into the ranks of prodigious super-companies. Corn Products Company, National Starch Company, and New York Glucose Company (financed by Standard Oil) were the prominent front-runners in the field at the turn of the century. In 1906, when the Staley company was incorporated, New York Glucose combined with Corn Products to emerge as the celebrated Corn Products Refining Company, accounting for 74 percent of the nation's starch and glucose output. Indeed, bigness per se later led to problems such as that in 1913 when Corn Products Refining Company was sued by the federal government for alleged unfair and monopolistic practices and was ultimately required to spin off some of its properties.

Why, one may have wondered, would Gene Staley of 1906 want to get into a business where invulnerable heavyweight companies would be his direct manufacturing rivals? Why would anyone, really, want to joust with the blue-chip giants that led from a position of depth, breadth, and overall strength? Why would any upstart David take on such established Goliaths?

In a world where it's always risky to play someone else's game, why did Staley think he'd be able to outplay the seasoned competition in such specialties as the grain market, manufacturing, and distribution?

Without much study he knew he'd not be able to afford to build a sparkling new manufacturing facility from scratch. It would be rough enough to scrub up funds for a rundown relic that no one else wanted.

Anyway, the principal job at hand was summed up by Staley in a two-word manifesto to his staff: Sell stock! His Baltimore salesmen were instructed to make every mission in behalf of selling starch also serve as a mission for selling preferred shares at $100 each. Staley said, "If a retailer is a Staley stockholder, he'll work even harder selling Staley starch."

He trained his salesmen over and over. The idea of raising capital through stock sales was new to all of them. After several indoctrination sessions had been completed, Staley asked his salesmen to submit in writing the actual language they would use in their sales presentations. He did this in order to make sure the material had "two essential qualities—forcefulness and honesty." He believed "No one can sell effectively with a canned sales talk prepared by someone else. So write your own and use your own." As boss, he retained the right to edit. And he had an additional piece of strategy as part of the campaign. He gave each salesman copies of letters containing character endorsements—letters that lauded Gene Staley's virtues and which were written by bankers, brokers, and vendors he had dealt with.

Regardless of the stock-peddling challenge, there was one powerful asset of the new company that was not to be overlooked, namely, the company had an evangelistic president and promoter whose vision and idealism were balanced and bolstered by a streak of pragmatism and a resolve not to disappoint those newly anointed stockholders who were willing to share his risks and rewards.

In those long-gone days before the federal government imposed regulation upon regulation, transactions in the stock market were uncomplicated. Any reliable and conscientious corporation which decided to gain financial support by inviting stockholder participation found the ground rules simple and the market inviting. In the instance of Gene Staley, he felt a personal obligation to provide an attractive return for each investor and felt duty-bound to fulfill his personal part of the bargain.

A typical Staley stock subscription contract went like this:

> I (the purchaser) hereby subscribe, and agree to pay for, <u>ten</u> shares of the Preferred Stock of the A. E. Staley Manufacturing Company (incorporated), bearing a 7 percent cumulative annual dividend, at the par value of One Hundred Dollars ($100) per share, total of $<u>1,000</u>, payable <u>July 1st, 1907</u>, twenty percent in cash and each thirty days thereafter until paid in full. It is further understood that with each

TWO shares of Preferred Stock purchased as above, there is to be given as a bonus ONE share of Common Stock of said company of the par value of One Hundred Dollars, which shall be fully paid and non-assessable.

The above sample was, in fact, a transaction entered into by a purchaser named Arthur E. Richards of Royersford, Pennsylvania, on March 4, 1907, only a few months after the Staley incorporation. The stock subscription form was signed at the lower left in the flowing penmanship of A. E. Staley and at the lower right by the purchaser.

Preferred shares on the installment plan! In five easy payments! With common stock thrown in free on a 1-for-2 basis!

By mid-1907, almost 2,000 preferred shares were in the hands of stockholders. Dividends were scheduled on a semi-annual basis. The stock was sold mostly in Maryland, Pennsylvania, Delaware, Virginia, and the New England states at the start, moving later into Ohio, Indiana, Illinois, and Michigan.

In the autumn of 1907, Staley learned of an available manufacturing site at Lafayette, Indiana, but the nation's economy was in a turmoil and he felt it would be prudent to wait for another site another day.

But he didn't stop investigating. In an era when statistical market research was still a novelty—almost a toy—he engaged the services of experts and instructed them to develop criteria for the selection of an affordable factory and for projecting sales and earnings once operations would get under way. Inexperienced in the world of corporate balance sheets and auditors' audits, Staley believed in getting advice from experts qualified to give it—a belief he never abandoned.

Early in 1908, he learned that a 13-year-old inactive starch plant in Decatur, Illinois, was in receivership and was about to be purchased, as abandoned distressed property, by Standard Oil Company. The information came to him privately but not so privately that it couldn't be investigated. Off to Decatur he went. A meeting with receivership trustees was the first order of business. Hoping he'd be able to come up with a purchase price a bit above that contemplated by Standard Oil, he took an option to purchase the Decatur facility for $45,000. This turned out to be $2,000 more than Standard Oil had in mind.

What was the plant's true value? A few clues:

The prior owners—Pratt Cereal Oil Co. and Wellington Starch Works—had installed almost $600,000 worth of machinery. The plant had been idle for two years and much of the machinery would be inoperative without repairs.

An expert engineer from Evanston, Illinois, who was hired by Staley to inspect the property, said the manufacturing buildings on the site would cost $175,000 to reproduce and that the plant's 6 acres and its water and sewer systems represented an additional asset of $50,000.

The appraisal expert also observed that "coal is at your doorstep" and "all the corn you'll ever need is within 75 miles of Decatur." He added "freight rates from there are favorable" and "Decatur is served by five railroads" and "labor is plentiful." He concluded by saying that an additional investment of $150,000 for plant improvements, plus the $45,000 purchase price, would give Staley a package of assets with a potential worth of approximately $375,000.

Sold!

Staley knew a bargain when he saw one. The financial details were arranged later in 1908 and Staley took title to the Decatur property early in 1909. Knowing he'd be doing a lot of commuting between Baltimore and Decatur during the period of getting the plant in shape, he knighted Charlie Schuster as overlord of the Maryland operation. Staley emphasized that Schuster's chief priority would be to sell more stock and that Schuster's other priorities would involve packing and selling starch, keeping corporate financial records, handling the payroll, and tending to the various day-to-day activities that had mushroomed since the simple life of 1906.

Was Staley welcomed with bugles and drums by the Decatur citizenry and business community once the news got out that the Baltimore visitor would be operating a starch plant at the east end of the city? Answer: Not quite. Actually, Decatur gave him a bit of a chilly reception.

Why? Well, his predecessors at the plant site hadn't been very successful and he, as a newcomer getting into the same line of business, would be cast in the shadow of their negative reputation. Staley understood this. He knew that when a plant site seems hexed, a new out-of-town owner automatically picks up some of the curse. One of the local papers called the site "jinxed."

A self-sufficient community of 31,000 in 1909, Decatur was not inclined to go all out for an upstart stranger in a perilous business whose corporate headquarters were far away in Baltimore, whose specialty was promoting preferred shares, and whose demeanor seemed a bit overpowering.

Staley observed to a friend that "some people seem to think this town ought to have a wall built around it and be for Decatur people exclusively and that no outsider has a right to come in." He added that "gossip is everywhere and it was circulated that we do not propose to employ any Decatur people but instead we intend to employ a lot of Italians, Greeks and Poles, and other foreigners. It was also circulated that we do not intend to employ Protestants but to employ only Catholics." This latter gossip was particularly upsetting because Staley was a card-carrying Mason, as was the redoubtable Charles J. Schuster in Baltimore, and as would be his general superintendent and foreman—all of the same Masonic persuasion. To whatever degree, if any, that Staley believed in discrimination, he most assuredly had no policy of favoring Roman Catholics during the period of his early Decatur experiences—or at any other period. He wondered who might be at the root of the rumors and gossip. He also wondered why.

And so it went.

In 1910, he was able to set some things straight in a press interview. The *Decatur Herald* of August 21 carried a headline reading "Staley Tells of Plans in Decatur" with a subhead reading "President of Starch Company Says His Plant Will Be Showplace of City." That helped. The story quoted Staley as saying the plant would begin operations in 1912 with a $25,000 weekly payroll for almost 1,000 local workers. That also helped.

In subsequent opportunities Staley mentioned the appropriateness of having a corn refining plant in the heart of the central Illinois Corn Belt. Also, he declared—perhaps in an optimistic mood—that within three years he would be making a $2 million capital investment for additional production facilities, aiding the overall economy of the community and bringing employment to hundreds of construction workers and other tradesmen. As the result of his earnest assurances, some of Decatur's chilly skepticism began to vanish and he felt more welcomed as a new man on the local business scene.

That corny old joke about "bankers putting out their right hands for shaking and their left hands for taking" was inapplicable because Gene Staley found Decatur's bankers among the first to drop by and offer their services and support. Their institutions were rather small and parochial in 1909. The local bankers knew that the new man in town would probably want to deal with his own Baltimore banks or with the major Chicago banks in order to swing the kind of big deals he'd need. But the local bankers seemed cordial and community minded. Staley's only objection to their attitude was "they didn't want to give me credit beyond 30 days," a limitation fated to be short-lived.

During 1910 and 1911, the plant's old equipment was gradually repaired and some new machinery was added. By early 1912, Staley felt sufficiently established to justify bringing to Decatur his wife, Emma, and five children—Ione, Ruth, A. E. Jr., Mary, and Rollin. The family moved temporarily into a two-story home on Prairie Avenue prior to Staley's purchase of the "home of my dreams"—which he had admired during his 1897 Royal Baking Powder days—on College Hill.

But the company headquarters stayed in Baltimore, where Charlie Schuster and his colleagues remained under great pressure to provide needed funds through the sale of stock.

Then came the big day. On March 12, 1912, at 7 a.m., the first corn started its parade through the mill. Staley could hardly wait to press the button. More than 8,000 bushels of corn had been put into the steeps (soaking tanks) the two prior days and the start-up plan called for grinding 5,000 bushels on the first day. Yet a few mechanical problems developed and only 1,000 pounds were ground on day one.

Technicalities aside, the Decatur plant was on stream. Gene Staley was a manufacturer at last.

Aware that reconditioned old machinery occasionally tends to misbehave, Staley was not too surprised when parts of his plant sputtered and sagged during the initial operating period. Despite the presence of a few pieces of new equipment, he was relying heavily on some very tired 17-year-old hardware.

Into the picture came George E. Chamberlain, an engineer who had designed the Corn Products Refining plant at Argo, Illinois, near Chicago. Gene Staley brought him into the Decatur plant as general superintendent—and in those days the title of general superintendent amounted to a major accolade. The responsibility of a general superintendent was running the plant, with a guarantee of no front office interference. Such was the crucial assignment given to Chamberlain, who was destined to be Mr. Manufacturing for 14 years.

Staley was obviously relieved when Chamberlain took over. He told his superintendent, "You run the plant and I'll worry about the other worries." Fair enough. But Staley didn't sufficiently comprehend what the "other worries" would be in the immediate years ahead. Financial worries, of course.

Here was the picture: Back in Baltimore, Schuster was scrupulously minding the shop. He was, furthermore, on a program that would ultimately sell the entire initial issue of authorized preferred shares.

However . . .

Neither Staley nor Schuster had properly perceived the amount of capital that would be required to fortify and operate the Decatur installation—and to maintain the Baltimore headquarters operation—and to buy corn—and to distribute finished products—and to meet payrolls—and to pay dividends —and to sell more stock—and to pay off debts—and to do all the necessary things to maintain a healthy balance sheet. Even Staley's own personal salary—$2,000 a month—had to be paid by a check from the Baltimore payroll account, a check that was sometimes on time and sometimes not.

The fledgling company survived, of course. But it almost didn't. Plagued by debt, it lived a day-by-day existence, getting to the bank within literal minutes of deadlines.

The following excerpts from correspondence provide an intimate insight into the nervous period of 1912–1914. The excerpts contain a perspective into what it took to nurture and sustain a shaky enterprise during a period of almost unbearable stress. Some of the touch-and-go tension can be felt in these verbatim comments as exchanged, in memo form, between Staley in Decatur and Schuster at Baltimore headquarters.

> *March 4, 1912—Staley to Schuster:* Things here are not in the best of shape. There are a number of changes to be made in the plant. We'll be buying more corn in two or three days and will need money to buy it with. It will be necessary for you to commence forwarding us money (from stock sales or packaged starch sales).
>
> *April 10, 1912—Schuster to Staley:* Our stock sales since April 1 are 246 and collections so far this month are $11,950 following March subscriptions of 648 shares and cash of $32,835. But we are in a very serious condition regarding starch, as our supply has been used up and there is none in Baltimore. So it is necessary for you to ship starch immediately.
>
> *May 9, 1912—Staley to Schuster:* Last night I went into Greider's Cafe, looking for another party, and found one of our accountants under the influence of liquor. He talked in front of everyone, in a loud voice, about the bills we owe. An embarrassing situation.

May 16, 1912—Staley to Schuster: I hope you will be able to send us a good sized check Saturday so that it will reach us Monday when our payroll obligation will be $6,000.

August 28, 1912—Staley to Schuster: Today is circus day in Decatur as the Ringling Brothers show is here. Naturally, I'll have to take the kids even though I don't care anything about circuses myself. We are shipping out a car of corn oil today and will deposit a draft for it tomorrow. We'll also ship this week eight or ten cars of feed and will deposit a draft against these.

January 28, 1913—Staley to Schuster: I am pleased to advise I have today purchased the Ennis house on College Hill—for $16,500. Buying a home will show the people of Decatur we are part of a permanent proposition.

July 16, 1913—Staley to Schuster: On Saturday I wrote you and explained we would need a check for $10,000. I had expected to receive it today without fail. Our two bank accounts are overdrawn, one for $466.41 and the other for $654.01. Send money by telegraph irrespective of the amount of expense involved.

January 15, 1914—Staley to Schuster: Our bank account here is now about $20,000 overdrawn. The financial worry is breaking the writer down. We sincerely hope your stock collections are good and that you will be able to send us large sums of money.

March 10, 1914—Schuster to Staley: When any company like ours gets into such a hole, it certainly must be the beginning of the end—but I hate to think of such a thing. Please watch your purchases and expenditures in Decatur.

June 30, 1914—Staley to Schuster: We are in desperate need of immediate funds. We need $20,000 to pay the Millikin National Bank and we have $16,000 to pay in freight charges. We have no money on hand and not much to come from Baltimore because you'll need that money to pay dividends. We are liable to be jumped on at any moment and put into the hands of a receiver. We are in a very dangerous and distressing condition. I get no sleep. I am simply all in.

August 25, 1914—Staley to Schuster: I am going to the ball game this afternoon and watch a double-header. I hope my nerves will feel more settled so I can put up a good, strong proposition to the Millikin Bank tomorrow. [Author's note: the Millikin Bank—Staley's last hope—refused to issue any more credit. It did agree, however, to help Staley sell his inventory of corn, which had not been paid for.]

October 11, 1914—Staley to Schuster: I have got to have money for my personal living and travel expenses and cannot continue without compensation as has been the case the past few months. If this company is not able to pay me a salary, or pay up my back salary, I shall be obliged to seek employment elsewhere. [Author's note: Staley wasn't blaming Schuster. He was simply crying on the shoulder of his Baltimore colleague. And, oh yes—Staley remained at Staley.]

A bleak period. The Decatur plant was finally shut down. Yet Staley managed to show a bit of optimism by saying the shutdown would be for only a few months and that the office would remain open. To help cut family costs, his wife, Emma, offered to serve macaroni instead of meat at the dinner table at home. Even though her heart was not in it, she even agreed to selling the house—heavily mortgaged—if such became necessary. Her husband invited several real estate people to come by and make appraisals. Yet, desperate as things were, the house was not sold.

Perhaps the most crushing blow was that which fell on December 31, 1914, when Staley decided his corporation would be unable to pay the regular semiannual dividend on the preferred stock, which was due January 1, 1915. Considering that Staley had personally assured so many stockholders, this turn of events was nothing short of catastrophic in his judgment. The overall gloom was exacerbated when Charles C. LeForgee, prominent Decatur lawyer and valued advisor, reported that he was having problems trying to persuade several Decatur businessmen to come onto the company's board. Plainly, the company's predicament, known all over town, was bad news in every quarter. The unhappy situation was occasioned by the company's undercapitalization and by the sudden glut on the market of corn feeds, resulting from the drying up of the European market as war threatened overseas.

On the one hand, Staley felt friendless. On the other, he felt gratified by the loyalty and support of his key salaried employees—such as Schuster, Pritchard, and Chamberlain. Yet he was $250,000 in debt.

Then he had an idea—an idea that he discussed with his outside auditors, Ernst & Ernst, and which he promptly took to Chicago for a "financial reorganization meeting" with Continental Trust and Savings Bank.

Realizing that additional short-term loans would be an inadequate remedy for his financial malady, he proposed floating a $600,000 bond issue which would—if successful—bring in sufficient new capital to enable him to pay all existing debts and put the plant in first-class condition in preparation for a fresh start.

Board minutes tell the story of what occurred: "The company gave a $313,000 mortgage on its property and plant in Decatur to Continental Trust and Savings Bank of Chicago to secure an authorized issue of $600,000 First Mortgage Six Percent Gold Bonds." The bonds were spelled out as an obligation due in 1935 —20 years later!

That did it.

But not without difficulty.

Furthermore . . .

Gene Staley assured the Chicago bank's officers the bond issue would be successful because the offering would be promptly snapped up by his retailer friends and others who had purchased the original 7 percent preferred stock.

His confidence turned out to be only partially justified. After all, he had defaulted on the promised semiannual payment of stock dividends. It should not have been surprising, therefore, that some stockholders quite adamantly reacted by saying they'd prefer not to be bondholders.

Yet even before the new bonds could be put on the market, majority approval by common stockholders was required. When Staley wrote stockholders, requesting their proxies, he got some nasty replies. One stockholder responded, "Your letter is at hand and contents noted, along with proxy to be signed, both of which are respectfully consigned to the waste basket, meaning no offense to the waste basket." Another stockholder wrote, "If the thing is a fraud, tell us so." Something less than enthusiasm from the field, to be sure.

Financial World magazine ridiculed the company's desperation effort. It called Staley's letter of appeal to stockholders "very touching, including a touch for more cash."

Staley had not counted on endorsement from the world of journalism, but he had counted on substantial stockholder loyalty.

During the process he learned that in fact most stockholders were primarily interested in the return on their investments and that loyalty was not always the major motivating factor in the cold and impersonal world of business. Yet, despite the insults by mail and magazine, a majority of the stock was voted in favor of the refinancing plan and bond offer, the obvious reason being that proprietor Staley controlled more than 70 percent of the outstanding common shares and had the outcome in his pocket all along. A victory? Yes. But it was not the kind of victory the founder wanted. He would have far preferred to have had some positive public support. He believed in his company with a passion, despite what he referred to as "temporary setbacks." He would have liked others to have shared his faith when the chips were down. However, even a hollow victory was a victory.

Only $400,000 of the $600,000 in bonds were ultimately sold, but Staley was able to pay off his short-term debts and also able to rejuvenate and open the plant—and he had $27,000 left over as a surplus.

The refinancing, based on funds raised by the sale of bonds, was not only successful but heroic in Staley's judgment. And there was a fascinating extra touch to the upbeat tone of the 1915 dramatics.

The extra touch was recalled in later years—much later—by the founder's daughter, Ione Tressler Staley. It should be explained that in 1915, Gene Staley was speculating actively in the grain market at the Chicago Board of Trade. He had taken a so-called short position in corn futures and he was understandably concerned about the consequences of his investment. Ione Staley remembered, "I'll never forget the night on College Hill. The whole family was at home, including my father. All of a sudden we heard thunder. Then lightning flashed all over the sky. Then the rains came—heavy rains. My father was jubilant. We had a great family celebration." What had happened was this: Gene Staley—using what he called his "sixth sense"—had earlier taken a strong position in corn futures, convinced that prices would soon decrease. And the beneficial rain on that memorable night was an indication that cornfields in central Illinois would deliver bountiful yields and that the increased supply of corn would inevitably translate into lower prices—which was Gene Staley's bet. Daughter Ione, who shared in the elation of that summer night at home in 1915, recently remarked, "My father's gains on that good fortune also helped him reopen the plant."

So, mostly through bonds but also through welcome summer rainfall, Gene Staley went back into production in November, 1915, after a 15-month period of idleness.

In retrospect, the founder looked back on "the great shutdown," as he called it, as a test. He observed that "I feel I have just about completely exhausted myself." Yet when the refinancing plan was wrapped up, the old adrenaline began to surge through his veins and he reverted to his old confident self.

Schuster, in Baltimore, had struggled along with only occasional salary checks for himself during the dark days. Now that financial sunshine was again prevalent, he found himself again under the gun. "Help sell the new bonds" was the order from Decatur to the man who had earlier helped sell the stock. Schuster responded by promising, "We'll do our best."

In 1916, the A. E. Staley Manufacturing Company even went so far as to take on a multinational character—in the days long before the word "multinational" was born. Gene Staley made several trips to New Orleans and Galveston for the purpose of expediting exports. On one Britain-bound freighter 30 carloads of Staley starch were the principal part of the cargo. The obscure and struggling company from the Corn Belt was beginning to make worldwide tracks.

But the big news on the global scene was that frightening scourge called war. Ominous clouds over Europe had appeared for a time to be no more than a threat to Europe itself. But the pox proliferated and by 1917 the United States entered "the war to end all wars," sending soldiers, sailors, and marines to fight in the fields, trenches, skies, and waters of Europe "to save the world for democracy."

Isolated as the Staley company may have seemed in the far-off reaches of central Illinois, it found its priorities rearranged by the force of war-related events. So-called normalcy went by the boards. Foreign markets for starch were cut off and domestic business felt the repercussions in terms of transportation crises, manpower shortages, and uncertainties in financial circles. Starch had still not fully matured as an essential raw material for other industries, but its usual placid role was nonetheless shaken by the tremors of war.

Yet despite wartime pressures, Staley was able to get his company organized. Thanks to George Chamberlain, the plant's machinery began to grind and hum and purr in what the general superintendent called "music to my ears." By the time the Armistice was signed on November 11, 1918, the Staley organization had undergone a major expansion. By 1919, plans were under way for moving strongly into corn syrup and for adding several varieties of modified starch.

Because a great volume of water would be required for expanding the corn grind, the company installed a pumping station, with a capacity of 12 million gallons of water a day, on the Sangamon River more than a mile distant from the plant, along with a 24-inch conduit alongside a railroad right-of-way, from river to plant.

As the company approached the twenties, its initial 6-acre property in Decatur had grown to 47 acres and its original 8 manufacturing buildings had grown to 41. Positive as these developments may have been, the financial reports were even better. Following a $76,000 deficit in the somber year of 1915, the next four years were heartening. They showed respective sales of $4 million, $6 million, $9 million, and $13 million. Of greater importance, pretax profits were respectively $285,000, $1.2 million, $1.3 million, and $2 million.

And perhaps it should be mentioned that the 1910–1920 decade had brought some shocking new subtractions on Gene Staley's corporate and personal income statements. Dating back to an act of Congress in 1909, the 1910 finances of the corporation had to reckon for the first time with federal income taxes. Then in 1913 came that old "debbil" called the Sixteenth Amendment whose language proclaimed, "Congress shall have power to lay and collect taxes on incomes, from whatever source," etc. That meant a levy also on personal incomes across the land. During the war, a corporate excess profits tax was also added to the mix. Alas, Uncle Sam's chain-reacting services could no longer be supported by excise levies, property taxes, and other tributes which had earlier been sufficient to underwrite the cost of a then-modest federal infrastructure in Washington, D.C. By decade's end, the era of big government had, for better or worse, arrived.

Gene Staley may have been able to escape from other financial exigencies, but the new phenomenon of across-the-board taxation was a new way of life he'd simply have to learn to live with.

And lest there might have been any misunderstanding about the nature of Gene Staley's willingness to bear his share of the nation's burden, he demonstrated his patriotism whenever an opportunity arose. For example, in 1917 he was a pioneer in developing an internal communications program, the feature of which was a bimonthly magazine called the *Staley Journal* (with type on its masthead copied in unsubtle fashion from the top of the front cover of *The Saturday Evening Post.*) The front covers on early issues of the *Staley Journal* included a photo of President Woodrow Wilson; a photo of Stephen Decatur, 1815 naval hero, accompanied by his famous quote of "Our country, right or wrong"; a picture of the Statue of Liberty, and a plea, "Buy Liberty Bonds."

Beyond doubt, that 1910–1920 decade was the most exciting period of Staley's life, highlighted by a manufacturing debut that almost turned out to be his financial funeral.

Staley had had other problems before, of course, during his days as a salesman when the rigors of the road were rough. He would have still other problems later on. But those formative years in Decatur were a test of his endurance.

As things turned out, he not only endured, but he prevailed.

CHAPTER THREE

STALEY MAKES HISTORY IN SPORTS

O. Henry, the celebrated author—referred to in Chapter One of this narrative because he was a pharmacy apprentice in Greensboro, North Carolina, at precisely the same time that Gene Staley was a hardware store apprentice—had a special knack of withholding the "punch line" until the end of an engrossing story.

Some unsung journalistic hero at the A. E. Staley Manufacturing Company had to have been a disciple of O. Henry, as evidenced by the way the Staley "house organ" writer held his snapper until the finale in the following summary in 1920:

> The A. E. Staley Manufacturing Company is one of the largest producers of corn products in the world. It grinds 30,000 bushels daily. Products include starch, syrup, gluten feed, meal, and oil.
>
> The corn starch is used in the manufacture of textiles and also in laundries and in foods. The corn syrup provides texture and a sparkling appearance in hard candies and confections.
>
> The table syrups are white or golden—also maple-

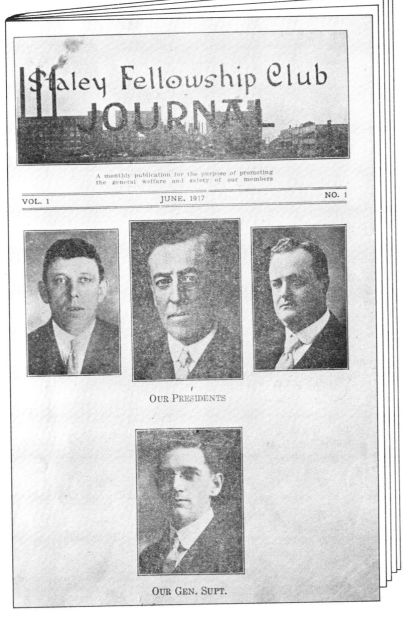

Staley Fellowship Club

JOURNAL

A monthly publication for the purpose of promoting
the general welfare and safety of our members

VOL. 1   JUNE, 1917   NO. 1

OUR PRESIDENTS

OUR GEN. SUPT.

The *Staley Fellowship Club Journal,* forerunner of today's *Staley News,* was first published in 1917. Pictured on the cover, top row, from left, are C. G. "Boob" Keck, a foreman in the plant who was president of the fellowship club; Woodrow Wilson, president of the United States; and A. E. Staley, Sr., company president. Pictured below them is George Chamberlain, general superintendent of the plant.

These were attendees when the first sales meeting was held in Decatur in December, 1922. Front row, from left, Reginald Pope, W. H. Randolph, Jr., New York; L. R. Dickinson, Boston; G. A. Dean, Spartanburg, S.C.; Don J. Houran, Jack Hixon. Second row, from left, Theodore Jones, Tommy Webb, George Diamond and J. W. Pope, Atlanta.

These were the members of the Staley Fellowship Club, formed in 1917.

Addition to Mill House, circa 1919.

Under construction in 1920 was the syrup refinery, which in this photograph is mistakenly labeled the Bone Black Kiln house. The building is now known as No. 10 and is still in use.

The Syrup Packing House, or
Building 17, under construction in 1919.

A. E. Staley, Sr., pictured above, generally recognized as the founder of soybean processing in this country, opened the first soybean expeller plant in Decatur on September 30, 1922. Mr. Staley had to use all of his persuasive skills to convince corn farmers, who used soybeans solely as a nitrogen replenisher for the soil between corn plantings, that there was money to be made in rotating the two crops.

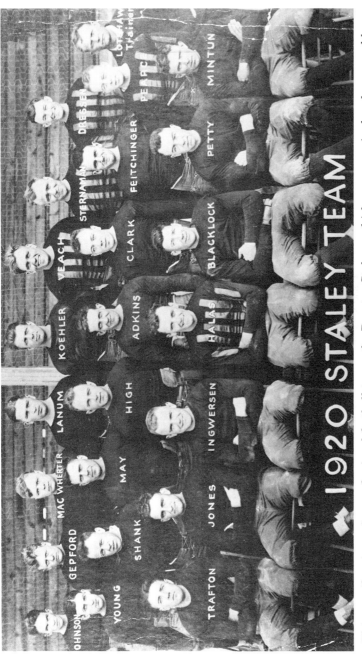

1920 STALEY TEAM

JOHNSON · YOUNG · GEPFORD · MAC WHERTER · LANUM · KOEHLER · VEACH · STERNAMAN · DRESSEN · LOTSHAW Trainer

SHANK · MAY · HIGH · ADKINS · CLARK · FEITCHINGER · PEARCE

TRAFTON · JONES · INGWERSEN · HALAS · BLACKLOCK · PETTY · MINTUN

This was the pioneering professional football team, the Decatur Staleys, which was organized and managed by George Halas starting in 1920. This legendary team won the national professional championship in 1920 with ten victories, one loss and two ties. Most of the players had achieved fame at colleges before signing on as Staley football-playing employees who had additional duties to perform in the Decatur company's office and plant.

A.E. Staley Manufacturing Company
CORN PRODUCTS

Decatur, Ill., October 6, 1921.

The Staley Football Team,
Decatur, Illinois.

Gentlemen:

Confirming our verbal agreement with you, we agree to place the names of all your football players (Total number not to exceed nineteen) on our payrolls at a salary of $25.00 per week with the exception of those already being taken care of in that manner on regular jobs.

We also agree to enter into an advertising contract with you whereby we undertake to pay you Three Thousand ($3,000.00) Dollars for such advertising in your score book as you have suggested.

It is our wish and plan that when the football team goes to Chicago on October 15th, it remain there until the end of the season.

In this event while the team is in Chicago we will maintain on the payroll the entire nineteen men on the team at $25.00 per week until this Company shall have paid you in total, including both advertising and salary amounts, the sum of Five Thousand ($5,000.00) Dollars.

In consideration of these various payments, it is agreed that the team is to operate under the name of "The Staley Football Club". That you are to use your best efforts to disseminate information regarding, and to facilitate the business of the A.E.Staley Manufacturing Company; that you are to secure the utmost publicity in the newspapers for the team and the Company; that you are to so conduct the team, its playing and management as to reflect credit upon the A.E.Staley Manufacturing Company; that you will enter into no contracts or obligations in any way binding upon the A.E.Staley Manufacturing Company with this present exception.

It is understood that this arrangement shall terminate at the end of the present football season.

Please indicate your acception of the provisions of this agreement. I remain

Yours very truly,
A.E.STALEY MANUFACTURING CO.

Accepted by
Staley Football Club
_by_
Geo. S. Halas

Mr. Staley gave Halas $5,000 "seed money," allowing him to move the team to Chicago. He asked only that Halas continue to call the team the Staleys for one more season.

Joe "Iron Man" McGinnity, left, joined
the company as manager of the Staley
baseball team in 1919. He had set major
league pitching records for Brooklyn and
Baltimore in 1900 and 1901, and ultimately was enshrined in the Baseball
Hall of Fame at Cooperstown, New York.
George Halas, above, better known for
his football exploits, was a hard-hitting
outfielder on the Staley team. Halas
earlier played briefly for the New York
Yankees.

For many years the Staley field, located at the corner of Eldorado and 22nd Streets in Decatur, was the center of the city's sports interests.

Founder Staley (in derby) and Judge Kennesaw Mountain Landis, on his left, at the 1927 dedication of Decatur's Three-I League ballpark, Fans Field.

flavored. They are packed in many sizes of tin cans.

Feed, meal and corn oil are used in a variety of ways and along with our other products they go to Great Britain, France, Germany, China, Scandinavia, Turkey, Egypt, South Africa, India, Japan, South America and Australia.

The A. E. Staley Manufacturing Company believes in frank and friendly relations with its loyal employees, and in the support and encouragement of clean athletics of every kind.

We trust that our football team may merit your approval.

Football team?

One might rightly wonder, "What's a football team doing there?"

One might further observe that the founder, Gene Staley, had barely managed to survive during the rough years of the 1910–1920 decade. Granted, he had experienced healthy growth over the 1916–1919 period. And in the immediate postwar period he was grinding more corn, broadening his product line, and making money. He was on his way!

Wasn't such startling and unprecedented progress sufficient?

Was this really the time and place for an anachronistic diversion like (of all irrelevant things) football?

For better or worse, Staley was a sports fan. Period. Never having had the opportunity to go to high school or college, he consequently had missed the chance to sit on the sidelines and to root for fellow students competing in baseball or football.

The city of Decatur had a minor league baseball team which occasionally lured Staley to an afternoon of escape, and it also had a spirited football team at Millikin University which created some excitement on Saturday afternoons. Yet Staley was not content simply to sit on the sidelines cheering for players affiliated with other organizations.

He wanted involvement.

He wanted to own his own teams!

In 1918 and 1919, an employee organization called the Staley Fellowship Club had the founder's encouragement and financial backing when it decided to sponsor baseball and football teams in action against a scattering of industrial teams, as they were called, on a 2-acre vacant lot adjacent to the Staley plant, on the north side of Eldorado Street—and at opponents' locations as well.

The founder felt that participation in sports would provide a boost for worker morale regardless of whether the Staley workers would be observers or actual participants.

Further, the founder was sensitive to a relationship between sports and sportsmanship. He felt that sports were not just fun and games but were, in fact, a positive force for developing human character and for stimulating a wholesome attitude of spirited competition. And the founder was, above all, a competitor—on or off any field. He was that special stamp of man who always dared to dare.

But those 1918 and 1919 teams didn't have the razzle-dazzle Staley was looking for. The coaches and players did their best, but they were principally starchmakers and secondarily athletes who performed only on infrequent occasions. A few had earlier established respectable credentials in sports, mostly at colleges and mainly in football.

Founder Staley was less than satisfied. He checked with several corporations in Ohio and Pennsylvania that had introduced so-called industrial sports as an employee pastime and as a way to enliven the ambience in drab company towns where weekends could be boring.

Sponsoring corporations in Ohio and Pennsylvania reported that their industrial leagues were getting along nicely despite the parochial, low-key nature of their efforts. Expectations were realized largely because they were modest. Fair enough.

But Staley had always found it difficult to mount modest expectations and to settle for modest results. He wanted his company to be biggest and best and he was impatient with anyone in his organization compromising on moderate goals.

40

High aspirations were essential for high accomplishment, in his view.

Long before Goodyear envisioned a fleet of airborne blimps to be its symbol and long before Anheuser-Busch opted for Clydesdale horses, Gene Staley envisioned that a proficient and colorful sports team could effectively carry the company's name far beyond the limited environs of Decatur, Illinois.

"He dreamed big—and then he set about to make his dreams come true," observed Thomas W. Samuels, partner in the Decatur law firm of LeForgee, Vail and Miller, who had come to Decatur in 1914. "Staley wasn't the kind of person who could think big in corn and think small in sports. He was all-or-nothing-at-all, all the way."

Without abandoning the idea that employee participation would enhance employee morale and loyalty, the founder moved sharply ahead on a singular piece of strategy, namely, the sponsorship of championship teams to carry the name and glory of the Decatur enterprise to distant points.

In the implementation of this crusade, Staley knew he'd have to upgrade one sport, football, and worry less about baseball. This realization was a blow in itself. To be sure the 1919 Staley baseball team had a 50-year-old manager named Joe "Iron Man" McGinnity who in 1900 had pitched 29 major league victories for Brooklyn and in 1901 had scored 26 triumphs for Baltimore. "Baseball was my first love," Staley confided to a colleague, "and I'd prefer not to de-emphasize it." Indeed, a good case could have been made that starchmaker Staley was a frustrated shortstop at heart but was either too busy or too portly, or both, to suit up.

In embarking on a serious football program Staley realized that he'd be able to attract first-class athletes to the degree he'd be able to assure them adequate compensation. Amateur athletes playing "for the fun of it" would not meet his expectations. The thought of using mercenaries in football was a bit outrageous all by itself considering that professional football (unlike professional baseball) was not yet formally born. Staley's concept was simple: He would hire top-flight athletes to

41

work in the plant and pay them an additional fee for their performance as football gladiators. The athletes would not be strictly amateur nor strictly professional. They'd be semipro.

Staley also realized that big-time charisma would be achievable only with big-time sports leadership on the scene. Staley knew he needed a whirlwind of a man to come in as athletic director for the corporation. And he picked a man named George S. Halas who was uniquely suited to the Decatur challenge and who, later on, moved into national fame as a star player, coach, and owner of the Chicago Bears professional football team.

"Without Gene Staley, there never would have been the Chicago Bears," Halas told this author a few days before Papa Bear's eighty-fifth birthday in 1980. "Decatur, Illinois, was the real birthplace of the Chicago Bears, and the Staley company was indirectly and partially responsible for the founding of the National Football League."

George Halas, class of '17, studied engineering at the University of Illinois, where he played football, basketball, and baseball. Upon enlisting in the U.S. Navy after graduation, he was dispatched to Great Lakes Naval Training Station where he was promptly inducted into a vigorous, no-nonsense football program.

"This was a good news situation all the way," he said. "Several months earlier at the farewell football banquet at Illinois, Bob Zuppke, the great coach, had asked, 'Why is it that just when you players are beginning to know something about football, I lose you—and you stop playing? It makes no sense. Football is the only sport that ends a man's career just when it should be beginning.' "

If it had not been for the war and a desire to serve in the Navy, Halas would have turned pro as a baseball player as soon as he graduated. But it was football with a flourish at Great Lakes and he reveled in it. Emmett Keefe, a guard from Notre Dame, was captain of the team. John "Paddy" Driscoll from Northwestern and Jimmy Conzelman of Washington University were strong-running stars of the backfield. Halas played right end. The Great Lakes team was so prodigious against college teams (and even defeated the Naval Academy at Annapolis) that it was chosen for the 1919 New Year's Day Rose Bowl game at Pasadena where Great Lakes upset the undefeated Mare Island Marines, 17–0. It was the only Rose Bowl event in history played by military service teams and George Halas was awarded the Most Valuable Player trophy.

After being discharged as an ensign, Halas returned to civilian life with baseball—not football—in his career plans. After a spring training session with the New York Yankees in Florida, he won the right field position for the regular season. Yet, alas, he was injured in a thundering slide into third base at Yankee Stadium, was sidelined, and was eventually farmed out to St. Paul.

One wonders if Halas would have gone on to baseball glory with the Yankees if he had not twisted his hipbone and torn the ligaments in a leg while diving into third base. It's a moot point in the assessment of his early career. As it so happens, shortly after right fielder Halas was injured, the Yankees brought in a right fielder named Babe Ruth, purchased from the Boston Red Sox for $125,000.

Then Halas got a 9-to-5 job as a bridge engineer with the Chicago, Burlington and Quincy Railroad in Chicago at $55 a week. His mother was delighted. "A railroad job," she said, "is secure—and safe."

But sports competition called. Halas learned that some of his Great Lakes buddies were playing football for a semipro team at Hammond, Indiana—including Paddy Driscoll and Jimmy Conzelman—so he arranged his schedule to include practice sessions at nearby Hammond on Thursday evenings and competition against other semipro teams (which were few in number) on Sunday afternoons.

It was during his Hammond football career that Halas had the opportunity to play against the formidable Carlyle Indian, Jim Thorpe. Halas recently recalled that being blocked or tackled by Thorpe—of the Canton, Ohio, Bulldogs—was like being

43

hit by a falling tree. Halas said, "Thorpe had sheet metal inserted around his shoulder pads and around his rib cage. He was faster than the wind and as sure-footed as Indians are reported to be."

In January, 1920, Gene Staley had been advised that there was a fidgety bridge engineer working for the C. B. & Q.—a man named Halas who seemed happiest when moonlighting in football. So Staley asked his general superintendent, George Chamberlain, to take the train to Chicago and to make a date with the young man. Halas recently recalled, "Chamberlain made a date with me and we met at the LaSalle Hotel."

Would Halas be willing to move to Decatur to organize a first-class big-time sports program?

Considering that the Indian Meat Packing Company in Green Bay, Wisconsin, was paying its employee-athletes extra compensation to play football and further considering that a few other companies were going the same route, would Halas be willing to introduce semipro football in Decatur under the sponsorship of A. E. Staley Manufacturing Company?

Would Halas be willing to recruit outstanding football players following their senior year in college and perhaps also bring in some of the stars he had played alongside at Great Lakes and Hammond, Indiana?

In return for sound corporate support, would Halas be willing to coach football and to play football and to try to win some sort of a national championship under the Staley banner?

And during the summer lull, would Halas be willing to captain the Staley baseball team under the managership of "Iron Man" McGinnity?

And, finally, would Halas enjoy such an assignment at a weekly salary $5 lower than the $55 he was getting from the C. B. & Q.?

The answer to all questions was a resounding, enthusiastic, immediate yes. Halas had only one condition. If his semipro football players were also to be full-time employees at the Decatur starch plant, would the company assure him he could have two-hour practice sessions every day—on company time?

George Chamberlain, knowing how bossman Staley would have responded, said okay.

So it was a deal.

Without totally forsaking that great national pastime called baseball, Halas gave it limited attention upon moving into Decatur in March of 1920. Nonetheless, Halas had great respect for McGinnity and was anxious to find out whether he and McGinnity remembered the fundamentals they had learned playing in major league ball. Yet Halas assured Gene Staley that greater opportunities existed in blazing a pioneering path toward pro football via the semipro route. Pro baseball was a bit old hat. It had been around since 1876, when the National League was formed.

Firm friendship flowed fast and felicitously once Halas and Staley started having one-on-one sessions in the latter's office or in the "blackboard meeting room" at the end of the playing field alongside the starchworks. Shortly after Halas signed on as a scale house clerk, responsible for weighing deliveries of corn, he began checking into the credentials of those employees who had played amateur football for the Staley Fellowship Club in 1919—amateur in the sense that they had received no extra off-the-job compensation for their athletic endeavors.

Halas was pleased to note that he had inherited a Decatur native and employee-quarterback named Charlie Dressen, who ran at lightning speed on the gridiron and who later transferred his affection to baseball to become a legendary manager of major league teams. Halas also noted that several other holdovers from the 1919 football team merited the switch from industrial league amateurs to semipro gridiron luminaries.

During the summer of 1920, Halas played shortstop on the Staley baseball team through July. Then he set off on what he described as "probably the first professional football recruiting journey in history."

Wearing five hats—employee in the Staley starchworks, athletic director, football coach, football player, and talent scout —Halas stopped first at the University of Wisconsin at Madison where he signed up Ralph Scott, an All-America tackle. At the

45

University of Nebraska he latched on to Guy Chamberlain (no relation to manufacturing superintendent George Chamberlain), a 6-foot, 3-inch All-America end.

Next in line were Jimmy Conzelman and Hugh Blacklock, who had played with Halas at Great Lakes. He wanted Paddy Driscoll but learned that Driscoll had signed a contract elsewhere.

From former University of Illinois teams he acquired Burt Ingwerson, Ross Petty, and Edward "Dutch" Sternaman and from Notre Dame fame came Jerry Jones, Emmett Keefe, and a great center named George Trafton. Others came from Millikin, Northwestern, and the University of Pennsylvania.

Upon the completion of his recruiting swing he told boss man Staley, "We're really going to have a team." And he explained, "I assured the players they'd get paid at the end of the season for their football, depending on the size of the gate, and I also told them they'd get paid weekly wages for the various duties they'd have in the plant. They all seemed to like the prospect of stability in a corporate set-up."

Halas also told Staley, "I'll bet we'll draw standing-room-only crowds." This was a reasonably safe prediction considering that Staley Field, next to the starchworks, had a grandstand that would accommodate only 1,500 people—with standing room available for an additional 1,000.

So the stage was set.

Now all the Decatur Staleys (and that was their name) needed was some opposition for the fall and winter season.

But opposition on a regular basis was hard to come by considering there was no league.

In August, 1920, Halas contacted Ralph Hay, manager of the Canton Bulldogs, and several other semipro friends and suggested that a full-scale professional organization would be the solution to the problem of scheduling a full season of games. Hay called a meeting for September 17, 1920, in his Hupmobile and Jordan showroom in Canton, Ohio.

Two Staley employees attended that meeting with authority to speak for the corporation—George Halas and a company engineer, Morgan O'Brien, who was strong in administrative and budgetary matters.

The circumstances of the birth of professional football—at that milestone meeting in an automobile showroom in Canton —were described in detail by Halas in his book, *Halas by Halas* (McGraw-Hill):

> The showroom, big enough for four cars—Hupmobiles and Jordans—occupied the ground floor of the three-story brick Odd Fellows Building. Chairs were few. I sat on a running board. We all agreed on the need for a league. In two hours we created the American Professional Football Association [to be renamed the National Football League, at Halas's urging, two years later].
>
> To give the Association some financial standing, we voted to issue franchises on payment of $100. Twelve teams (all represented at the meeting) were franchised on the spot—Akron, Canton, Cleveland, Dayton, Decatur (Staleys), Hammond, Massillon (Ohio), Muncie (Indiana), Chicago (Cardinals), Racine (Wisconsin), Rochester and Rock Island (Illinois).
>
> The Association needed someone with a name. Our minds turned to Jim Thorpe, the biggest name in sports. Unanimously, we elected him president.
>
> When I told other managers about the top players I had lined up, there was great eagerness to meet us on the field.

George Halas and Morgan O'Brien returned promptly to Decatur and enthusiastically reported to Gene Staley that "We're ready for the kickoff."

Such was the scenario in the dim and distant dawn of professional football.

Such were the roles of a starch company and its trusty corn-weigher.

Now all they'd have to do is go out and win some games.

The scoreboard, all of a sudden, became an additional "bottom line" for the founder to worry about.

On Sunday, October 3, 1920, more than 2,000 local fans turned out to see the Decatur Staleys play the Moline, Illinois, Tractors. The Staleys won, 20–0.

It was an auspicious start for the starchmakers.

The game against the Rock Island Independents was at the opponents' field. Decatur fans chartered a train. The attendance was a booming 5,000. Conzelman ran 40 yards for the only touchdown of the game. The Decatur Staleys won, 10–0. Making corn syrup had never been as exciting for sportsman Staley and his colleagues.

The results for the 1920 season were euphoric—10 victories, 2 ties, and 1 defeat (at the hands of the Chicago Cardinals). The Decatur Staleys quite properly proclaimed themselves world champions!

George Halas recently commented, "That first season was the real test. Gene Staley sat on the bench and sweated out every play of every game. But he never second-guessed my strategies and never interfered. One Sunday I insisted he accompany me up and down the sidelines. Wearing his dark blue business suit and stiff bowler he was an unusual sight along the sidelines. And he found there was a lot of walking to do—back and forth, back and forth. But he was happy, mainly because we had a team he could be proud of.

"We charged only a dollar for admission to Staley Field, which maybe wasn't enough. Employees got in at half price. When the season ended, the 18 players on our squad received $1,800 each for three months of action—their share of the agreed-to 50 percent of the total take. This was a lot of money considering they were making only $50 a week as plant and office workers. All this plus a winning season was almost too good to be true."

The overall financial picture was less exciting for the sponsoring corn refining company. The "bottom line" in the corporation's accounting department showed a football loss of $14,406.36. All but three of the games had been played at opponents' locations, mainly because opponents' fields had room for larger crowds. The final game of the season, against Akron, was played at Wrigley Field in Chicago with 12,000 fans in the stands.

Founder Staley was so encouraged by the 1920 season's victories that he was not inclined to take the $14,406.36 corporate thumping too seriously. Sensing his quandary, the team gave a victory dinner for its starchmaker boss at Decatur's St. Nicholas Hotel on December 17. Halas and the players picked up the tab. Staley was emotionally stirred by the experience. After he stood at the head table to express his gratitude, a local newspaperman commented that "A million dollars couldn't buy the pride he feels. He has accomplished a genuine first."

And it should be added that the boss's remarks included an expression of confidence that the Decatur Staleys of 1921 would be even stronger than that pioneering first contingent of 1920.

Yet, as things went, 1921 was a sweet-sour year for the Decatur Staleys. On the sports pages they were victorious—winning 9 games, achieving 1 tie, and registering 1 loss. But only 2 of those 11 games—the first 2—were played at home.

The American Professional Football Association, duly noting the season's performance, officially declared the Decatur Staleys the national champions of 1921 (a formality that somehow never officially occurred in the prior hectic year).

That was the sweet side of the story—plus an all-time honor no other sponsor would ever be able to claim.

Then there was the sour side. With expenses up substantially for travel, insurance, equipment, maintenance, and other necessities, Gene Staley had commented, early in the season, that the restricted capacity of the Decatur field was continuing to limit the opportunity to match greater expense with greater income. At the very time his team—and he called it "my team" —was poised for an official national championship, Staley had to face up to the fact that big-time football belonged in a big stadium in a big city, where big crowds could generate a big gate to support the big expense of fielding a championship football team.

Of all reverses, this was the hardest to bear for starchmaker Staley. His idealism suggested keeping the winning team in Decatur. His pragmatism suggested finding a new home where the team's stars could run, pass, punt, and drop-kick before massive crowds of cheering fans.

Plus . . .

There was something called the 1921 Depression—a latter-day spillover from the financial and production imbalances caused by the nation's shift from war to peace. There were perilous predicaments in the starch business. There were stock-holders. There were customers. There were employees complaining—perhaps justifiably—of the favoritism granted to privileged, prima donna football-playing colleagues. There was a fierce high noon of reality more intense than the dawn of a new American sport.

When Staley talked things over with Halas early in October, Halas understood. Staley explained that the company was running heavily in the red (headed toward a $692,000 loss for the year). Both men agreed that the football success so far had, indeed, lived up to their impossible dreams. The football team had gained (and would continue to gain) national recognition for a starch company in the cornfields of rural Illinois. And, most importantly, the team was a dramatic front-runner in the vanguard of an emerging, spectacular, new style of football destined to be an all-encompassing, captivating, overpowering passion in American sports—down the road.

But . . .

A new assessment was required in the fall of 1921.

In six words: Staley sports would have to go. They were a frivolous luxury in light of more pressing priorities.

Traumatic as the situation may have been to the company's founder, he played it quietly, coolly, softly. He didn't panic— if for no other reason than he had had plenty of earlier experience at suppressing the pangs of panic.

He proposed to Halas (and to the football employee-athletes) the following:

1. That effective with the next road game, at Wrigley Field in Chicago, the Staleys would remain in Chicago and not return to Decatur.
2. That the entire football squad—now up to 19 players—would remain on the Staley payroll for a certain period of time.
3. That the team would operate in Chicago as "The Staley Football Club."
4. That the new arrangement would terminate at the end of the 1921 season.

A remarkable arrangement! A $5,000 bonus for the team was involved. In effect, Gene Staley paid $5,000 to get the Decatur Staleys out of town. In the doing, he literally rewarded George Halas for taking the Decatur Staleys' official franchise to Chicago, not realizing, of course, that 60 years later a professional football franchise would be worth $30 to $40 million plus $5 million annually in television rights! (To quote NFL Commissioner Pete Rozelle, "A franchise is like a Picasso. There are only a limited number of them available.")

Halas and his heroic players went to Chicago on October 10, 1921. They moved into the Blackwoods Apartment Hotel at 4414 Clarendon Avenue, within walking distance of Wrigley Field. Rent: $2 a week per person. For the team's October 15 encounter with Rochester at Wrigley Field, they called themselves the Staley Football Club; they drew 7,500 patrons; they won, 16–13. Their semipro days were over. Unleashed from the starchworks, they basked in the limelight of being 100 percent professional and they rapidly became convinced that pro football was really here to stay.

Halas brought in Dutch Sternaman as a front-office partner for the first few years but wound up with total ownership of the franchise. Halas commented that he "sorely missed working alongside Gene Staley, whose first obligation was to his corporate stockholders and employees and customers." Halas added, "Staley had no legal or moral responsibility to assure the continuation of the football team. Later, whenever he could, Staley came to Chicago to root for what he called 'the transplants.' If it had not been for him, the team would never had existed. He had the respect and affection of all of us."

Halas came up with some adroit footwork on his own after arriving on the Chicago scene, such as:

1. He promptly visited William Veeck, Sr., president of the P. K. Wrigley–owned Chicago Cubs baseball team, which played in Wrigley Field. Persuading Veeck that continuity in professional football would always assure a supplemental season of revenue, Halas agreed promptly when Veeck suggested that Halas's fee for using Wrigley Field would be 15 percent of the gate receipts.

2. Ever the deal-maker and bargainer, Halas added a condition. He told Veeck, "Okay, if I can keep the program rights." (Programs sold for 10 cents in those days.) Veeck capitulated to Halas's minor demand.

3. Following the victorious 1921 season, the Staley Football Club needed a name change. With his obligation to the Decatur corporation finished, Halas considered calling the team the Chicago Football Cubs. Yet he noted that "football players are bigger than baseball players, so if baseball players are Cubs then certainly football players must be Bears." The baseball Cubs organization felt relieved—and Halas felt fine.

When the Wrigley organization's executive committee contacted Gene Staley in Decatur to make sure there were no legal snags, Staley confirmed he had transferred the franchise to Halas and that the corn-refining company was abandoning its sports program. After all, sports were fascinating, but starch came first.

The 1922 Bears came out running—and have been running ever since. They've had successful seasons more often than unsuccessful seasons and they've become almost synonymous with that sensational sport called pro football. They stayed at Wrigley Field—unique in that it has never installed artificial illumination—until 1971 when they moved to Soldier Field.

Halas played on the Chicago football team for only a brief period after moving from Decatur, but he remained the Bears' coach until 1955 when he stepped aside in order to bring in his old friend from the days of the 1918 cadets at Great Lakes— Paddy Driscoll. But Halas very much remained the Bears' owner. By 1955, his record as coach was 368 victories, 117 defeats, and 27 ties.

In the interim, Staley alumnus Halas became one of the legendary and inspirational impresarios in the world of sports. When he was enshrined at the Canton, Ohio, Football Hall of Fame, he was ushered in under the real-life fable, "Once upon a time there were three Bears"—owner, coach, and player. And it should be noted that three other football greats with Staley roots have also been admitted to the Hall of Fame: Chamberlain, Conzelman, and Trafton. These were among the high priests in the emergence of a revolutionary sport.

But the honorary embellishments don't end there. Staley alumnus "Iron Man" McGinnity has been permanently enshrined at the Baseball Hall of Fame at Cooperstown, New York.

Indisputably, no company in industry can match the record of the Staley stars. In particular, the post–World War I adventure at Decatur remains a singular episode in both business and sports annals. It was a fragile Camelot moment, glorious in its concept and conquests but brief in its duration.

What accrued to the corporation as a result of the experiment? This question is often asked. Fleeting fame? Of course. Short-term or long-term profits? Not quite. Exemplification of innovation and courage? A thousand times yes.

Gene Staley was a mortal man who had many worlds to conquer, many hills to climb, many dares to dare. Honed by adversity, he lived for the purpose of reaching toward the sun, moon, and stars. He did it in sports and he did it in his industrial endeavors at Decatur, Illinois.

53

CHAPTER FOUR

SOYBEANS COME TO THE U.S.

In 1922, the city fathers of Decatur, Illinois, never envisioned their community hosting such organizations as Soy Capital Bank & Trust Company, Soy Capital Electric Inc., Soy City Electric Supply Co., Soy City Marine Inc., Soy City Motel, Soy City Tire & Retreading Inc., Soy City Towing Co., Soyland Power Cooperative Inc., and Soyland Service Center, Inc.

Not to mention radio station WSOY.

Back in 1922, Decatur was a beanless sort of place, content to be in the heart of the Midwest's sprawling farm belt where corn ruled as king of the realm, and content to have the Staley company spearheading corn's golden era.

The lowly soybean was both old and new in 1922. In the Orient, where meatless diets were commonplace but where protein nourishment was obviously as essential as anywhere else, the soybean had been a staple for many centuries. But in the United States it was a strange, new, experimental legume growing within a pod on a bushy plant and inviting investigation by farmers whose fate and fortune had always depended on such tried-and-true crops as corn, wheat, and oats.

Especially in the Midwest flatlands, farmers were becoming

increasingly aware of the virtues of rotating crops. Corn farmers in particular were eager to tap any emerging bits of knowledge that would be helpful in increasing yields and fighting such blights as bugs, weeds, and disease in an era prior to the development of chemical fertilizers, herbicides, and insecticides. County agents and university extension specialists were beginning to mention soybeans as a solution—or at least a partial solution—to some of the farmers' problems. Many of the Midwest's finest farms had been intensively "corned to death" and they plainly needed some sort of balanced program that would bring about better year-to-year productivity per acre.

Farmers' questions about soybeans were many, including:

"Where will we get the beans to plant as seeds?"

"What implements should we use for planting and harvesting?"

"How far apart should we plant our rows?"

"Who'll buy our soybeans once they're harvested and for how much a bushel?"

"Where will the purchasers come from?"

"Should the soybean plants be used mainly for hay and forage or for plowing under to serve as a nitrogen supplement for a subsequent crop of corn?"

"To what end-uses will the beans be put by processors?"

"Will the experiment be worth the time and trouble?"

A broad body of practical knowledge existed—in northern China, for example. But in the United States there were more questions than answers. In 1922, the U.S. Department of Agriculture was still two years away from the simple process of keeping statistics on soybeans. Thus, the ancient bean was not only a newcomer on the U.S. scene but, as with most new things, it was often greeted with skepticism. The average farmer was understandably more comfortable following the traditional paths of his father and grandfather.

Yet news about soybeans began to circulate. The news not only included the role of soybeans in rotation planting and in providing soil nutrients, but it also included the powerful fact that soybeans when processed could be an unparalleled source

55

of protein—for animal feedstocks and, down the line, also for human foods. At agriculture-related universities there was discussion to the effect that soybeans had been a part of the regular diet in the Orient for many centuries.

Historical literature indicates that soybean meal and oil—the two principal derivatives—were initially produced on a small scale in the United States in 1911 through a crushing process in Seattle, Washington, using beans imported from Manchuria. American-grown beans were initially processed on an even smaller scale in 1915 by several cottonseed oil mills in North Carolina.

The literature also points out that in the 1920s "several Illinois farm-related groups" and "an Illinois processor" were ready to give guarantees to provide a market for "all the beans grown on 50,000 acres" in the Illinois Corn Belt.

That "Illinois processor" was the Staley company, of course, and the one-man committee making the company's decisions was Augustus Eugene Staley, Sr., of course. The ever-restless, ever-inquisitive, ever-innovative founder was motivated by the pure and simple desire to achieve profit and growth through corporate diversification. Yet he had a less pragmatic and more idealistic instinct as well. He felt the soybean needed advocacy. He felt the western world had neglected it. He felt it needed a father—a champion. And he felt his "sixth sense" was pointing in the right direction.

Corn refining by the "wet milling" process would, of course, continue to be the principal line of activity at Decatur, but Gene Staley insisted that the soybean side of the business should not tiptoe in as a lowly orphan. In an effort to demonstrate his confidence and his intent, founder Staley declared in 1922, "The day will come when our plant will process more soybeans than corn."

(Author's note: This was an on-target prediction. In 1950—28 years later—soybean facilities at Decatur handled up to 50 carloads daily, whereas corn facilities handled up to 30 carloads. In 1950, the company boasted, "We are the world's largest in soybeans and Number Two in corn. It takes 3,500 acres to grow enough soybeans to keep us operating for a single day."

And the community of Decatur could justifiably boast, "We are 'The Soybean Capital of the World.'")

Despite the soybean excitement during 1922, despite the corporation's bid for a leadership role in a new product line, despite the founder's forecast that someday the company would process more soybeans than corn, there were some employees at Decatur who didn't like to see refined corn products upstaged by an experimental wonder bean from the Orient.

That the Staley company didn't really forget its corn-bred roots was demonstrated in the April, 1922, issue of the *Staley Journal* in a story entitled "After Ten Years," which reminded one and all that the company's corn refining operations had started in 1912. The story included the following huzzahs:

> Since 1912 we have ground 35 million bushels of corn. If all that corn were to be loaded into freight cars the train would be 400 miles long. Our products are shipped to every part of the globe. On the streets of Cairo, it is not uncommon to see a fallaheen wearing a Staley starch bag for apparel. In Constantinople, many a rain barrel displays the Staley brand. We now have 4,000 employees looking to the company for their living. We have the second-largest (behind Corn Products) starch factory in the world, containing 750,000 square feet.

But the soybean glory was just around the corner.

The soybean road from 1922 to 1950 was a rough one, replete with chuckholes of challenges, problems, setbacks, complications, disappointments, and occasional splashes of red ink—plus triumphs that were tall enough to make believers out of the most obstinate cynics.

Gene Staley, founder and president, picked 1922 as the year for a soybean start-up only because he had been thwarted earlier by internal and external conditions that were not conducive to flirtations with expensive experiments.

As far back as 1918 he had begun his own soybean investigations and in 1920 he had ordered two pieces of heavy hardware, called expellers, from the V. D. Anderson Company of Cleveland, Ohio, a leading manufacturer of hydraulic equipment used for crushing corn germs and sunflower seeds. When the expellers arrived, George E. Chamberlain, general superintendent and Staley's "right-hand man," suggested that some modifications be made on the expellers before any production schedules were set. But his big worry concerned several pieces of machinery called bean dryers which were fashioned by his own well-meaning people.

In 1921, Chamberlain had the manufacturing equipment somewhat squared away, but several new reasons for delay became apparent.

Delay Number One involved building a ramp for use by trucks bringing soybeans to the plant—trucks being used because the loads would be less than the amount needed to justify use of railroad freight cars. To solve the problem of providing access for trucks, the ingenious Chamberlain commandeered hundreds of creosoted railroad ties and constructed an improvised ramp inclined at a 10 percent grade leading up to the area where soybeans would be dumped. Improvisation had always been among Chamberlain's virtues and the ramp was in fact nothing more than a new manifestation of the manufacturing superintendent's day-in, day-out ingenuity.

Delay Number Two was more serious, involving not only the corporation's economic plight but also the nation's economic plight. The year 1921 had been gravely imperiled by an ominous downturn and many business institutions had been shaken by the tremors of a nationwide depression. Expenses in corn refining had exceeded income at the Staley plant—the net loss for the year 1921 amounting to $692,000. It was obvious that this was no time to be adding new expenses which would inescapably be part and parcel of a pioneering venture into soybean processing.

Even though the corporation was "sound as a dollar, long-range," in the founder's words, it had to exercise caution in its expenditures. A young man named Edwin K. Scheiter, who had joined the company as a manual laborer in 1918 and who would someday become its president, demonstrated the tenor of the times in assignments he undertook in 1921 and 1922.

Scheiter reported later that quite often "finances were so tight that it was necessary to take each day's invoices to a financial discount company in St. Louis. I was selected to personally carry certified copies of these invoices on the afternoon Wabash train. On arrival in St. Louis I was given a check for the amount of the invoices, less the factoring fee. I brought each check back to Decatur on the midnight train. Each check was then deposited in Decatur when the bank opened in the morning. That way we were able to cover corn drafts and payroll checks which were waiting to be issued."

It was the good old "touch and go"—a circumstance in which the company had amassed substantial experience. And of course there was no cushy reserve sitting snugly in the back room, waiting to be tapped for the purpose of staging a debut party in Decatur for a new bean called soy.

In 1922, Gene Staley was ready to go, risks notwithstanding. Thornton C. Burwell, longtime traffic manager and vice president of the Staley company who retired in 1957 after 40 years of service, reminisced by saying, "I knew the boss was determined to get into soybean processing, regardless of the problems of the times."

Burwell—known as Chase—added, "Gene Staley used to come into the offices of the various department heads every day when he wasn't traveling, always wearing a flower in his lapel. I remember one day he came in and sat down across from my desk after returning from a trip to his birthplace state of North Carolina. He reminded me that he had once planted some soybeans on his father's farm near Julian, North Carolina, when he was a boy. These beans had been brought to America by a Baptist missionary who had returned from China.

"Well, on the day of that particular visit to my office—in 1919 —Staley reached into his pocket and pulled out a handful of beans he had picked up several days earlier during his North

Carolina trip. He showed me the beans and said, 'Thornton, do you know what these are?'

"I asked him, 'Are they cowpeas?'

"He said, 'No, they're North Carolina soybeans. Farmers need something to rotate with corn and I think soybeans are the answer.'

"I'm sure Gene Staley had already made up his mind to become a soybean processor. When the company finally got around to putting in the machinery for crushing the beans, we had some trial runs to see how everything was working out. The beans were dried and then dumped into a hopper at the end of one of the expellers and they were carried along a horizontal path on a corkscrew sort of shaft. The revolving shaft squeezed out crude soybean oil through the openings around the circumference of the housing and it forced out soybean cake, or meal, at the end.

"It was a rather primitive device by today's standards but it worked. We didn't know it at the time but we were getting into a product line in which we'd be the biggest in the country."

Two formal announcements in 1922 told the story—but not all the story—of the company's plans and activities.

Announcement Number One (June, 1922) said: "The A. E. Staley Manufacturing Company announces that in response to the general and urgent desire on the part of the farmers of Central Illinois, it has been decided to install a soybean plant in conjunction with the Decatur starch and glucose manufactory.

"A satisfactory building is now in readiness. Several expellers have been purchased and delivered. Bean dryers are under construction. Storage for 150,000 bushels of beans is ready for use. The plant is planned so that large increases in capacity may be had without expensive changes. The first unit will have a capacity of about 500 bushels a day. It will be finished in ample time for the 1922 harvested crop."

But the announcement didn't say that the "general and urgent desire" of the farmers was brought about, to some degree, by the Staley company's founder's own stirrings.

Gene Staley plainly had a chicken-and-egg puzzle to solve. Which should come first—the soybeans or a guaranteed market for soybeans? That was the question.

Announcement Number Two (October, 1922) said: "On September 30, the new soybean plant of the A. E. Staley Manufacturing Company was put into operation, thus inaugurating a new industry for Central Illinois and providing the growers of this territory with a market for their beans."

Central Illinois farmers had created some of their own problems. Productivity of cornfields had been diminished by the farmers' reluctance to rotate crops during World War I when corn prices rose to all-time highs. In the 1918–1922 period, many affected farmers told their tales of woe to Gene Staley and his colleagues when the farmers dropped in at the Staley plant where their corn was the one and only raw material the plant needed.

Staley was no technical man, no agronomist. But he was attuned to the needs of farmers. "I'm just an overgrown North Carolina country boy myself," he'd tell the visitors. And then he'd pass along information on soybeans—information he picked up at the University of Illinois and at other centers of learning where soybean experiments had been started and where fundamental literature on the subject was being developed.

Initially, Staley had what one of his colleagues called "a bum steer" and, consequently, he passed along some information that was less than 100 percent correct. He advised some farmers that they'd benefit by plowing in green soybeans, removed from their pods, as a nitrogen nutrient for a subsequent corn crop. Yet with not too much delay he learned, and the farmers learned, that nodules on the roots of a soybean plant—not the beans themselves—contained the maximum amount of fertilizer. Thereafter, this new knowledge was promptly put to use.

In experimental fields prior to 1922, growers used their soybeans for seeds and, in addition, they used the entire bushy plants—pods, beans, roots, and everything else—for soil conditioning. Yet it became obvious to all, in short order, that industrial processing would be the high reward for getting into the soybean business. The pot at the end of the rainbow was plainly at a processor's plant, far beyond the fence of the farm.

The noteworthy element in the case of Gene Staley's entry into soybean processing had to do with one important factor: timing. If he had been able to afford an earlier entry, he would have encountered even more primitive technology and manufacturing equipment; if he had chosen to delay for several years, he would have been a "me, too" operator following the footsteps of other processors and would have been in a weaker position to establish a commanding franchise in a promising field. That valuable "sixth sense" he often referred to—the one that enabled him to "get well" playing the futures market at the Chicago Board of Trade—was Staley's prod to plunge into the risks and rewards of being a soybean pioneer. He had not really been a path-finding pioneer, in the true sense, in the refining of corn. But in soybeans he had the distinction of starting the first major processing plant—or, better stated, the first plant destined for such glory—in the United States.

For corporate profitability and growth? Of course. For the glory of it all? Yes—but to a lesser degree. Importantly, both his pragmatism and his idealism were served by the noble experiment.

And while on the one hand he was trumpeting his company's ability to meet the "urgent desire" on the part of farmers to have a market for their beans, founder Staley knew very well that on the other hand he would have his own "urgent desire" to obtain enough beans to keep his factory operating. And as things worked out during the introductory period, he needed beans more than the farmers needed a factory outlet.

His first actual purchase of beans occurred on September 28, 1922, from the Andrews Grain Company of Walker, Illinois. The transaction involved 1,547 bushels at 99¾ cents a bushel. In subsequent weeks Staley located and purchased an additional 5,764 bushels. However, the expellers were out of beans after staying in operation for only 16 days. They turned out

209,300 pounds of meal and 42,036 pounds of oil during that initial operation. Then came a shutdown. No beans was a disappointment for Staley, but it was a boon for George Chamberlain who had time to make a few more mechanical modifications on his homemade dryers. As things turned out, the new facilities were in operation for a total of 74 days late in 1922 and 57 days early in 1923.

By the time the 1924 season approached, beans were rather plentiful—at $1.50 a bushel. In Illinois, threshed bushels had increased from 813,000 in 1922 to 1,380,000 in 1924.

A letter written by Staley in May of 1924, in response to an inquiry from West Virginia, said, in part: "The result of our experience in the soybean industry so far has been both unprofitable and very discouraging, but it is our intention to leave the machinery in our plant for another year. If the operations are not profitable, we'll dismantle the plant and discontinue the soybean business altogether.

"We are forced to pay $1.50 a bushel but some new companies which have entered the processing field have paid $1.70 to $1.80 in order to get a supply to maintain their operations. Our company refused to pay over $1.50 but on 34,000 bushels we lost more than $12,000."

The real upswing came in 1925. And the good news, albeit temporary, was that the company was able to buy beans for $1.30 a bushel. With the supply side up, the company brought in almost 70,000 bushels for conversion into almost 3,700,000 pounds of meal and more than 600,000 pounds of oil. Operations were maintained for seven months. By 1926, operations were upped to eight months.

All was well—relatively speaking. Yet Gene Staley felt there was more spadework necessary with users and with suppliers.

Users, including companies that became Staley customers for the first time, were not taking advantage of the inherent qualities of soybean oil and meal, Staley felt. The oil—unrefined and crude—went into soaps and paints, competing with linseed oil, from flax, and with cottonseed oil. But Staley saw the future of oil in widespread uses, including human edibles.

He didn't like it when observers said his soy oil was only a cheap substitute for existing products. Such comments made him snort. To be sure the soybean oil would have to be further refined and purified, and Staley knew that someday this would be inevitable.

The meal, rich in protein, was ideal in mixed feeds for cattle, hogs, and poultry, but feed formulators were reluctant to try new mixes. They were doing nicely with what they had. Anyway, coming up with new formulations would entail the expense and nuisance of registering new analyses in various states.

In addition to worrying about the market for oil and meal, Staley also was worried about farmers' willingness to "plant more acres, plant more acres, plant more acres." Forecasting that his company would need more than 300,000 bushels of beans by the mid thirties, he felt more missionary work was essential to convince growers—especially corn growers—they were "missing a sure-fire bet."

So what did super-salesman Staley do? He hired a train!

Feeling the need for a massive educational program throughout central Illinois, he announced that "the newest thing on rails will be the Soybean Special."

Granted, nostalgic railroad buffs may never rank the Illinois Central Soybean Special along with the Santa Fe Super Chief, the Pennsylvania Broadway Limited, and the New York Central Twentieth Century Limited, but the Soybean Special opened up what was called a new era in railroading. Planned in 1926 and operated in the spring of 1927, the Soybean Special was whistle-tooting proof that Gene Staley was a salesman, an "operator," an entrepreneurial innovator, and a spirited crusader for the lowly bean.

In his desire to spread the word "broader than ever and more persuasively than ever" throughout the rich farmland of central Illinois, the Staley company's founder enlisted the help of the development department of the Illinois Central Railroad Company in Chicago, which ultimately took over responsibility for physical arrangements and logistics.

Among those who cooperated in the venture were the U.S. Department of Agriculture, the College of Agriculture of the University of Illinois, and Southern Illinois State Normal University (now Southern Illinois University—Carbondale).

When the Soybean Special was rolled out for inspection March 28, 1927, in Decatur, all in attendance agreed they had never seen anything like it. The train consisted of an engine and six cars. At the rear was an office car containing dining and sleeping quarters for officials. Then came two cars with exhibits and displays on soybean planting, cultivation, processing, and end-uses, these having been prepared in Decatur with the assistance of Professor J. C. Hackleman of the University of Illinois. Then came two cars converted into motion picture theaters. Then came a lecture car.

To keep the project from being a total symphony to soybeans, there were, at interspersed locations, several exhibits showing damage done to corn by the European corn borer and also suggested measures to be taken to combat the problem.

Between March 28 and April 17, a total of 33,939 people passed through the train. The exhibits and lectures and film showings attracted guests on a seven-days-a-week schedule from 7:30 A.M. to 9:30 P.M. The train traveled 2,478 total miles. It made 105 scheduled stops.

Supplies of literature were insufficient, necessitating putting such reading material back on the presses in Chicago and Decatur. Manufacturers of farm equipment also added their literature, as did a paint manufacturer whose exhibit included large photos of a house resplendent in soybean oil–based paint.

A special touch of showmanship, suggested by Staley, was a contest—with prizes awarded in seven districts of the 19 counties visited by the train. Each prize was the same—50 tons of soil-enriching limestone. The game involved guessing the number of soybeans in a 5-gallon glass jug.

Frederick Wand, articulate expert on soybeans, was the Staley company's principal and constant representative on the train, but Gene Staley went aboard for some parts of the excursion. When a young visitor asked Staley if he was the "inventor" of soybeans, he said no and displayed a sense of modesty which was appropriate under the circumstances but otherwise atypical. And when a newspaper reporter asked Staley if he ever had time to cultivate a hobby, he replied, "Sure." When the reporter followed through with the question, "What might your hobby be?" the Decatur entrepreneur answered, "Soybeans—just soybeans, I guess."

The year 1927 showed the Staley company far out in front in the soybean industry, crushing 216,000 bushels and accounting for 39 percent of all beans processed by an industry that by now was up to 18 processors. (This leadership role was destined to be staunchly maintained by Staley until 1957 when Cargill, Inc., the formidable Minneapolis company, unceremoniously jostled Staley off the peak.)

In the late twenties, the Staley company pressed ahead on three soybean fronts. It exhorted growers—and beans became plentiful. It exhorted customers—and new uses materialized. And it exhorted its own production people and its own research and engineering personnel—and the internal synergism which resulted became the real key to progress.

Encouraging breakthroughs occurred when an edible grade of soy flour was developed for the baking industry and when semirefined soybean oil began to open up new markets in oleomargarine and mayonnaise and in other end products where the oil's yellow coloring was not a disadvantage. And further refining of soy oil was not far away.

Other developments included a "vegetable casein" from soybeans for the paper and adhesives industries, but the big news was the sudden acceptance of soybean meal by feed formulators who recognized that soy protein in mixed feeds was simply too big a benefit to miss.

Kenneth J. Maltas, who was in the Staley ranks for almost 40 years and who was hired in 1927 at 25 years of age, recently recalled some of his experiences as a traveling salesman for soybean meal in the late twenties.

"My territory was mainly anything west of the Mississippi

River but I also had the state of Illinois," Maltas remembered. "When I began my travels in 1927 I met some feed formulators and elevator owners who said they had never seen a soybean in all their lives. *Prairie Farmer* and other magazines had used articles on soybeans but seeing magazine stories was one thing and seeing soybeans was something else.

"It wasn't my job to talk farmers into growing beans. It was my job to sell Staley soybean meal. It was also my job to sell pellets which were made in Decatur. Each pellet was about as big around as a broom handle and about two inches long. The pellets were developed by Staley when ranchers and farmers said they wanted special feed for cattle and sheep for use in wintertime when the fields had been covered by snow and the pasturage had been consumed.

"The pellets were mostly soybean protein but also included a little molasses to serve as a binder plus a little limestone and bone meal. Some ranchers bought small supplies at the start but I wound up selling pellets by the ton. Perfecting the formulation for pellets at the Decatur plant was not an easy job. The pellets had to avoid crumbling during shipment to Colorado and other cattle states. They had to be hard enough so that they wouldn't soak up moisture and disintegrate. But they also had to be soft enough for cattle and sheep to eat.

"I used to enjoy seeing a cowhand, with sacks of pellets across his pony's back, dribbling the contents in a path through the snow or using a light truck to scatter pellets off toward the horizon—thousands and thousands of pellets. One of the most picturesque sights on a snowy range was to see cattle and sheep strung out, single file, over a great distance, munching the special winter diet from Decatur, Illinois."

By 1930, the soybean processing industry had expanded enough to feel it needed a trade association. The Staley company was represented at an organizational meeting held at the City Club in Chicago as were Archer Daniels Midland Company, Allied Mills Inc., Funk Bros. Seed Co., and Spencer Kellogg & Sons, Inc. By the time the National Soybean Oil

Manufacturers Association was completely organized, it had 12 processing companies in its ranks. It subsequently changed its name to the National Soybean Processors Association.

In the early days, Gene Staley remarked that he felt vindicated when other companies decided to get into the soybean business. Also he realized that soybeans would multiply dramatically in acreage to the extent that processors would provide a market.

"But I worked hard and wound up losing money on soybeans in the start-up years," he added, "even though I always knew we were on the right track and would need perseverance and patience in order to achieve profits."

Meantime, back at the rest of the company, it was nice to have an ongoing corn refining operation to support the cost of those experimental distractions, and general activity proceeded apace within the halls and walls of the Staley office and plant.

Following an operating loss in 1921, the corporation leaped forward the following year, posting more than a half million dollars in net earnings on sales exceeding $9 million. With the exception of a less profitable year in 1925, the rest of the decade showed encouraging results with 1929's numbers exceeding $2 million in net profit and approaching $20 million in sales.

In addition to focusing on product development and profit development, the twenties were a powerful decade in people development. Indeed, three of the corporation's five presidents (over the life span of the company's first 75 years) were directly involved in important management changes in the 1920–1930 period. Here are the principals:

Augustus Eugene Staley, Sr., founder and first president. He not only was involved, but he was the prime perpetrator of the management changes. By the mid-twenties he was approaching 60 years of age. "Energetic but tired," he said of himself. Never one to take a vacation—except that he talked a lot about "doing it someday"—he was a workaholic on a seven-day beat.

Bothered increasingly by diabetes and its incessant discomforts, he tried to stay on a rigid diet but was not often success-ful. Gaining weight (to a high of 278 pounds) didn't help. When he was at home in Decatur, his wife, Emma, was a beneficial influence, but when he was on the road—which was often—sleep came in short snatches and food was not always nutri-tious.

He was both Mr. Inside, as administrative officer and chief executive officer, and Mr. Outside, as salesman, business devel-oper, financier, and soybean missionary. Not averse to the art of delegating responsibilities, he was nonetheless frustrated by not having an adequate cadre of senior people to help share the load.

Augustus Eugene Staley, Jr., who in 1932 would become the second president. The founder's older son, born in 1903, went onto the company's payroll in June of 1922 as a part-time worker in the plant while on summer vacation from the Whar-ton School of Commerce and Finance of the University of Penn-sylvania. His first summertime job involved duties as a machinist's helper.

After his graduation in June, 1925, he came aboard on a full-time basis and had a stint as a salesman for a retail product —table syrup. He also served as an administrative assistant to his father and as an assistant to George Chamberlain, the gen-eral superintendent.

Unquestionably the saddest news of the twenties was the death of Chamberlain in 1926. After having served the com-pany since 1912 as the founder's principal associate and as "the man who runs the plant," 56-year-old Chamberlain succumbed suddenly and unexpectedly following a siege of acute indiges-tion. Young Staley, known as Gus, succeeded Chamberlain in the important general superintendent post and was promoted to vice president and treasurer two years later and to executive vice president three years later. Did his father push him ahead too rapidly? There were some who so believed.

Edwin K. Scheiter, who in 1958 would become the third pres-ident and in 1965 the vice chairman. This is the remarkable nonfamily achiever who had had a high school education in

Decatur before becoming a member of the Staley plant's "bull gang" (general purpose labor) in 1918, after which he further boned up on scholastic matters at Brown's Business School on an upper floor over a downtown Decatur store. He specialized in accounting. He became a clerk in the company auditor's office in 1919—at $60 a month.

The management changes of the twenties also involved Scheiter. In 1922 at age 20 he became sales manager and two years later he became a vice president. He was elected to the Staley board in 1925 to enjoy ultimately an unprecedented 53 years as a director of the corporation. His ascendancy was therefore almost as meteoric as that of Staley Jr.

These were the major management situations on the Staley scene in the twenties—transcending the continuing adventures in corn refining and the bothersome, fatiguing zigs and zags of soybean pioneering.

In sum: Chamberlain's loss was beyond comprehension. Founder Staley Sr. used to say he never worried about plant operations, modifications, additions, hirings, firings, and other related considerations as long as George Chamberlain was on the job. But the new young men in the wings were a counterbalancing source of assurance for the founder.

And it shouldn't be forgotten that throughout the tempestuous twenties, Charles J. Schuster continued to serve as corporate secretary in the original Baltimore office. The founder had a sentimental attachment to Baltimore and he bridled whenever anyone mentioned the costs and inefficiencies involved in supporting an eastern branch. "Baltimore is where the company started and that's where I packaged and sold Cream starch," Gene Staley would say, putting an end to the subject. (But ultimately he relented when the realities of the Great Depression necessitated permanently closing the door at the unnecessary Baltimore location.)

And how did son Gus work out during the late twenties as he moved up and up? Example: Gus Staley, on his own, took a deep interest in the company's Fellowship Club and in the workers who contributed a dollar a month to support the dances and dinners and picnics sponsored by the Fellowship Club. In 1927 he suggested the monthly dues be increased by 25 cents to support a group insurance program, to which the company would also contribute.

The son's entry into such a matter was recognized as "something 'the old man' may not have had time to attend to." In proposing a group insurance program with broad benefits for employees and their families, including a $1,000 life insurance policy, young Staley found that most of the plant people had never heard of group insurance. He suggested they take a vote as to whether the benefits seemed worth an additional 25 cents a month. The vote turned out to be overwhelmingly favorable. The employees recognized a bargain when they saw it.

Ed Scheiter also demonstrated he could move in on his own and advance the company's cause—without waiting for the founder's instructions from on high. He developed and spelled out, in writing, specific sales strategies for the broadening line of corn products.

Board members in 1928 included the two Staleys, Scheiter, and Schuster. They also included Chase Burwell, a vice president and traffic manager who was destined for a long and illustrious career, and R. O. Auger, the on-the-scene assistant secretary (compared with Charlie Schuster 650 miles east in Baltimore). J. H. Galloway served as general superintendent, monitoring the manufacturing operations much in the same spirit as the indomitable George Chamberlain.

In those days there were no outside, nonemployee board members (and there would be none until 1941). In those days there was no chairman of the board, per se. As the undisputed chief executive officer of the corporation, Gene Staley signed his mail "president" and was listed in the bylaws as "president and general manager." He chaired board meetings, of course. In the late twenties he personally owned 80 percent of the company's common stock. No one inside or outside questioned the nature of his role.

But, needing strong backup as he did, he encouraged second-echelon executives to "make your own tracks." He managed to generate a little extra optimism during ad hoc meetings with his subordinates, partly because he felt that somehow his usual good luck would add a tail wind to the company's progress.

And he even had some shaky evidence that Lady Luck was on his side. One day in 1928, after he had stopped to "shoot the breeze" (his words) with some townspeople in front of the St. Nicholas Hotel, he yielded to a longtime temptation and dropped in to visit a fortune-teller.

The fortune-teller amazed him by telling him, "You've got a lucky coin in your pocket." He did. It was a dime with a cut-out wedge. He had once found the dime on a sidewalk. It was like a miniature apple pie with a slice removed. It was a keeper, he thought. So he kept it.

Upon showing it to the not too surprised (or surprised) fortune-teller, he heard her say: "That is your lucky coin. Wear it upon your person as long as you live."

And he did.

CHAPTER FIVE

WHAT'S GOOD FOR DECATUR IS USUALLY GOOD FOR STALEY AND VICE VERSA

Ever since the Staley corporation purchased property in Decatur, Illinois, in 1909, there has been a rather reciprocal relationship between the company and the community. Granted, during the early years Gene Staley was an unwelcome outsider —or at least he felt like one. He saw Decatur—population then only 31,000—as being parochial, smug, and inhospitable. And there were undoubtedly many Decaturites who had negative reactions when the self-confident entrepreneur blew into town as a Baltimore baron intent on taking over a defunct corn-refining plant which under prior owners had become a community liability and eyesore.

Yet over the years the city of Decatur and the A. E. Staley Manufacturing Company have developed a relationship founded on mutual interests. Each has contributed substantially to the other in recognition of a strong bond of interdependence. Every now and then there have been examples in which one party seems to have been expediently opportunistic, but by and large there has been an awareness that what is good for Decatur has usually been good for Staley and what is good for Staley has usually been good for Decatur. In sum:

Public and private interests have been simultaneously served.

Over the years the Staley company has been a major employer in the area. From 1912, when it started operations, through 1980, the company has paid millions of dollars in local taxes. Its employees have been active in just about every civic, fraternal, welfare, cultural, and educational project. And the company has helped make Decatur "The Soybean Capital of the World," which is not an inconsequential distinction.

Decatur has often gone to great lengths to accommodate Staley. It has made adjustments to provide a favorable climate for the company's operations. It has contributed public funds to help the company—while helping itself, to be sure.

For its part, the company has tried hard to project a positive image—and has usually succeeded. It has tried to avoid appearing paternalistic, uppity, haughty, demanding, or elitist.

And for the city's part, it has tried hard to project a cooperative and progressive stance—and has usually succeeded. It has tried hard to avoid appearing political, impersonal, populist, and high-handed.

Despite the predominant tone of cooperation, however, there have been occasional disputes. Happily, in all cases compromises were arranged and a spirit of accord again became the order of the day as Decatur inched up and up to its current (1981) population of almost 100,000.

The partnership environment involving Staley and the city of Decatur would have been difficult to achieve if the company had been much smaller and/or if Decatur had been much larger. In New York or Chicago or Los Angeles, such an ongoing private sector/public sector relationship would have been improbable at best and perhaps impossible.

As O. T. Banton, Decatur journalist, pointed out in his 1976-published history of Macon County, the village of Decatur was founded in 1829 when agriculture was the only game around. The first big-time industrialist to pick Decatur for his operation was not A. E. Staley. It was Hieronymus Mueller, who had been an apprentice gunsmith in Mannheim, Germany. Mueller opened a gun shop in Decatur in 1857. He not only repaired guns but also took care of clocks and sewing machines. Ultimately his shop grew into the Mueller Company, headquartered midtown on Eldorado Street, for the manufacture of fire hydrants—the world's largest in this item—and distribution equipment for water and gas. In 1981, the Mueller Company's assets were in the multimillion-dollar range.

But back at the turn of the century it was the railroads, not manufacturing, that started Decatur on its way to becoming a hub of commerce. Rich farmland on all sides helped to nourish the city's roots. And during the past 50 years, manufacturing companies, together with warehousing and distributing organizations and service industries, have been principally responsible—via their payrolls and taxes—for the city's growth and progress. Plus agriculture, of course. Stores, banks, schools, and hospitals have increased in number to accommodate a growing community's needs.

There have been many Staley episodes that have directly impacted the city's well-being, but three in particular are noteworthy. All three took place during the twenties. One episode involved a lake. Another involved a viaduct. And the third involved "The Castle in the Cornfields." All three have involved the establishment of Decatur landmarks. And each has its own little story.

The Lake

As noted near the end of Chapter Two, in 1919 the company began to deal with the very real problem of needing more water to sustain its operations. During that year it built a pumping station, with the capability of handling 12 million gallons of water a day, on the Sangamon River more than a mile distant from the plant. It also installed a 24-inch conduit alongside a railroad right-of-way, from the river to the Staley plant.

It would have been advantageous, of course, if the ramshackle plant Gene Staley purchased in 1909 had been located immediately adjacent to a river, considering that a supply of water, in large quantity, was as vital as a supply of corn for a "wet milling" plant. Yet even if the plant site had been on the banks of the Sangamon River, the company would still have had problems because the Sangamon was only a medium-sized stream, characterized by fickle tendencies. It ranged from a trickle during times of drought to a flood basin during heavy rains.

As early as October of 1916, Staley wrote his longtime associate, Charlie Schuster, in Baltimore, as follows: "We have learned that a farmer upstream has dammed up the river and created a lake, two or three miles in length, on his farm. City authorities plan to visit him and ask him to open his dam and allow the water to come down the river. If he refuses, the dam will be dynamited.

"If the dam is not holding much in volume, as has been reported, we will employ a gang of men to go up the river and open up the sandbars that are holding up considerable water. This will be expensive for us but not as expensive as shutting down the plant at this season of the year."

The pumping station which was installed three years later, together with the large conduit leading directly to the plant, enabled the company to bring in more than twice the water as ever before, assuming the river would be high enough and full enough to serve as a source of supply—a shaky assumption, at best.

The Staley numbers were impressive. "We need a Niagara of supply—10 million gallons a day, including 5 million for glucose syrup alone," founder Staley said. Then came the Sunday punch. He added, somewhat dramatically, he'd have to abandon his adopted hometown and pull stakes if "dry Decatur" could not arrange to provide a "Niagara" for his current and future expansions.

Aided by George E. Chamberlain, his general superintendent, and by Charles C. LeForgee, his general counsel, Staley prepared his case thoroughly and presented it to Mayor Dan Dineen and the members of the City Council. He suggested that a large dam be erected near an existing Sangamon River bridge and that water be impounded in a massive lake in order to permit his plant and others to grow hand in hand with the community.

Was Gene Staley's presentation to the town burghers a plan or a ploy? Was he indulging in a bit of gamesmanship? Was he, the eternal "plunger," making an easy-odds bet that he could cajole the city into capitulating to his demands? Would he really pull up stakes at a location where his company's physical assets were almost $10 million?

The response to these questions, and to other asked, unasked, and implied questions, came when he revealed, again somewhat dramatically, that his company had actually purchased, for $200,000, an "ideal 72-acre site" on the free-flowing Illinois River at Peoria, 70 miles northwest. That revelation made the local folks sit up and take notice. Staley wasn't kidding! And there was a "hometown pride" element to deal with—one that worked out in Staley's favor. Did Decatur want to feather rival Peoria's industrial development nest? No. A thousand times no. It was a classic "does Macy's help Gimbel's?" story in spades in the fast-growing economy of central Illinois.

So what happened? The situation was properly stabilized in 1920 when the City Council announced that Decatur's citizenry and its industry would need an increased supply of treated, filtered water for all, at the city reservoir, and an increased supply of raw, untreated water not only for Staley but also for Mueller and other taxpaying, payroll-creating industrial institutions.

Gene Staley was delighted with the outcome, of course, but he wasn't surprised. He felt the city had no other viable alternative. Anyway, he remarked that both his personal and professional instincts tilted strongly toward remaining in Decatur. In addition—and not unimportantly—he knew he had picked up the Peoria property at an attractive price. He knew that the riverfront property there would escalate in value.

In his persuasive closing arguments before the City Council in Decatur, he even went so far as to guarantee establishing a water-return system to the Sangamon River, downstream.

It was, in retrospect, simply another "Allah be praised" chapter in the founder's career of precipitating—or at least participating in—"cliff-hanging" scenarios long before Hollywood had any such predilections.

Scenarios without conflict, opposition, fist-shaking? Of course not. Owners of bottomland adjacent to the Sangamon River were incensed when they learned that the pro-Staley, impoundment proposition had passed. They felt they'd be disadvantaged by having their property condemned and fated forever to be nothing more than the unseen floor of a lake. One Council member, harkening to the fears of the property owners and unmoved by the long-range economic aspirations of his peers, stated: "I am not in favor of granting anything to unborn generations."

But the opposing view lacked weight. As things turned out, the City Council pressed ahead with finalizing the impoundment plan—a $2 million project. To help achieve adequate financing the city of Decatur sold $376,000 in "waterworks bonds," as they were called—issued at 5 percent in 1920, under a sinking fund arrangement, with payments to bondholders to start in 1930.

To keep costs down, the city opted for installing a 500-foot-long dam reaching 610 feet above sea level, even though some proponents demonstrated the far greater virtues of going to 615 feet. In the haste to get the new project established, some of the area was not sufficiently cleared away. The *Staley Journal,* the company's internal magazine, expressed regret. It said, "Inasmuch as this is part of the permanent basin of the lake, the failure to clear it is a matter of serious import."

Yet by 1922, there it was—Lake Decatur, the largest artificial body of water in the state of Illinois. It contained a total of 2,800 acres and it created a shoreline of 30 miles. The lake was immediately recognized as an important civic asset, lending new ambience, beauty, and recreational activity to a prairie region not noted for fishing and boating and various forms of water fun. Contained totally within Decatur's city limits, the lake soon became something for the city fathers to shout about.

Henry H. Bolz, secretary of the Decatur Association of Commerce, commented: "A. E. Staley has literally kicked the community upstairs. The lake is a monument to his wisdom."

But George Chamberlain, the Staley company's trusty general superintendent, went a bit too far in his partisan commentary. Dipping deep into hyperbole, Chamberlain spoke to the Transportation Club of America banquet March 2, 1922, and said: "Historians of the future will tell the youth of that day that A. E. Staley was the Moses of his generation. The rod of his foresight struck the rock from which the unfailing water supply gushed forth."

That was a bit much. But the founder, in attendance, offered no objections.

The big celebration came on July 4–7, 1923, when Lake Decatur was officially dedicated, featuring speeches, parades and pageants, plus aquatic events in a community where speeches, parades, and pageants had been numerous but where swimming contests, diving events, and speedboat races had been virtually nonexistent.

World and national swimming champions were among the participants in the competition. Perhaps the most famous celebrity was 19-year-old Johnny Weissmuller, who would later go on to claim five Olympic gold medals in swimming and who would go even further in renown as Hollywood's Tarzan, King of the Jungle.

In the 500-meter freestyle competition at Lake Decatur in 1923, Weissmuller—wearing the colors of the Illinois Athletic Club of Chicago—swam the distance in 6 minutes, 55 seconds for a new world record, clipping 11 seconds off the old mark.

It was an exciting holiday for a city that had never had a lake before. And in all the jubilation it was easy to forget that the lake was created in part to help grind corn, not just to provide a setting for a splash and a bash.

The Viaduct

When the Staley company began operations in 1912, it had a small plant near the northwest corner of Eldorado and Twenty-second streets. No one knew at the time it would grow in all directions—mainly toward the north and toward the east.

No one knew that in less than 70 years it would sprawl over 400 acres and would become one of the most formidable manufacturing sites in central Illinois.

Back in 1912, Twenty-second Street was called Seventh Street. It was a major north-south artery even then. But there were two problems: (1) Motorists had to cross the busy Wabash railroad tracks, immediately north of Eldorado Street, and (2) a streetcar line terminated at the area south of the tracks, converting thousands of daily riders into pedestrians who would have to cross the tracks on foot. The situation not only presented safety hazards, but it also involved a large measure of inconvenience for one and all.

By the early twenties, the Staley company's expansion and increased traffic in the neighborhood made the situation intolerable. Also, the Wabash railroad announced it needed additional tracks.

The first two "solutions" went to the extremes of being too modest and too daring. The modest proposal involved building a footbridge over the tracks so that pedestrians wouldn't have to wait for freight and passenger trains to pass. The daring proposal involved the construction of a million-dollar subway for north-south automobile traffic. Neither proposal was considered for long.

So a viaduct was proposed. In the words of A. E. Staley, Sr., "In all plausibility, I first conceived the viaduct idea." In fact, he not only had the idea, but he began implementing it long before viaduct plans were finalized. Sensing the need for substantial open space to accommodate the structural supports for a two-lane upper roadway, Gene Staley began purchasing property along Seventh Street. He knew a corridor without obstructions and encumbrances would ultimately be needed to enable a massive viaduct to take form.

Once the viaduct idea became widely known, the entire community voiced approval. With Decatur's growth moving briskly to the northeast—beyond the bothersome east-west railroad tracks—it was obvious that a viaduct would be the ideal solution to the worsening predicament alongside the Staley plant.

But who would pay for a bridge providing safe and gratis access to the land beyond the noisy trains? The answer to this question and an overall commentary on the project was recently (in 1981) provided by Thomas W. Samuels, 95-year-old attorney who came to Decatur in 1914 and who spent the better part of his life with the law firm of LeForgee, Vail and Miller.

Samuels remembered, "Since the proposed project would benefit not only the Staley company but also the Wabash Railroad Company, the City of Decatur and Decatur Township, such an undertaking would require the cooperation of all four parties. After some preliminary negotiations, they all agreed to work out a joint contract, with each party paying its proportionate share of the viaduct's cost."

(The total cost, $250,000, was finally split as follows: one-third Staley, one-third Wabash, and one-third divided equally between the city and the township.)

Back to Samuels: "The negotiations were prolonged and not without difficulty. When we had ironed out all our problems, Lee Boland, counsel for the City of Decatur, threw a bombshell into the whole proceeding. He pointed out that the southern half of the viaduct and the southern approach to the viaduct would be in the City of Decatur and the northern half would be in Decatur Township, a distinct and separate municipality. We had all known this all along, of course.

"Boland admitted there was no question about the City's authority to help build and help pay for a bridge within its boundaries, but he said he could find nothing in the statutes which authorized the City to help build only a half of a bridge within its boundaries and certainly no authority to help pay for one half or any part of a bridge outside its boundaries."

Attorney Boland's technical analysis was not without an inadvertent ripple of humor. He was objecting to the prospect of using municipal funds for construction of a half of a bridge—and this commentary conjured up a caricature of the viaduct's center leading to an exit in midair, as though poised as a takeoff ramp for some early-day Evel Kneivel. He was also postulating that the city had no business aiding a cause in which half would be physically located in someone else's backyard.

Appreciating the letter if not the spirit of the city counselor's nit-picking, Tom Samuels found it necessary to haul out his own landmark documents in order to persuade the committee of negotiators not to be enmeshed in the web of alleged legal constraints in old statutes. These statutes obviously had not envisioned the need for accommodation and cooperation among two private companies and two municipal units in planning for the erection of what Gene Staley called "a modern vehicular skyway."

Samuels recently said, "Boland was a good lawyer but was flawed by his own propensity to come up with technical objections to anything desired or proposed to be done. I reminded conferees on the negotiating committee that Thomas Jefferson had entertained serious doubts about his constitutional authority to purchase the Louisiana Territory but that 'like all wise philosophers,' as has been said of him, 'he turned his back to the doctrine and did the act.' I suggested that we do likewise. We did. And the viaduct was built. So far as I know, neither the wisdom nor the legality of what we did has ever been questioned."

Whew! That was close. Actually, it was so close that a narrow interpretation of language in—or not in—an old statute threatened to thwart the whole viaduct project. There was even thought, for a time, of considering a new "solution," namely, abandoning the key north-south artery and closing off Seventh Street, thus forbidding easy public access to a new northeast region of promise and opportunity.

As things turned out, final plans were announced in 1925. Construction started in 1926. And on July 3, 1928, a ribbon was cut signaling the opening of "the Staley Viaduct, the great, safe, expediting route to the northeast." Since that time, areas beyond the tracks have blossomed into shopping centers, subdivisions, and new hubs of commercial activity. The dangerous grade crossing adjacent to the Staley plant thus moved into ancient history much in the same way as the Wabash steam

82

engines ultimately were relegated to the obscurity of the past.

"The Castle in the Cornfields"

The place: A construction shack on the northwest corner of West William and Church streets in the heart of Decatur, Illinois.
The year: Summer of 1928.
The project: A new Masonic Temple, to cost approximately $750,000.
The time: Dusk.

As daylight dimmed, an assistant superintendent in the J. L. Simmons Company construction shack began to light up several dozen kerosene lanterns. It had been a long, hot day. The employee's final chore would involve taking the lanterns to various positions around the site so that the burning wicks, glowing through the red barrel-shaped glass chimneys, could warn passersby to steer clear of the construction impediments.

The employee was E. L. Simmons, 31-year-old great-grandson of the construction company's founder. While he was igniting the wicks in the drab and dusty quarters alongside the Cecil B. DeMille–type Masonic fortification, he heard a knock on the door.

"Come in," Simmons beckoned.

And in came a portly, perspiring visitor named A. E. Staley, Sr. He was carrying rolled-up papers under his arm. "I've got some architectural plans I'd like to show you," the visitor said.

"Who are you, please?" Simmons asked.

"My name is Staley," the uninvited guest replied. "I run a company at the east end of town. We're in the corn refining and soybean crushing business. We need a new office building."

"Do those drawings show the way you want to go?"

"I think so."

"Who prepared them?"

"Aschauer and Waggoner, a local architectural firm. But the

plans are rather preliminary. They're far from final. Yet I've been doing some investigating. I've learned that the Simmons people have been doing a marvelous job with the Masonic Temple. Maybe they could do a marvelous job for me."

Simmons explained he was only a middle-management employee whose superiors were in Chicago and Bloomington, Indiana, prompting the visitor to say, "You're the type of person I want to talk to. Let me show you my plans."

Inasmuch as the drawings were only floor plans, with no elevations and no overall perspective of the proposed building's exterior, Simmons asked, "What's your building going to look like?"

"Come to my office tomorrow morning at eight o'clock and I'll show you," the visitor said.

"I'll be there," Simmons responded. "I know about your company. I know where you're located. I'll be prompt."

Next day, as the meeting started in the then-existing two-story office building at the east end of town, Staley explained that his casual drop-in the prior evening was not as inadvertent as it may have seemed. He further explained he had done a "little checking" and had learned of the construction company's credentials.

And then he hauled out the rest of the drawings.

Simmons recently (in 1981) recalled what then occurred:

"I wasn't prepared for what I saw. Actually, I doubt if anyone would have been prepared. As we sat around a table in that old, frame office building alongside the company's football field, I was amazed by what Gene Staley showed me. Actually, I had expected to see somewhat of a nice structure—something surely a lot better than that old wooden office building which leaned firmly to the east.

"But I surely didn't expect to see a drawing of a mammoth building with a giant tower—a building more imposing than many new office structures in Chicago. I remember my first words were, 'It looks like a state capitol.' I was tempted to ask, 'Are you sure you want to consider something this large?'—but I kept this thought to myself.

84

" 'What do you think?' Staley inquired sharply.

" 'Such a building would be extremely costly,' I commented.

"I'm not sure Staley heard this observation. If he did, he didn't acknowledge it. Perhaps he had discussed costs with his very fine architects or perhaps some of his people at the plant provided estimates but he seemed unwilling to discuss costs with me. The main thing he wanted to talk about was granite. 'I want to use granite from Mt. Airy, not too far from where I was born in North Carolina.'

"Trying to clear my own mind, I said to myself that if this is a million-dollar building it would cost another half million to buy granite and bring it in from North Carolina. But on that first day it was no time for me to be bringing up negative reactions. He asked me to take all the drawings and to study them for a few days and to come back and give him an estimate of how long it would take to finish the job. And as I left he warned me not to forget about the North Carolina granite.

"On my second visit, I told him that it would take maybe a year to a year and a half to build the monster, even on a hurry-up schedule. And it was plain to see he wanted a hurry-up schedule. Then came my bravery. I told him the structure should be built of Indiana limestone. I even told him of a supply of beautiful limestone, unusually dense in texture, available at the Shawnee Stone Company quarry near Bloomington, Indiana. And I stressed the fact it would be foolhardy to use North Carolina granite unnecessarily.

"Here was a man who wanted the best. 'Granite is best,' he said, over and over. But, somewhat to my surprise, he finally seemed willing to compromise. When I suggested we could use granite sparingly—for the areas around the main entrance—and limestone everywhere else, he countered with 'Let's use granite for the wide array of steps at the main entrance and also let's use it for the visible part of the foundation beneath the elevation of the main floor.' I said okay. But I had the feeling that he was leaving a dream by the wayside when he agreed, reluctantly, to go mainly to limestone. But there was no doubt in my mind that an all-granite structure would have been a luxury beyond common sense, beyond need. When I assured him there would be no compromise in beauty and no compromise in structural integrity, he gave in.

"The most unbelievable part of the experience was the fact that he never asked for a detailed estimate. He knew and I knew and the architects knew and his accounting department knew we were talking about a new administration building which would cost a million dollars or more to build and equip. But during our planning sessions he never asked for cost breakouts. He seemed interested only in the quality of the job. 'I trust you,' he told me. And, believe me, his assurance of trust translated into a heavy burden of responsibility our company felt throughout the job.

"Those plans which he showed me at the Masonic Temple shack and at his office the following day were good enough to use when the Simmons company put out for preliminary bids from subcontractors. When we got to the point of needing detailed drawings and specifications and supply requirements, all Gene Staley talked about was expediting the job. 'Let's avoid delays,' he ordered, over and over again."

The Staley company's board minutes of December 31, 1928, show the approval of a contract with Simmons "for the erection of an office and administration building, to cost approximately $1,200,000, to be completed about May 1, 1930." At the next meeting of the board a resolution was passed concerning the "uncompleted portion of the Simmons contract including the costs for plumbing, heating, elevators, electrical wiring, and interior decorating amounting to a total of $492,366."

In sum, an amount of $1,692,366 was allocated to underwrite the venture.

And what a venture.

J. L. Simmons moved his residence and office from Bloomington to Decatur once the project was approved, and he took over as unit manager. After a short spurt continuing as assistant superintendent he became superintendent, working closely with the architects and with a group of Chicago engineers in setting forth the logistics for the biggest construction job in

Decatur's history. On one occasion when a Chicago engineer was informed about the Staley project, the engineer blurted out "Decatur, Illinois? A building like that in that hick, high-grass town? An edifice like that is worthy of any city in the nation."

Ground was broken on February 16, 1929, and the new offices were occupied April 19, 1930.

When the local newspapers used illustrations of the heroic, spectacular Aschauer and Waggoner drawings, showing that the proposed structure would be like a mammoth birthday cake with tapering insets at several levels of the 206-foot-high building, the editors began to call it "The Castle in the Cornfields." Yet very few people realized that ultimately the building's interiors and its landscaping would be as dramatic as the high-rise silhouette.

Perhaps the best early description was that used by Ruth E. Cade, editor of the monthly house organ called the *Staley Journal*. Eager to spread the good news to those administrative and clerical employees who would, one day soon, be occupying the spectacular structure, editor Cade provided a rundown of the wonders to come:

> The new building, 14 stories high, will be the tallest structure downstate.
>
> From the ground to the top of the observation tower, it will rise 206 feet, more than twice the height of the Standard Life Building, the tallest in Decatur now.
>
> It will front 264 feet on the north side of Eldorado street, and run back parallel with Twenty-second street, 104 feet. It will set back 200 feet from the Eldorado street line and 250 feet from the viaduct.
>
> It will house all the administrative and executive offices of the company, the grain department and the clerical force.
>
> The architecture is distinctively American in the perpendicular style. The exterior finish will be of Indiana limestone.
>
> An observation tower will be the striking feature of the building. The topmost observation platform will be en-

closed in glass. The dome of the tower will be roofed with gilded tile to enhance the effect obtained from viewing the structure at a distance. The grounds surrounding the structure will be landscaped by Jans Jensen, nationally known landscaping artist of Chicago.

The principal portion of the building will be six stories high. The main entrance will be in the center of the Eldorado facade. The entrance will be reached by a flight of steps 60 feet wide. There are to be five doorways, surmounted by bronze arches in the entrance. Over the doorways will be four bronze lanterns, each six feet in height. The doorways are to open into a rotunda treated in marble and bronze. The rotunda will be 100 feet long and two full stories high. That part of the main floor not occupied by the rotunda is to be devoted to general and private offices. Offices also will be on the floors above.

The president's suite, to be panelled in walnut, and the assembly room of the board of directors, with offices of minor executives adjoining, will occupy the eighth floor. Part of the ninth will be given over to a cafeteria for employees. A kitchen to serve both the employees' cafeteria and a restaurant for executives is to be attached to the cafeteria. The executives' dining room will be on the tenth floor, opening onto a lounging room.

On the east and west terraces outside Mr. Staley's private suite will be flower beds, which may be reached through French doors of bronze. All exterior doors of the building, and all window frames, are to be of the same metal. Inside doors to private offices are to be of Art Metal (sculptured bronze). These doors will swing on ball bearings.

Three elevators, two for passengers and one for freight, will be of the high-speed type, powered by electricity. They are to be equipped with push-button controls and automatic floor levelers.

A system for heating and ventilating with washed air will be provided. This system will cool the building in the summer, keeping the air inside eight or ten degrees lower in temperature than outside. Both the heating in winter and the cooling in summer will be under positive thermostatic control. In summer it will not be necessary to open the windows for ventilation.

The pneumatic tube system for conveying inter-department messages will be built into the building. Steam and power will be conducted to it through underground tunnels from the present power plant. A private telephone system and exchange sufficient to serve a small town is being planned.

All the floors of the building are to be underlaid with ducts containing telephone and power wires. In every five square feet of floor space will be an outlet, kept covered when not in use by a cap sunk to floor level. Wherever a desk may be placed, one of the outlets will be near it, ready to furnish current for lights and fans, and wires for telephones.

Furniture built of steel is to be bought for the building. Present office equipment of wood will not be moved into the new structure.

The office building was hailed as "Staley's showplace" long before it was finished. As an extra touch of class, the founder added a fountain at the north (rear) of the building—this decision coming when the project was well under way—and he also summoned General Electric Company to install "theatrical illumination to make the tower a rainbow of beauty, visible for 20 miles."

After the headquarters site was dedicated and occupied, the main thing people talked about was the vivid, multicolored illumination which provided a nocturnal decoration for the towering edifice. Families would drive into Decatur from many miles around. One description went like this: "Visitors would drive up to the five-acre park, with that jewel of a building as the centerpiece. They'd find a nearby location and they'd just sit there—enthralled by the beauty of the brilliant light and marvelling at the sight of an office building more majestic than anything they had ever seen."

Beyond doubt, such comments were precisely what Gene Staley had in mind when the project was still on the drawing board. And that spectacular light show, an innovative phenomenon for which General Electric had to design special control panels, was the most talked-about frosting on Gene Staley's birthday-cake-shaped edifice. "It's an automatic Thyratron-activated Polychromatic floodlighting wonder of the world," a company booklet bragged. The founder proclaimed, "We're more than a company. We're a symbol. Macon County corn and soybean farmers already know where we are, but we've made it possible for them to look from afar and see Staley in all its glory."

Less visible than the 160,000-square-foot industrial fortress was that rear courtyard featuring a reflection pool 40 feet in diameter with a fountain in the center. Around the circumference were 58 bronze frogs, each squirting its own little stream of water inward, plus five bronze herons toward the middle of the pool, squirtless. "There's never been a fountain like it," the founder observed—an unchallenged statement.

The most important aspect of the showplace was often lost in the excitement of the external theatrics. In a recent retrospective, Simmons said, "Gene Staley wanted a place his employees would be proud of. He wanted them to feel they were part of a special sort of empire. He was confident his company would grow and he wanted the right environment for the future. Even the workers out in the dusty factory seemed proud of the new office building. If they were cynical or envious, they usually didn't show it. A plant foreman—not aware of my role in constructing the building—once told me at a dinner: 'I'm from Staley—out where the lights go on.'

"Granted some people, who no doubt didn't know Gene Staley as well as I knew him, probably thought he was out of his mind. When the October, 1929, Great Depression came, some people probably wondered how the Staley company would ever be able to afford that fancy castle at the east end of town.

"Actually, all through the construction period there never seemed to be any concern on Gene Staley's part when I went in, on the last day of every month, and handed him an invoice for the payments needed. Only on one occasion did I find myself worrying a bit. This happened to be in 1929 when the monthly invoice I had in my pocket was pretty stiff. As I handed it to him, I said: 'You'll have to dig pretty deep in your pocket to find the funds to handle this one.'

"He did frown a bit when he saw the amount. But not for long. He called in his accountant, Ray Scherer, and told him, 'Here's the bad news. Got enough in the till to handle this?'

"I'll never forget what that accountant said. He told his boss, 'We made more on the "call market" [playing grain futures at the Chicago Board of Trade] last week than that.'

"I shouldn't have worried, I guess. Staley had his financing fully planned and I'm sure he even factored in the escalations and, of course, the risks. He knew what he wanted and got what he wanted—except for all that unnecessary North Carolina granite. Every now and then when I look back over the years I find myself wondering if I shouldn't have let him realize the fullness of his dream by bringing in that granite from Mt. Airy. When I got to know him better I found out that no luxury was too great if he thought it was best for his company."

The question has since been asked, over and over: "Was 'The Castle in the Cornfields,' among other things, a monument to the vanity, vitality, and vision of the castle's monarch?"

And the answer is "of course."

The foregoing adventures were immensely successful. Yet in an imperfect world each had its own telltale imperfections. In all three instances, short-term needs were obviously easier to perceive than long-term needs. Ultimately, all three projects had to go back to the drawing board.

The Lake—Later

The lake turned out to be too small and too shallow. Silting problems developed shortly after the 1923 dedication. Thirty years later, in 1953, bascules were installed and the height of the dam was raised to 615 feet above sea level. As a result, the lake's surface was increased from 2,800 to 3,300 acres, but its shoreline remained essentially the same—30 miles in total.

A conflict, city versus the Staley corporation, developed as the "new lake" was being planned with the city attempting to levy a charge for the company's use of untreated water despite an earlier written agreement to the contrary. The company wound up voluntarily contributing $250,000 to help underwrite the cost of the new civic improvement.

The Viaduct—Later

The Twenty-second Street viaduct became its own worst enemy. By serving as a gateway to the north and northeast and by helping create new pockets of population where farmland had once quietly flourished, the two-lane viaduct ultimately became an occasional bottleneck and scene of heavy traffic. Latter-day horn honking by impatient motorists and truck drivers was not exactly what founder Staley and the other pioneers had in mind.

Under the philosophy of "the more things change, the more they remain the same," the old problem of access resurfaced forcefully in the late seventies with a latter-day encore of the earlier demand, "We need a better roadway to the north and northeast." Accordingly, plans were developed in 1981 for widening the viaduct's southern approach, where traffic tieups were most frequent.

The "Castle"—Later

When the editor of the *Staley Journal* predicted the new non-air-conditioned office building would have cool air in the summertime and that there would be no need for opening windows for ventilation, her commentary was perhaps the most incorrect forecast in the company's history. Granted that in 1930 air conditioning was a rather new phenomenon, found mainly in motion picture theaters, but it is obvious in retrospect that insufficient attention was paid to the inescapable discomforts in a virtually airless, monolithic summertime "oven."

The fact of the matter was that "The Castle in the Corn-fields" was termed a "sweltering mausoleum" by those working in it during the hot summers. Not until 1970 did a merciful breath of refrigerated air arrive in the otherwise exemplary offices and hallways. (A behind-the-scenes description of the heat created in the halls of management, generated by pro and con arguments on air conditioning, will be found in Chapter Eleven.)

CHAPTER SIX

TRIALS AND TRIUMPHS
OF THE THIRTIES

When President Herbert Hoover was inaugurated early in 1929, he radiated optimism while declaring, "In no nation are the fruits of accomplishment more secure." Forecasting that poverty would be eliminated and that Americans would have "two chickens in every pot and a car in every garage," Hoover equated the Republican party with prosperity and he underlined the crucial role of the business system in a nation whose economy is nourished by the private sector's payrolls and taxes.

Son of an Iowa farmer, the new president also sensed the importance of agriculture to the country's well-being, illustrating his attitude by promptly calling Congress into a special session during which a Federal Farm Board was created in order to deal with agricultural surpluses. Also he led the fight for adoption of the Hawley-Smoot Tariff Act, which increased duties on some farm imports and which provided a temporary period of protectionism under the U.S. flag.

Gene Staley and his Decatur colleagues were delighted. Rose-colored glasses were the accoutrement of the day. All seemed right with the world.

Then came October and the Great Depression.

Unanticipated by those confident Americans coast to coast who'd soon be engulfed in its disastrous consequences, the Great Depression was a monstrous catastrophe that started with a stock market crash in the United States, sending its shock waves toward every corner of the earth. The devastating situation for the American business community was a thousandfold worse than that during the infamous Panic of 1907 when founder Staley doggedly peddled stock in his one-year-old corporation despite the economic turmoil of the time.

No one in the nation was untouched by the effects of the Great Depression, which stalked forward from late 1929 into the decade of the thirties. During the early period of the crisis, a large proportion of the American financial community was in disarray. Thousands of banks failed. Mortgage foreclosures became commonplace. Thirty billion dollars in stock values vanished.

By 1931, total wages fell to 60 percent below those of 1929. "Brother, Can You Spare a Dime?" became a mournful national theme song. Well-educated men sold apples on street corners. Unemployment jumped to 13 million—almost a third of the nation's work force.

The Staley company's customers, representing many industries, were immediately affected by the course of events. Yet the Decatur corporation withstood the economic tremors better than most. This was largely attributable to what founder Staley called "a fundamental product line centering on food." Even in a depression, people had to eat, cattle had to eat, poultry had to eat. Corn and soybean products loomed more importantly than ever before. They were nonfrivolous, nonluxury necessities.

The Staley company's depression era arithmetic went a zigzag course starting with a net profit of more than $2 million on sales of $19 million in 1929 and falling to less than a half million on almost $18 million in sales in 1930 before plummeting to a $160,000 loss on $13 million in sales in 1931. Heavy expenses involved in occupying the new office building were responsible in part for the decline in 1930 and 1931.

Then came five successive profitable years before 1937 brought a return to the loss column to the extent of a $71,000 deficit on almost $23 million in sales, the loss having been caused in part by a drought and high costs of scarce corn and soybeans.

Importantly, the Staley enterprise was staunchly enough established to withstand the trials of the thirties, and in fact, the period provided an opportunity for market development, manufacturing improvements, and technological break-throughs. In sum, the terrible thirties were a test—a test enabling the company to "pass with flying colors." That test has obviously been more pleasant to perceive retrospectively than was the actual day-by-day struggle, considering the nature of the nation's lingering economic malaise as the Depression wound down and as a new war began stirring on the European continent.

As evidence of Gene Staley's confidence when the tempestuous thirties dawned, he amazed his fellow workers by announcing—in January, 1930—that he was heading for a two-month vacation in Miami.

If his timing during the Depression seemed a bit eyebrow-raising to some, his actual decision to "vacate" was even more surprising. He had always insisted he "didn't have time to take time off." Yet now he was 63 years old and his diabetic condition was surely not improving. "Who'll take over the reins when the founder ultimately fades away?" was a favorite question inside and outside the company walls—almost a parlor game. And the founder was sensitively attuned to what others were thinking and saying. Even when he hadn't appeared to be listening, he was listening.

So off to the sunny south he went. He and his wife, Emma, traveled by train. They left the cold climate of Decatur several days after their chauffeur and cook departed in the family Pierce Arrow, a cumbersome but stylish sedan with its headlights poised at the tips of the front fenders.

For that first Florida holiday the Staleys rented a large

apartment. Despite its comforts, Gene Staley was edgy, the result being his decision to "buy a home of my own, on or near the Miami waterfront," a decision he implemented the following winter when he purchased a mansion on Biscayne Bay.

Ostensibly, the founder went to Florida in 1930 to see if he could learn to relax and to bask in the warm sunshine of the semitropical zone. But in fact he had another purpose. He wanted to trigger a transition period that would enable a new and younger management team to run the show at Decatur. Somewhat weary and wary of being a constant one-man-band and, also, concerned about the possible trauma of management succession, he knew he'd be looking over everyone's shoulder if he remained always on the home-front scene. He also knew the stay-at-homes would have to learn to endure various burdens if he'd get out of town on a voyage more extended than a round trip to the Baltimore office.

Candidates for the succession process were few in number. Far and away out front as the odds-on favorite was the founder's older son, Augustus Eugene, Jr., executive vice president, who was then 27 years old. Yet there were two others who were theoretical candidates on the basis of overall prominence. One was not a member of the family but the other was. There is no evidence that Gene Staley gave too much thought to these candidates at the time, but nonetheless they were plainly in view, for all to see.

Allowing that "the old man" (as many of his closest friends respectfully and affectionately called him) may have considered a non-Staley for successor, the one and only nonfamily standout in management ranks was 28-year-old Edwin K. Scheiter, vice president and board member, who had joined the company in 1918 and who had moved rapidly into prominence as a skilled strategist in sales administration.

The senior Staley's attitude concerning Ed Scheiter was best expressed in the following Staley-endorsed comments published earlier in the internal publication, the *Staley Journal:*

"Mr. Scheiter is a young man. He is in fact so young that we refrain from printing his age for fear that it might lead someone to err in underestimating his ability. His progress in the sales department has been astonishing. We don't wish to advertise Mr. Scheiter to the point that we might lose his services to some other company but we cannot refrain from the statement that his future opens on a broad horizon."

Some testimonial! "Don't let him be pirated away by some competitor" was what Gene Staley had in mind.

Thus, a case could be properly made that Ed Scheiter stood high as the elder Staley's fair-haired boy and was possibly worth consideration for a top job if avoidance of nepotism was to be a controlling factor in the boss's judgment.

(Later on—much later, in 1958—Scheiter did indeed become president—for seven years. He retired from the board in February, 1978, and died eight months later.)

Then . . .

On the other hand, allowing that in the early thirties the founder may have been leaning toward keeping management control within the family, there was not only the older son, Gus, to consider. Among the senior Staley's four other children there was an additional son on the scene, more prominent locally than Gus.

The second son was A. Rollin Staley, who was 23 years old in 1930—almost four years younger than his brother. Rollin had attended the University of Illinois and had shown only modest enthusiasm for business pursuits.

Rollin Staley had marched to a different drumbeat. After leaving college his interest turned to flying airplanes and driving fast cars. His extracurricular adventures worried his father, particularly when compared with other son Gus's conservative behavior, prim decorum, and distaste for public displays of any sort.

In fact, Rollin had not completely settled down by 1930 and was actually—if not theoretically—a noncandidate for succession. But he was there, highly visible as a Staley scion in a town where any Staley was ipso facto a factor not to be ignored. Such was the price of prominence in a smallish sort of community.

(Unpredictable in nature and often defiant in stance, Rollin

Staley did ultimately choose a serious, narrow path. He joined the company in 1931; he became a vice president; he resigned as an employee in 1956; he served on the board for 27 years. Moving in 1957 into an extravagant Polynesian-style home in Naples, Florida, he showed his colors by christening his showplace "Rebel's Rest." He died in 1968.)

So those were (in sports terms, not unfamiliar to the founder) the executive "reserves" of the early thirties. Those were the potential management "substitutes" who were available for the call to move upstairs. In one way or the other, Gus Staley and Ed Scheiter and Rollin Staley had to be dealt with—or not dealt with—if any top-level readjustments were to be made.

Did Gene Staley, therefore, deal promptly with the problem early in 1930 as, indeed, had been his plan? No, he didn't. Instead, he brooded about the problem. But he took no immediate action. Despite his penchant for impulsiveness, he decided against impulsiveness.

His early 1930 absence from Decatur did serve as somewhat of a test period. It provided an opportunity for the "substitutes" in the Decatur snow belt to show what they could do while the founder basked in the Miami sunshine. Yet there was hardly a day when Staley wasn't on the phone—asking questions, giving counsel, providing encouragement.

During the next winter season, starting in November of 1930, there were rumors that "now he'll act." But he didn't. By the time he left for his second sojourn in Florida he had decided simply to entrust his executive vice president son, Gus, with a few extra responsibilities and he had also decided to mark time before making any formal adjustments in the company's high command. Realizing, however, that adjustments were inevitable he stewed and fretted about the situation, but was nonetheless reluctant to take himself out of the driver's seat which he had occupied since the company was founded prior to the turn of the century.

The only new element in the 1930–1931 winter period was the founder's decision to spend three months instead of two at his southern retreat. After all, his reasoning went, making a change in his company's management infrastructure was a postponable decision as long as his health remained firm despite the discomforts of diabetes. Yet, he fussed and worried about the situation throughout his three-month vacation. The long-distance telephone bill, reflecting frequent calls between Miami and Decatur, reached an all-time high.

Not until the founder's 1931–1932 Florida trip did he decide it was time to act. Early in 1932 he confided to intimates that —unsurprisingly—the Number One son, Gus, would move into the presidency.

The change became official upon Gene Staley's arrival home when the well-tanned founder presided at the March 15, 1932, meeting of the board. The company's announcement said: "A. E. Staley, Sr., was elected chairman of the board of directors at the board's Annual Meeting. Until this year he has been president. His son, A. E. Staley, Jr., was elected president." The scenario, which belatedly unfolded, was as simple as that.

Even though the latter-day term chief executive officer was not used during the board's discussions, observers rightly noted that the new chairman would continue to be the primary boss and the president would be the secondary boss. In other words, Gene Staley would in actuality remain chief executive officer and Gus Staley would be chief administrative and operational officer, one step down the ladder. Fair enough.

Did the young Staley relish the new job? No. Had he campaigned and strategized for the presidency? No.

Then why did he take it? More out of duty than desire. He had profound respect for his father, and he was concerned about his father's health. Also, he was very much concerned about the future of the company. Above all things he was diligent, trustworthy, responsible—and able. Charismatic and personable? No. Serious and stern? Yes.

With a mixture of resolve and reluctance, the second generation thus moved into the front office, a move which strongly suggested that upon the father's retirement or death, the junior Staley would take over the helm of the growing empire.

The elder Staley added a special dimension to the situation

100

when he revealed to friends and business associates that he very much enjoyed Florida and that he'd stay down there for a longer period during future years.

Yet those who knew Gene Staley knew he'd never totally relinquish his hold. They knew that Miami would never really be a thousand miles from Decatur in actual remoteness as long as the senior Staley could pick up a telephone or dictate a letter.

"It was his company," a longtime friend observed. "He alone created the corporation, delegating responsibilities only to those he personally hired and implicitly trusted. The company's blood was in his veins. He was a magician who cajoled, wheedled, pleaded, borrowed, persevered. He fashioned and formed the substance of the corporation. He thought, ate, and slept corn and soybeans. Even from Florida he knew he'd be able to keep an eye on Gus, not out of distrust or lack of confidence but out of habit. He had confidence in Gus. He was determined that Gus would succeed and he felt a responsibility to nudge Gus along, step by step. But the big decisions of the thirties were always made by the founder. His title wasn't important. He could have been without title or portfolio, but he still would have ruled the roost. He could have been in Zanzibar with a shortwave radio and he still would have found a way to coach his son and to call the major signals from the sidelines."

The early thirties brought in a new system to further refine corn oil and also brought in improved processes for soy meal and soy flour and soy oil. Soy flour for use as a binder in the manufacture of sausages was greeted by the meat processing industry, and soy oil began to work its way into oleomargarine, an emerging wonder of the world preparing to compete presumptuously all-out against butter.

The dairy states, notably Wisconsin, took a dim view of oleomargarine's emergence. They lobbied effectively and insisted that the federal government levy a tax of 10 cents a pound on colored margarine. They referred to the new substitute spread as "like lard—or worse." Ultimately they didn't keep margarine out, but they did fight strenuously, and successfully, for regulations that forced margarine manufacturers to make their product white, and that brought about the insertion—in each package of margarine—of a capsule of yellow food color which enabled housewives to stir up a yellow spread looking very much like—but not quite tasting like—butter.

In a less controversial area, the University of Illinois dramatized its campaign for soy oil utilization by painting all of its agricultural buildings with soybean-based oil paint.

And at the Staley company, soy sauce—hitherto an import from the Orient—was added to the product line.

Depression hangovers notwithstanding, the Staley company broke out the horns and confetti in 1934 in recognition of its twenty-fifth year of Decatur presence. In the *Decatur Herald,* Gene Staley was hailed as the builder of the "world's largest independent corn products company." Wearing an ill-fitting suit in a photo appearing in the *Herald,* the founder nonetheless sported a smile plus a rose in the lapel of his coat.

The *Herald* story saluted "the men and women employed in the production of 80 different varieties and fluidities of starch, corn oil, corn sugar, soybean flour, meal, oil, feed and other products." The newspaper's story added, "Today, the Staley property comprises 56 buildings on 300 acres."

On the national scene, politics were on page one. Gene Staley, a lifelong Democrat, had reservations in 1932 about Franklin Delano Roosevelt's New Deal and was equally unenthusiastic about Herbert Hoover. Even though Staley had always believed in the importance of voting, he had decided to abstain in the presidential election in November, 1932. But he had gone to the polling place to cast a straight Democratic ballot for congressional, state, and local candidates.

President Roosevelt, in Staley's view, was a potential dictator with socialistic tendencies. During the first two years of Roosevelt's initial term in office, Staley and his colleagues made several trips to Washington, D.C., to oppose newly established reciprocal—or so-called reciprocal—trade treaties, especially the treaty with the Netherlands under which no import

102

This headline from a *Decatur Review* of 1930 told of an explosion at Staley. Note misspelling of the word "receive."

Early quality control was conducted in small but adequate quarters in Decatur.

Immediately following World War I, Staley glucose syrup was shipped to England in large barrels.

In 1920, when he was chosen as the Democrats' nominee for vice president of the United States, Franklin Delano Roosevelt visited the Staley plant in Decatur, accompanied by Mrs. Roosevelt. The visitors are flanked by A. E. Staley, company founder (right), and George E. Chamberlain, general superintendent (left). Roosevelt and James M. Cox, the presidential nominee, were defeated by Republicans Warren G. Harding and Calvin Coolidge. Roosevelt later was elected to four terms as president in 1932, 1936, 1940 and 1944, the only man in history to hold that distinction.

Thornton C. "Chase" Burwell, top left, was a long-time vice president and manager of transportation. Edwin Scheiter, above right, joined Staley upon graduation from Decatur High School and rose through the ranks to become the first non–Staley-family president of the company. James H. Galloway, below left, was the company's first plant superintendent, while C. C. "Dok" Hollis, below right, was placed in charge of the firm's Chicago office in 1927.

Officers of the Staley Sales Corporation in the early years included, seated from left, Roy M. Ives, Ray C. Scherer, A. E. Staley, Jr., and Edwin K. Scheiter. Standing is Company President A. E. Staley, Sr.

Members of the early grocery products sales force drove their own delivery trucks, in an attempt to assure customers of prompt, individual service.

Lake Decatur has for many years provided an important supply of water to the Staley company. The upper floor of the pumping station, at the shoreline, formerly served as headquarters for the Staley Fellowship Club.

Some early delivery trucks displayed signs identifying the company they represented.

The Staley Viaduct, a "great, safe route to the Northeast," was opened on July 3, 1928.

The viaduct, which carries traffic over the plant site, was built as a cooperative effort among the Staley company, the Wabash Railroad, the City of Decatur and Decatur Township.

A. E. Staley was proud of his 1929 touring car and prouder of the Administration Building erected at the east end of town.

Ground breaking for the building took place on February 16, 1929. On April 19, 1930, employees moved in. At 206 feet, the structure was the tallest and most modern in downstate Illinois. It has been referred to in print by such names as "The Castle in the Cornfields" and "Lighthouse of the Prairie."

The seal of the A. E. Staley Manufacturing Company is embossed in granite on the face of the company's Administration Building in Decatur.

The lobby of the Administration Building is a favorite spot for visitors, many of whom are noticeably impressed by the architectural style of the building's interior. Founder Staley insisted that no expense be spared when he commissioned the building's construction.

duty would be placed on sago and tapioca starches, which Staley called "substitutes to compete against American corn starch."

In 1936, the company's founder decided to switch his allegiance to the GOP. When Governor Alfred M. Landon of Kansas, the Republican hopeful, passed through Decatur by train, Staley went aboard to contribute $5,000 in his own name and $1,000 in his wife's name to Landon's campaign.

In explaining to reporters he said, "I'm a million miles away from the New Deal variety of Democrats" and "Governor Landon has the ability, the integrity, the trustworthiness, the intelligence, and the desire to serve America for the good of all the people."

He added, "I was born and raised in North Carolina where you are born a Democrat and stay a Democrat but I won't support Roosevelt and his crowd." When Landon was overwhelmingly defeated and when Roosevelt went triumphantly into office for a second term, Staley was incensed and he resolved to work all the harder in the future for the Republican cause.

On the industrial front, 1936 brought a bit of good news to the soybean scene when the Chicago Board of Trade opened trading in what it called a "new commodity." The National Soybean Processors Association announced "the new market in futures will encourage banks to finance investments in soybean crushing capacity due to greater security through the opportunity of hedging."

The Staley company welcomed the prospect of seeing soybean futures as well as corn futures on the "big board" at Chicago, but the company felt, with justification, that it had been on top of the commodities picture all along, chiefly because the Staley buyer was a man named Horace J. Kapp who had attained national prominence as "the Decatur wizard." Kapp had joined the company as Grain Department manager in 1930 for what developed into a 23-year career, using statistics, judgment, and a bit of intuition in the important job of purchasing the company's raw materials "at the right price, at the right pace and with the right inventories." (Perhaps the greatest tribute ever paid to Kapp was one voiced by a competitor, Howard Wascher, chairman of the prestigious Corn Products Company. When asked to comment on the Decatur-based second largest corn refiner, Wascher said, "Staley? They've got Horace Kapp."

The year 1936 also brought about a development that demonstrated the elder Staley's concern for his own longevity and for the future financial stability of his immediate family. With the guidance of his principal attorney and longtime friend, Charles C. LeForgee, Gene Staley created a trusteeship for the benefit of his children. A. E. Staley, Jr., his older son, was named cotrustee along with the Baltimore Safety Deposit Company, a bank with which the founder had dealt for more than 30 years.

The trusteeship gave 6,000 shares of Staley common stock each to A. E. Staley, Jr., A. Rollin Staley, Ruth Staley Hunt, Mary Staley Annan, and Ione Staley Dunlap. In addition, 1,000 shares went to the founder's wife, Emma.

Provision was made that during the founder's lifetime the 31,000 trusteeship shares would be voted by him and that upon his death voting rights would pass to A. E. Staley, Jr. Those 31,000 shares represented approximately 72 percent of the corporation's 42,000 common shares outstanding at the time. In addition, the founder retained 5,254 common shares in his own name. He also held ownership of an undisclosed number of preference shares—a dominant majority amount.

Feeling secure in the knowledge that his family's future had been meticulously planned, Gene Staley and his wife left for Florida in November, 1936, for a stay lasting almost six months. Despite the distance, Gene kept in close touch with Gus by phone and correspondence.

Following the founder's return to Decatur in the spring of 1937, his son—not known for rash actions—did something rash. Along with vice presidents Ed Scheiter and H. P. Dunlap, young Gus Staley flew to Indianapolis to see the 500-mile auto race, making the trip in a single-engine Bellanca which a Chicago dealer was heralding as an ideal plane for corporate use.

The trip in itself wasn't really rash but the circumstances were. To begin with, young Gus Staley and Ed Scheiter and Hay Dunlap—all members of the board—didn't check things out with the founder before departing. In Scheiter's words, here's what happened:

"We had left early in the morning and we saw no need to bother the chairman. That afternoon in Indianapolis, after the race concluded, we went to the airport where the pilot reported that due to a storm west of Indianapolis he would fly back to Decatur by a circuitous route to the south. Even though we avoided the storm, the turbulence was severe. We arrived back in Decatur two hours later than scheduled.

"About a half hour after I got home, a friend phoned to advise he had heard that the senior Staley was 'wild.' The boss was at the St. Nicholas Hotel that afternoon telling anyone within hearing distance that he was firing Gus Staley and Hay Dunlap and me because we had 'secretly' gone on an airplane trip, using poor judgment by having three company executives flying together, particularly in a private plane, and, above all, flying in a storm. He announced at the hotel that he could no longer entrust the conduct of his business to such stupid people.

"I phoned Gus right away. We agreed that his father was right. Gus went to see his father late that evening. The next day, after we all had received a well-deserved lecture, we were reinstated in our jobs.

"I learned an important lesson, namely, think first, then act. I had never seen the boss in such a violent display of anger. He never mentioned the matter again but I never forgot it."

The Staley annual report which was issued on February 20, 1937, and which detailed the company's performance for the prior year, indicated that the payroll numbered 1,702 employees. In discussing products, the annual report highlighted Cream cornstarch for use in cooking and baking, cube gloss starch for laundry use, and corn syrup in four flavors for pancakes and waffles—all retail items.

105

Yet these traditional grocery store products accounted for less than 10 percent of total sales. The heavyweight products were starches for many processed food and nonfood uses; corn sugars for rayon, vinegar, and leather manufacturers; gluten feed for dealers and mixers; soy flour for bakers and meat packers; soy meal for poultry and livestock; and soy oil for paint and soap companies and for an increasing variety of edible purposes.

In a year-later annual report, issued February 10, 1938, management's commentary on 1937 was in a blue mood. In fact, red was the color in the profit-and-loss column. An operating loss of $71,542 was a source of gloom for both the elder and younger Staleys. Not only had a drought, affecting supplies and prices, made things difficult, but imported tapioca and sago starches —466 million pounds—competed "unjustly" against U.S. starch products. To be sure, the Decatur company had earlier forecast that cut-rate starch products from overseas would imperil the stability of American manufacturers. Yet father and son Staley could find precious little consolation in earlier predictions at a time when their "bottom line" hit bottom with a thud.

"Chalk it up to the New Deal," was the senior Staley's sigh.

But there was a bright side ahead.

The year 1938 brought the announcement of an innovative proprietary corn syrup called Sweetose. In its earlier years the Staley company had accomplished some technological firsts in modified starches, but the processes for these had not been patented for two reasons: Their patentability was uncertain and, anyway, the company had not had a patent lawyer in its ranks. But by the time Sweetose leaped from the Decatur laboratory, a trusty patent lawyer had arrived and had set his sights on protecting a legitimate Staley invention that wound up making millions of dollars in sales and royalties, especially during its 17-year period of protection under patent law.

The Sweetose story was recently recounted by Dr. David P. Langlois, principal coinventor, who was aided in his efforts by

Julian K. Dale, research director. Langlois was a PhD organic chemist who was recruited from Penn State by Gus Staley in 1932 and who was an earnest and successful research leader for the company until his retirement to Edinburgh, Scotland, in 1966. Langlois recalled:

When I was interviewed by the younger Staley in 1932, he told me he wanted to start a research division. He hired me to take over on starch and he also brought in an organic chemist named Paul Schildneck from the University of Illinois. We had equal billing. We were research supervisors in a company where there had not been much done in the way of formal research programs beyond routine application research.

For a while several rooms in the plant were used as makeshift labs until a three-story research building was built alongside the viaduct. In prior years up to the early thirties the company had been successfully making corn syrup by what was known as the boiling process. I said to myself that if hydrolyzing starch with hydrochloric acid at high temperatures resulted in a good product, the use of enzyme powder might result in a much better product. (Keep in mind that an enzyme is a natural organic substance which catalyzes reactions well below boiling temperature.)

In early experiments I was able to come up with a very good syrup. One day Gus Staley came over to the lab and I asked him to test the taste of my discovery. "Pretty good," he reacted, "but it tastes like any other corn syrup." That was a limited endorsement, of course, but a limited endorsement was better than none considering I had not expected a lot of enthusiasm in the first place.

But as I thought about it, I decided that I had had a pretty discouraging critique. And I knew I'd have

107

to have the president's backing if my research work was to be recognized. When the elder Staley was in town he hardly ever visited the lab. He simply wasn't interested in research. Ed Scheiter never came by, either. Therefore I knew if I couldn't get encouragement from the junior Staley I'd be out in the cold. He was the only hope I had.

Then came the lucky day. Larry Trempel of technical sales dropped by to chat. He had been with General Foods. He was sensitive to the need for technological advances in food products. I asked him to taste my sample. "It's sweeter than our regular syrup," he said, without hesitation. "It's pretty close to the flavor of cane sugar."

Good old Larry. He helped talk things up and pretty soon I had management support. We had a product more than twice as sweet as regular corn syrup and it was three times more fluid. We found a ready market in candies and in fruit-packing at the outset and then we moved Sweetose into jams, jellies, preserves and ketchup.

Gus Staley was the person who came up with the trade-name and he was behind us all the way when Julian K. Dale and I applied for a patent in 1939. We sold a license for Sweetose to Corn Products and to several other corn refining companies. Sweetose was a major discovery and it helped gain acceptance for the research function within the company.

In the annual report dated February 24, 1940, the founder's flowing and flourishing Spencerian-type signature appeared—as was custom—at the bottom of the chairman's letter to stockholders. The message noted that "in recent years the size of the soybean crop in Ohio has increased materially" and that "the company has purchased a plant site at Painesville, Ohio, for soybean processing." This was the corporation's first move to a manufacturing location away from Decatur.

That early 1940 decorative (if shaky) signature of A. E. Staley, replete with appropriate curlicues, was in fact making its farewell appearance in that report sent to 625 owners of common stock and 1,921 owners of preferred. The signature was destined never to appear again in a company annual report.

CHAPTER SEVEN

COUNTDOWN FOR A WEARY PIONEER

"He was a dreamer who made his dreams come true." That was the recent one-sentence description of A. E. Staley, Sr., by the founder's longtime friend Thomas W. Samuels, who began to practice law in Decatur as far back as 1914.

Samuels then added: "He was a plunger and he was a pioneer."

In a world where people often slip away into eternity with insufficient prior knowledge of the world's acclaim for their accomplishments, one might rightly wonder, "Did Gene Staley correctly perceive the respect and affection of others?"

The answer is "Yes, he did." Particularly during the last 15 years of his life, recognition had proliferated. By the end of the decade of the thirties he had achieved national stature on the business scene—not just in agriculture, not just in Decatur, and not just in his newly adopted wintertime home-away-from-home, Miami, Florida.

Did he relish the acclaim? Yes. Did he court it? Not especially. Did he have a foot-shuffling "aw, shucks!" posture of feigned humility while basking in the spotlight? Never. Particularly on those occasions when he had the opportunity to sit in an audience as the centerpiece for pro-Staley applause, he beamed benignly. On that classic scale of one to ten, he scored five for humility and five for vanity.

Examples of recognition were many, such as:

1. In April, 1926, the Staley Fellowship Club presented their boss with a bronze bust which had been commissioned from a Chicago sculptor, Emil Zettler. The sculpture was later placed prominently in the lobby of the new office building. It was (and is today) an item of dignity and respect.

2. In December, 1928, when the Decatur Masonic Temple was dedicated, an oil painting of benefactor Staley by Robert M. Root, a portrait artist from New York, was placed in an honor position (and in 1981 it was still prominent over the large fireplace in the temple's main lounge). But a special ironic twist went hand-in-hand with the Masons' honor for their thirty-second-degree benefactor. Shortly after the painting of the senior Staley was installed, his Number One son, Gus, was refused admission into the Masonic order. A further irony was that Number Two son, Rollin, breezed in without a blip.

3. In November, 1937, when Harry Irving Shumway published a formidable book called *Famous Leaders of Industry,* Gene Staley was included along with such notables as Bernard Baruch, Harvey Firestone, Charles Kettering, and John D. Rockefeller.

4. In June, 1939, High Point (North Carolina) College presented the company's founder with an honorary degree of doctor of laws. Because Gene Staley felt less than up to the task of going to the city not far from his birthplace at Julian, North Carolina, he asked son Gus to attend the college's commencement ceremonies where the award was given in absentia. It was a salute to a North Carolina native whose total formal education had taken place in a nearby one-room schoolhouse and whose only supplemental education had been in devouring books and listening to people.

5. In June, 1940, the company's founder was in attendance, yet in marginal health, when James Millikin University of

Decatur presented him with an honorary degree of doctor of sciences.

6. And during the twilight of his life, late in 1940, Staley contentedly sat for a portrait by Tino Costa, a French artist who was engaged to do an oil painting that would hang in the tenth floor dining room, and eventually be placed beneath the giant chandeliers in the art deco lobby of company headquarters.

7. In the external public media, the founder was not ignored. When *Time* magazine had the effrontery in 1936 to cite Henry Ford as the nation's leading champion of soybeans, a dutiful reader in Baltimore named W. Carroll Mead took *Time*'s editors to task in the Letters-to-the-Editor section, mentioning the pioneering role of A. E. Staley. The editors of *Time* acknowledged, beneath reader Mead's comeuppance letter, that "Detroit's Ford may have been the most publicized promoter of soybeans but Decatur's Staley was the pioneer, longtime processor." (Henry Ford had simply experimented for a few years with soybean-based resins in the hope of making steering wheel rims, gearshift knobs, horn buttons, and other automobile miscellany from a replenishable natural substance.)

8. Later when the upstart neighboring Illinois village of Taylorville, center of rich corn and soybean farmland, challenged Decatur for the designation "The Soybean Capital of the U.S.," Decatur citizens rushed in and reminded their Taylorville neighbors, "Decatur is the soybean capital in the same manner as Detroit is the center of the automotive industry, instead of the ore field which produced the steel for the cars." That took care of that.

9. And in the August 15, 1940, issue of *Forbes* magazine, the statement was made that "curiously, a man who hated farming has done more for the American farmer than almost any other man alive. A. E. Staley is the great salesman of the soybean, the only new crop of importance in many years. In 60 days last fall, five railroads brought 9,400 carloads of beans to the four processors [by now, Staley and three smaller

processors] in Decatur." Featuring a photo of the Staley company chairman, the *Forbes* story carried the headline, "Soybean Pioneer." The story was subsequently reprinted, in condensed form, in *Reader's Digest.*

Pioneer is what he legitimately was. He made paths where paths had not been made before. He learned about business by listening to businessmen. He learned about finance, accounting, law, and production by associating himself with financiers, accountants, lawyers, and production people. He enjoyed listening as much as he enjoyed talking.

Yet the art of salesmanship was something special. He seemed to have had a knack, a feel, a hankering for moving the merchandise, for responding to purchasers' needs, for persuading others of the validity of his viewpoint. (An unsigned old memorandum in the company's archives file takes note of the fact that Gene Staley's salesmanship reached perhaps its most artful form prior to World War I when he persuaded a Post Office employee to sell him a sheet of 2-cent stamps—on credit!)

Timid? Not exactly. Perhaps the most appropriate illustration was found in a letter he wrote in September of 1940 before leaving for his final excursion to Florida. Corresponding with a North Carolina–born friend, the founder wrote: "I am getting older all the time. I tire quickly and easily. I am feeling my age [73] to a certain extent. But my mind is just as clear and as brilliant as it ever was."

Truth? Probably yes. Humility? Not quite.

On October 29, 1940, Gene Staley dictated a letter to a longtime resident of Julian, North Carolina. The letter said: "I am not so strong any more. I hope I can stand the trip to Florida. The Illinois Central Railroad is putting on a through Pullman direct to Miami for our accommodation. This was a nice thing for the railroad people to do because my wife and I won't have to make any changes. We will arrive in Miami at 2 o'clock next Monday afternoon."

That was the last letter he ever dictated to his secretary, Mrs.

113

Blanche McDonald. When he left his office at 2200 Eldorado Street that day and told Mrs. McDonald good-bye, it was the last good-bye from her boss she would ever hear.

Mr. and Mrs. A. E. Staley, Sr., had one more item of unfinished business to handle before going south. They picked up absentee ballots and voted with enthusiasm, if not confidence, for the Republican presidential nominee, Wendell L. Willkie, who—like Gene Staley—had recently bolted away from the Democrats.

It was good to be back in Miami. Gene and Emma Staley were proud of their bayfront property. The first task to deal with was seeking a stenographer to come in and handle correspondence. The woman Staley had hired in 1939 had become upset by the frequent invasions of pesky mosquitoes and sand flies so Staley felt it would not be appropriate to ask her to come back to his waterfront home. A new stenographer, who lived nearby, was promptly interviewed and engaged. She would find that much of her outbound mail would be heading for Decatur, Illinois.

That mansion at 1408 South Bayshore Drive was more than a home away from home. It was, in the proprietor's own words, "one of the leading showplaces of south Florida." Centered on a 3-acre plot behind a formidable seawall at Biscayne Bay, the main house had six bedrooms and six baths.

There were several pieces of sculpture in the yard. There were two greenhouses. There were separate quarters for servants. And there were even colored floodlights at night—an imitation, to be sure, of the rainbow illumination of the company's towering office building back home. There was even a separate gazebo-type pavilion called "the teahouse."

But the area that Staley loved best was his outdoor garden. The man who liked to have a rose or carnation adorning his jacket lapel found a sense of tranquility in his rose garden. In making plans for the observance of Christmas, 1940, he expressed two principal wishes: (1) to have as many family members as possible present at least for a few days during the

114

holiday period and (2) to have roses—thousands of roses—thriving in his garden.

Shortly before her death in 1981, Gene Staley's oldest daughter, Ione, recalled some of the activity focusing on the pre-Christmas period of 1940:

"My father never changed. He always wanted to have the biggest and the best. Sad to say but sometimes he sacrificed quality in order to get quantity. For Thanksgiving, he went out and bought the largest turkey he could find. I'm not sure it was the tenderest turkey but you could be sure it was the biggest.

"He was a regular customer at Uncle Tom's Fish Market in Miami. He'd go down to Uncle Tom's and ask for the biggest red snapper in the shop. The proprietor would explain that two medium-sized red snappers would be more tender and more tasty. But my father would hear no such talk. 'Give me the biggest you've got,' he would always say."

While Ione and her mother, Emma, were overseeing most of the daily routine that winter in Florida, Gene Staley kept busy with rapid-fire letters. Sample excerpts from those letters include the following:

To Texas Ornamental Nursery Co., Wells Point, Texas:

"I am enclosing a check for $175. Please ship the following 1,300 roses." (He listed 21 different varieties.)

To a friend in Detroit:

"I think Roosevelt is aspiring to become a dictator like Hitler in Germany, Mussolini in Italy and Stalin in Russia—except he's not as smart as any of those three." Also: "I have had a bad gall bladder attack and liver trouble that has kept me down and out. Florida's ultra-violet rays do a lot for old bones and muscles." Also: "I am glad you saw the article in *Forbes* Magazine. I feel I have contributed a great deal to humanity and that the record I leave behind will not perish when I pass on."

To a friend in Chicago:

"The doctor is concerned over the condition of my heart."

To his secretary in Decatur:

"I was in a fruit store today and saw a Southern fruit cake.

I had one mailed to you by parcel post. It looks good and will make you nice and fat." (Incidentally, this letter to his secretary—as all other such letters to her—was formally addressed: "Mrs. Blanche L. McDonald, secretary, A. E. Staley, A. E. Staley Manufacturing Company, Decatur, Illinois." The letter's salutation was: "My dear Mrs. McDonald." The closing line was: "With my kindest regards and best wishes, I beg to remain, very truly yours." Those were the days of formal, almost courtly demeanor, even in routine letters to a secretary and especially in the attitude and decorum of Gene Staley.)

One afternoon after the founder had finished with his mail, his daughter Ione came home from the Hialeah race track and announced, somewhat triumphantly, that she had won $125 on the daily double. She recently recalled that her father, upon hearing the good news, told her (and others nearby): "I'll never know where this family ever gets its gambling instincts." Recalling that sense of humor example on the part of her father, Ione remembered, "We all laughed and laughed when he said that. And pretty soon my father joined us in a long round of happy laughter." He was obviously plainly amused at his little put-on—a gentle jab at his own tendencies to go for the bundle.

Liquor? Gene Staley was temperate but that didn't mean sternly temperate. A brand of rye whiskey called Sherwood was his favorite, his daughter Ione recalled, adding: "Two drinks before dinner was his usual indulgence. He had a few dyed-in-the-wool Methodist tendencies, tracing back to his youth—like no dancing. But he also believed strongly in some personal freedoms. Take cigars. He loved cigars. When his doctor said he could smoke two a day down in Florida, he went out and bought the biggest cigars I have ever seen. They were almost a foot long. My daughter, Shirley Cowell, used to join me in delight when we saw 'Papa Gene,' which is what we called him, sit back and relax while he blew smoke rings high into the air."

As Christmas neared, lighthearted moments gave way to serious concern as Staley's health headed rapidly downhill. On December 18, 1940, he wrote Mrs. McDonald: "I have been sick in bed for the last three days on account of unusually high blood pressure but this afternoon I came downstairs to dictate the mail."

Then came a worrisome period. Staley was pale and weak. New pains were frequent. His physician in Champaign, Illinois, Dr. J. M. Christie, rushed to Florida to check up and to urge "take it easy" to a patient who had never taken anything very easy in his lifetime. When Staley seemed to improve, briefly, the doctor returned to Illinois.

By December 22, the founder was back in his upstairs bed, promising his wife, Emma, to come down when Christmas arrived. This was a promise he was able to keep.

On December 26, he was sitting in a chair on the porch. It was a balmy day. He seemed content. Then all of a sudden a jolt went through his tired body, the result of a massive heart attack. He slumped in his chair, unconscious. Emma and Ione and others rushed toward him.

He recovered consciousness briefly. Opening his eyes, he knew where he was. Looking straight into the eyes of his wife, he said firmly: "Emma, I have had 150 years of living." And then he died—at 73 years of age.

Illinois Central Railroad put a private baggage car on the Panama Limited to carry Gene Staley's body back up north. The casket, of solid bronze, weighed 1,800 pounds. On Saturday, December 28, more than 600 people attended the funeral service in Decatur's First Presbyterian Church. An overflow crowd of 500 at the Masonic Temple heard the church services through a sound system set up for the occasion.

The governor of Illinois and other notables were honorary pallbearers, but the distinction of accompanying the coffin to a mausoleum at the Fairlawn Cemetery went to the plant "bull gang"—laborers "the old man" used to visit in earlier days when he regularly toured the plant.

The man who had fashioned an empire out of his dreams was gone.

This was a North Carolina farm boy who almost single-handedly took a company from an insignificant lost ball in the high

117

weeds of eastern Decatur—from there to almost $28 million in sales. He nurtured the company and encouraged its people by beckoning "follow me." But from late 1940 onward, he'd never again be out on the street selling Staley stock, soybeans and Sweetose. People rightly said, "an era has gone."

CHAPTER EIGHT

NEW MANAGEMENT
AND A NEW WORLD WAR

Shortly after the legendary Alfred M. Sloan became chairman of General Motors Corporation in 1937, he noted that the perpetuation of leadership in a corporation—any corporation—is "sometimes more difficult than the attainment of that leadership in the first place."

More recently, in 1980, William F. May, dean of the Graduate School of Business Administration at New York University, observed that "one of the hardest things for a company [under new leadership] to do is remain a risk-taker. The temptation for innovative companies is to protect their past accomplishments and to look for a period of relaxation."

Measured against these generic commentaries, the Staley company of 1941 was tested somewhat harshly and its report card showed rather high grades in the momentum of leadership and lower grades in risk-taking. But there was no relaxation.

The new chief executive officer, A. E. Staley, Jr., was not the relaxing type—at least not during business hours. He was, above all, diligently scrupulous and superconscientious.

There was zero surprise, of course, when he took over as successor to his father. Upon returning to the administration building at the start of 1941, he made several decisions: (1) As the new chief executive officer, he would simply retain the title of president and would not assume his father's title of chairman; (2) he would stay in his own office on the eighth floor and would leave his father's nearby office vacant except when it would be needed for board meetings, considering it was equipped with a suitable board of directors' table; (3) he would ask Mrs. Blanche McDonald, the founder's secretary, if she would kindly work for him "for a brief period" to help sort out the various transitional details. (The "brief period" turned out to be 13 years.)

Young (37) Gus Staley knew he'd be flying solo for the first time in his life. Habitually comfortable in an atmosphere dominated by his father's benevolent influence, he realized he was about to experience what is often referred to as "the loneliness of the high command." No longer would his father's shadow extend from across the eighth floor or, during winters, all the way from Miami.

"I am the custodian of my father's affairs," he told his closest associates in 1941. Appreciating young Staley's great respect for his father and further appreciating that the corporation was the realization of his father's dreams, the new boss man's colleagues sensed that Gus Staley would probably never forget the past while walking alone into the future where ominous clouds of war seemed destined to spread more widely through the world.

Comparisons were inevitable. No one could resist contrasting father and son. The author of this narrative noted that in all of his dozens of interviews with old-timers, mainly alumni, discussions inevitably got around to mentioning the similarities and dissimilarities between Gene and Gus. Actually, the author kept a log upon which adjectives were entered—adjectives recited by people who worked with both Staleys for many years, people who knew them best.

The most frequently used adjectives, applying to both father and son, were the words "honorable" and "trustworthy." The old-timer interviewees also zeroed in on the word "stubborn" as befitting both generations of Staley leadership.

The informal scorecard for A. E. Staley, Sr., shows the following adjectives were most often used by people who knew him well: "Approachable, confident, daring, enthusiastic, friendly, gregarious, honorable, intuitive, outgoing, persuasive, stubborn, trustworthy, visionary, and warm."

The scorecard for the junior Staley shows the following adjectives were most often used by his former colleagues: "Aloof, aristocratic, cautious, cool, conscientious, distant, frugal, hesitant, honorable, quiet, reliable, reserved, responsible, shy, stubborn, thoughtful, and trustworthy."

The founder, Gene, unquestionably inherited many traits of his father, William Staley of Julian, North Carolina, who was an outgoing farmer, an extrovert, a man of action. The son, Gus, inherited many traits of his mother, Emma Tressler Staley, of Bryan, Ohio, who studied music and wrote poetry and who was essentially a very private person.

The founder's daughter Ione summed things up recently in her descriptions of her father, Gene, and her brother, Gus: "My father was always comfortable in groups of people; my brother demonstrated his timid nature in his early days when I used to see him stand at the front window of our home on College Hill when he peeked through the lace curtains and watched other children at play."

Examining both men from a business perspective, they were at opposite ends of any measurement involving their formal education. Gene Staley had only a few years in a one-room rural schoolhouse. He learned about life through reading, through that school known as experience, and through his willingness—even eagerness—to listen to the comments of other people. On the other hand, his son Gus had a blue-ribbon education, majoring in business administration at the Wharton School of the University of Pennsylvania (founded in 1881 as the first collegiate business school in the world).

The father had struggled to amass $1,500 when he incorporated the Staley company in 1906. The son inherited great wealth. The father specialized in the art of persuading others —bankers, stockholders, suppliers—to be broad-minded and supportive when he veered toward the precipice of bankruptcy on several occasions. The son was spared such adventures. The company had sales of almost $28 million and a net profit approaching $1.4 million when the son assumed the high command at the start of 1941.

The father was, in his own words, "just a North Carolina farm boy," with minimum sophistication. In business matters he had to struggle to learn the fundamentals of such essential functions as accounting and law. But he did learn, early on, that delegating authority and responsibility to trusted subordinates was advantageous. The son could visualize, without strain, balance sheets, debentures, depreciation schedules, and tax liabilities. Yet he was not prone to the art of delegating, choosing instead to play the game of business close to his chest.

In an extracurricular way, the father's principal hobby was appreciating roses. The son seemed happiest in five major non-business interests: duck hunting, deep-sea fishing, golf, wine collecting, and gourmet cuisine. (In golf, Gus Staley had the distinction during his life of having scored a hole in one on two occasions, once at the Country Club of Decatur and once at Augusta National, where the Masters tournament is annually played. In the matter of gourmet food, he not only relished partaking of delicacies but also preparation.)

As is always the case in the development of human characteristics, each man's attitudes, personality, capability, and values were molded by the circumstances of his era as well as by such factors as heredity, education, and experience. Within two generations, revolutionary changes had occurred on the social, economic, and political scene and in the business community. At the turn of the century, America had still been sorting out the trade-offs of the era of industrialization and mechanization. By the early forties, the maturing nation's industrial prowess had become the envy of the world. Automation had arrived; nuclear wonders and computer science were waiting in the wings.

In light of the various differences between the two Staleys, a strong case could be made that each was probably right for his time and that each would probably have been wrong if their careers had been flip-flopped. Probably, the son would have been insufficiently entrepreneurial to gain initial momentum, inch by inch, during the early periods of risk and stress and worrisome teeter-tottering at the brink of ruin. And the founder would have found it difficult to cope with the regimentations of business during and after World War II and would have been outraged by increasing government intervention into business affairs.

No offense to his father's evangelistic pioneering, but Gus Staley was never big on soybeans. In his view, corn refining was blue chip all the way. It was big league. It was high technology. It was respectable. It was prestigious. But soybeans were something else—a commodity with unexciting profit margins and a chancy future considering that "everyone and his brother had gotten in on the act" and further considering that the Staley company was putting in disproportionate effort to remain the Number One soybean crusher in the nation.

The numbers are interesting. In 1927, the Staley organization had accounted for the production of 39 percent of domestic soybean oil and meal. In 1933 the leader's (Staley's) share was 29 percent; in 1936 it was 21 percent; in 1940 it was 18 percent, in competition with 30 other U.S. soybean-crushing companies, some large, some small.

By 1938, when Adolf Hitler was widening his European blitzkrieg, almost 11 million bushels of American soybean products, out of a total crush of 30 million bushels, were going into export, with Europe as the principal customer. Beans used for processing at U.S. plants were increasingly domestic in origin —but beans from the Orient were still the major source of supply, a situation destined to change dramatically once the Far East would be cut off and isolated by war.

More self-sufficient with respect to supply, corn refining brought the biggest rewards to the Decatur corporation. At the end of the thirties, cornstarches and corn syrup remained the heavyweight products contributing most consistently to corporate profitability, whereas soybean oil, meal, and flour had to struggle to stay modestly in the black.

The year 1940 was only moderately successful. A decline in earnings was caused by three factors: (1) a sizable jump in federal income taxes; (2) a cost-price squeeze in soybeans, and (3) a precipitous drop in export business during the last half of the year.

But 1941, Gus Staley's first year at the helm, was close to being a record-breaker, due almost totally to gains in corn refining. Soybeans, on the other hand, were a problem. The down-side status of soybeans was exacerbated by two unhappy circumstances: (1) Because of heavy and incessant rainfall in growing regions, most of the soybean crop was not harvested until late November and December; (2) incoming soybeans had a high moisture content and required extended drying periods before they could be stored in the company's elevators.

Gus Staley's strategy was simple. He decided to get out of the soybean flour business, where the markets—a binder for sausage and use in some bakery products—were limited and the profits small. The soybean flour plant at Decatur was converted to additional feed processing from corn. Benefiting from no signals from the "Great Soybean Pioneer" above, Gus Staley didn't bat an eye as he lowered the boom on a product line that had been his father's pride and joy.

To those employees who watched the new boss in operation, the new era looked not at all like the old era insofar as the president's visibility was concerned. As much an introvert as his father was an extrovert, Gus Staley stayed pretty much to himself. Working behind a closed door, he was in full view only when business circumstances required. Disliking crowds, he often bypassed employee-filled elevators and used the back stairs. Arriving at the office early and departing late, he found privacy rather easy to achieve. His closest confidants were vice presidents (and directors) E. K. Scheiter, H. P. Dunlap, R. C. Scherer, T. C. Burwell, and F. A. Eakin.

"Buck" Scherer as corporate secretary and "Franzy" Eakin as comptroller were among the most frequent visitors to his

124

office, but the main confidant was sales-oriented Ed Scheiter, who had been the founder's favorite protégé. Scheiter was, above all, loyal. Adapting as he did, earlier, to Gene Staley's likes and dislikes, Scheiter was equally adaptable to the policies and idiosyncrasies of the new chief executive officer, who needed loyalty in his second-echelon ranks and who appreciated Scheiter's intelligence and dedication.

There was only one matter where Gus Staley and Ed Scheiter didn't see eye to eye. The former was lukewarm on soybeans. The latter thought they were wonderful. Yet when it came to shutting down the soybean flour operation to make room for more corn processing, Staley won and Scheiter lost. After all, Staley was Number One.

Yet as Number One he didn't rush into anything dramatic and didn't participate in anything resembling a rally among employees. At least not for a while.

Insofar as most employees were concerned, they had a "what's new?" attitude. They said, in effect, "the fellow who has been president since 1932 is still the same fellow in the same office upstairs." Acknowledging that Gus Staley wasn't the communicative sort, his closest lifelong friend, George H. Batchelder of Hampton, New Hampshire, recently remarked, "I used to ride 100 miles with Gus to a duck blind in Illinois. Not 100 words would be spoken on the trip."

Yet Gus Staley wasn't really as insensitive as he may have seemed. He knew—as, indeed, his father had known—corporate life imposed a relationship between communication and morale and, in addition, a relationship between morale and productivity. Further, he knew employees would feel more like they "belonged" if they were assured "you belong." Also, he knew he was a symbol and that silent symbols are difficult to perceive.

So he did something about it—something which, for him, was dramatic. Influenced greatly by the shock of Pearl Harbor on December 7, 1941, he decided to abandon, temporarily, his low-profile position and to come out into the open in a speech to all the foremen in the plant.

125

It was a speech he wrote himself. It was a state-of-the-nation and state-of-the-company manifesto, a patriotic call to duty, and a review more comprehensive than any earlier effort by anyone in the company's history.

It was the new boss's coming-out party. Delivered in a quiet, deliberate, measured tone, it was presented to the Foremen's Club and to most corporate officers and department heads January 20, 1942.

The speech follows:

I have asked that this meeting be called in order to give you a picture of what lies ahead of us for the duration of the war. I have just returned from a week in Washington, and I believe that the problems facing us are now clear.

America's major role in this war is that of production. If we can successfully organize ourselves, and if we are willing to make the effort, we can produce the munitions, guns, ships, planes, food and supplies that are necessary to win the war. We cannot, however, do it at our leisure and come out on top.

America must produce, produce, produce. We must make everything needed for our men in the armed forces. We cannot let them down. In addition, we must supply our allies their needs. Not only guns and planes are required, but supplies of all kinds, including food and clothing. So far as food is concerned, it is obvious that America can feed herself, but in addition we must feed England, Russia and a large part of the world. During this war, any manufacturer of any essential supply is going to more than have his hands full. A brief review of the job that we are undertaking will clearly show the size of the problem that is involved.

Today, England is calling on us for not only planes and guns, but essential materials of all kinds. A list of the various items that we are sending to England today would cover almost every field of American industry. England has always looked to the rest of the world for a major part of her raw materials, and today a large part of the burden is falling on America.

Russia also is calling on us for vast quantities of materials. We must remember that when Russia lost a large part of the Ukraine, she also lost her principal food producing section. America is trying to make up for that deficiency.

In addition to supplying these two countries, which in itself would be a major assignment, America is endeavoring to send all needed supplies to Egypt; to Iraq; to Iran; to the other Near Eastern countries; to the Dutch, who are doing such a splendid job today in the East Indies; to China; and to virtually all of the world that is not dominated by the Axis.

As if that problem were not large enough, America today is raising an army which present estimates indicate will range between six and eight million men. This means that that number of men will be taken out of this battle of production. It also means that those of us who are left have the job of supplying those men with the materials and supplies they need.

This war program is the greatest challenge ever presented to the American people. Every man in this plant is going to play an active part in it, and here, as elsewhere, our watchword must be—produce, produce, produce.

The soybean industry is primarily one which supplies vegetable oil and protein concentrates. In the past America has received a considerable portion of fat or oil requirements from the Philippines. Tremendous quantities of coconut and other oils have come into the country to be used in the manufacture of shortening, soap and other essentials. Obviously, the Philippine supply has been shut off, and America must find ways of increasing her domestic production of other fats. These fats are needed not only for food, but today America needs an increasing supply for the manufacture of glycerin, which finds its way into munitions. In addition, our allies are calling on us to supply them with fats that they require.

The shortage of materials such as soybean meal is not so acute, but all of the soybean meal that is produced will find a ready market for the feeding of livestock and increasing America's production of meats and dairy products.

Although soy flour represents a smaller part of the total soybean production, the need for that material has substantially increased. England is taking considerable quantities of this material under Lend-Lease. Soy flour is so similar to meat proteins that it is difficult to distinguish them by chemical analysis. In this country, the government is anxious to see that not more than three percent of soy flour is added to sausages, but in England the government is anxious to see that not more than the specified percentage of meat is added to the soy flour.

Our own company discontinued the manufacture of soy flour some months ago and used that plant to enable us to increase our corn grinding capacity. We are today in the process of equipping a new soy flour plant, which we hope will be in production in the near future. [Author's note: The new plant went on stream in March, 1942.]

The Department of Agriculture has already announced a program for increasing the total acreage of beans from 5,500,000 to 9,000,000 acres. Important as is this job in soybeans, the job in the corn refining industry is even more important. I believe a review of the factors affecting our corn operations will be of interest.

In normal times the Dutch East Indies produced and shipped large quantities of tapioca to the various markets of the world. The United States was the principal importer, and Great Britain the second largest. Due to the present uncertainty of shipping between the Dutch East Indies and the other markets of the world, it is quite improbable that as much tapioca from the East Indies will be available. Certainly the amount will not be more than the boats leaving there can carry after they have first filled their holds with rubber, tin and other essentials.

To the extent that tapioca imports from the East Indies are shut off from this country, the corn refining industry will be called upon to supply additional corn starch. In normal times we have objected to the flow of tapioca from the East Indies, but the present interruption of the flow comes at a time when our capacities are already almost completely utilized.

Furthermore, the discontinuance of tapioca shipments

from the East Indies will have a double-edged effect. Since the outbreak of the war, England has taken a considerable quantity of tapioca and has supplemented those purchases with corn starch shipped from America under Lend-Lease. If England does not get tapioca, America will be called upon to supply the deficiency, which will mean increased shipments of starch from here to England.

In addition, we will have a tremendous job in supplying the starch demand of the United States. The largest consumption is in the cotton textile industry. Next comes the paper industry and, in addition, such other uses as in the manufacture of shipping cases, adhesives, the chemical industry; and a wide variety of food uses, such as in the manufacture of baking powder, in the baking industry, the confectionery industry, and, of course, in the manufacture of starch for home consumption. The cotton industry must supply the clothing for our army, our allies and our civilian population. Paper is so widely used that it is today indispensable. There is already a shortage of shipping cases, which are needed for packing supplies for the Army, for shipment abroad, and, of course, for our civilian use.

The sugar situation presents a problem of crucial importance. Normally, the Philippines supplied slightly less than one-sixth of our requirements of sugar, and large quantities have also been brought in from Hawaii. Obviously the Philippine supply is no longer available to us, and it is uncertain just how much can be brought from Hawaii. This means our country must turn to our domestic production of beet and cane sugar, and to Cuba and the West Indies.

Furthermore, England formerly took part of her requirements from the Dutch East Indies and Malaya. Again, it is improbable that these areas will be able to continue to supply England with what she needs, which means that England likewise will have to turn elsewhere for such sugar as she requires.

In 1940, approximately fourteen billion pounds of sugar were distributed in the United States. It is estimated that in 1941 this jumped to almost sixteen billion pounds, but a portion of the increase was probably due to hoarding, both by consumers and by sugar consuming industries.

As if that were not enough, the present demand for sugar for purposes directly connected with the war has considerably increased. The manufacturers of smokeless powder require considerable quantities of alcohol. In the past most of this alcohol has been secured from molasses, but today there is not enough molasses to manufacture all of the alcohol that is needed. For that reason the Government has recently ordered the distillers to use 60 percent of their capacity for the production of alcohol, but even so, considerable quantities of sugar are being used in the manufacture of alcohol in order to fill the demand. The need for molasses and sugar for alcohol is so acute that the Government has recently ordered a considerable reduction or discontinuance of the use of molasses in many other fields, such as in the manufacture of sweetened feeds and in the manufacture of rum.

All together, the sugar situation has become so acute that in December the Government issued an order permitting no one to use more sugar than that used in the same month of 1940.

Our company has felt the full effect of the sugar shortage during the last two weeks. Up until then we had been producing our new corn syrup, Sweetose, at the rate of approximately four million pounds per month, but a deluge of orders has descended on us and we have stepped up our production to the full capacity of our Sweetose plant, which is thirteen million pounds per month, and we are still obliged to turn down orders right and left because we are unable to fill them.

We simply cannot afford to lose one single hour of production that can possibly be avoided. In fact, our job for the duration of the war is going to be to produce more than possible!

In summary, we have the most difficult job facing us that our company has ever encountered. We must produce absolutely every pound of product that it is possible to produce, and at the same time we must do it under conditions where materials and supplies are difficult to obtain. This situation is going to place a terrific burden on our personnel and on our foremen. During this period, each foreman is going to be faced with a number of difficult decisions. Shall he request a shutdown to repair a certain item of equipment, or shall he take a chance on the equipment continuing to operate a little longer until a scheduled shutdown arrives? He is going to have to improvise, to discover new shortcuts, new ways to increase our production a little bit, and new ways to find substitutes for things that are no longer obtainable. He is going to have to squeeze out a little more product, and at the same time avoid any chance that a major piece of equipment will be lost through inadequate maintenance.

Today our plant is well engineered and we are turning out about all that we can with engineering methods alone, but I believe that we have a reserve production that is not being utilized, and which can be obtained only with the whole-hearted effort of everyone in finding ways and means by which good engineering can be bettered and a little more produced. I feel that we have the resourcefulness and the ingenuity to accomplish this; namely, to do the impossible and to turn out more product than engineering says the plant is capable of producing.

From the standpoint of the company, I want to emphasize that our major interest under these conditions is production. If we have to face a question of whether we should increase costs which would increase production or produce less at a lower cost, there is no question what our decision will be. The production must be secured. In normal times, profits are the lifeblood of a company or an industry, but today production is the lifeblood of the nation. In normal times when we fell down on production schedules, the company was the principal loser and suffered the loss of customer good will and the loss of profits on the business. Today not only the company will lose, but, more important, others will suffer because we failed.

There is one other thing that we must keep in mind during this period, and that is the possibility of sabotage. We have tightened up our precautions, and we are going to tighten them up still more. We want everyone to help, and we want everyone to suggest to us any method that may occur to him by which our protective measures can be improved.

As I said at the beginning, this is a war of production, and we here at the Staley plant are in that war clear up to our necks. We are definitely on the firing line, and it is our job not only to do all that is possible, but, in addition, to go beyond that and do the impossible. I hope that you men will carry to every man in the plant this message— that we must, for the duration of the war, produce, produce, produce. And I also want you to convey to every man the thought that I have tried to give to you—that the work in which we are engaged is as essential to the welfare of our country as a munitions plant, and that we are regarded as being in exactly that position by our Government. The nation is counting on us. It is up to us to do our part.

"The old man" would have been proud of his son's virtuoso performance. When the speech was concluded, the applause by foremen and others was not simply polite, deferential approval. It was loud and long. The speech was an exemplification of leadership. It was probably as close to a blockbuster effort as Gus Staley had ever undertaken. The reticent, taciturn, sometimes-peevish aristocrat, impeccably dressed in custom-made finery from an expensive Chicago tailor, was almost a cheerleader—a dignified cheerleader to be sure—for the causes of country and company. The audience consensus was "I didn't know he had it in him."

Among the people in attendance at the 1942 foremen's meeting was a newly hired employee named William F. Allen, embarking on a Staley career that would extend for more than 30 years. Allen had gained a reputation at the Bureau of Standards in Washington, D.C., where he developed technical specifications for paper stock used in currency and postage stamps. He had also been prominent in work done for the domestic pulp and paper industry which was interested in developing the use of southern pine (instead of Canadian spruce and balsam) for the manufacture of newsprint, then selling for $35 a ton versus $400 a ton 40 years later.

Bill Allen listened attentively as speechmaker Staley mentioned the paper industry's reliance on starch. Allen was particularly interested in the corporation executive's reference to "a shortage of shipping cases, which are needed for packing supplies for the Army, for shipment abroad." Allen didn't know it at the time, but he was at the threshold of playing a major role in developing and testing fiberboard containers which would be washed ashore deliberately at Iwo Jima, Guam, and Okinawa, carrying butter and bullets for U.S. armed forces during the height of the conflict in the Pacific.

Later in 1942, when Allen was working out of the Staley company's office in Savannah, Georgia, he learned that the War Production Board had ordered International Paper Company, a major Staley customer, to develop a special fiberboard which could be fabricated into strong, waterproof boxes designed to be thrown overboard to float in—or otherwise wash and tumble in—carrying food, ammunition, medicine, and other supplies for the nation's fighting men on foreign shores. Such a method of delivery, it was determined, would be simpler than air drops and safer than carrying supplies onto potentially hostile beaches.

"Paper products were in short supply and so was starch," Allen recently recalled. "The need for strong boxes for protecting and conveying supplies was obviously a very serious matter. Delivering military shipments by deliberately throwing boxes into the ocean was a new idea—an idea which everyone thought was ingenious as long as the fiberboard boxes would survive after being tossed into the surf and into hidden boulders at every imaginable kind of beach. International Paper was told to develop new fiberboard in extreme haste. The War Production Board added, 'Even if 25 percent of the boxes never arrive on land, the project will be worthwhile.' At the outset, International Paper told the Staley company of a pressing need for a special formulation of urea formaldehyde and starch to serve as an adhesive for five-ply, laminated fiberboard strong enough to do the job.

"American Cyanamid furnished the urea formaldehyde and we at Staley were instructed to come up with a unique strain

133

of starch. Actually, the starch we came up with—which proved to be ideal—was a little-used formulation made for the textile industry. Anyway, we developed a starch-based adhesive which we felt was just right. We called it 'Staclipse KST.'

"By early winter of 1942, we were able to rush 29,000 pounds of Staclipse KST to our South Carolina customer which began pilot plant production of what we called 'the indestructible box.' Yet there was some serious oceanside testing to be accomplished before the War Production Board would accept the new container. It was my job to work on the testing program.

"We took several hundred newly-made boxes to a point south of Myrtle Beach, South Carolina, feeling that this shoreline would give us all the action we'd need. We filled each test box with 24 No. 2 cans of tomatoes. Then we tossed the heavy boxes into the ocean—from various distances off shore. We tied some boxes to anchored ropes to see how the boxes would behave during long confinement in turbulent surf. Most of the anchored boxes managed to survive the ordeal. Some of the unanchored boxes sank out of sight right away. Yet, they didn't stay submerged long. They were somehow caught up in the swirling waters and were buoyed and bounced to shore. A few loose boxes disappeared—a very few. Perhaps some ocean currents carried them out to sea. But no matter.

"Just when I was beginning to feel our problems were behind us, I got a tap on the shoulder from behind—from a man in uniform, who identified himself as a member of the U.S. Army Beach Control. It seems that some vacationing lady had been in a lounge chair, watching her daughter making sand castles. The lady evidently observed me as I was tossing boxes in the ocean. She had somehow learned the boxes were filled with cans of tomatoes. After all, we had not tried to make the tomatoes a military secret.

"Keeping in mind that early in the war seven Nazi saboteurs in a submarine had gone ashore near Jacksonville, Florida—and were all ultimately captured—the lady in the lounge chair had come to the conclusion I was possibly in the act of provisioning foodstocks to German U-boats offshore. In light of the earlier, highly publicized excitement not too far down the East Coast, and in lieu of any other logical explanation for my unusual behavior which involved dispatching tomato cans out to sea, it was perhaps reasonable for the vacationing lady to surmise I was in collaboration with a new wave of submarines from the Third Reich.

"She had relayed her suspicions to the military. And that's how I wound up with a tap on the shoulder from the Beach Control. You can bet I showed my various identification cards in a hurry. Also I suggested that a check-out at International Paper, at Staley and at the War Production Board would demonstrate I was not a Nazi collaborator. It was an unanticipated interval. Later I told myself, 'relax—this proves the effectiveness of the coastline's surveillance and security system.'

"A few weeks afterward, everything was stars and stripes when we had a full-dress demonstration in South Carolina for War Production Board and military representatives. We subjected 96 boxes to every conceivable oceanside test for a period lasting 72 hours. Then we took the wet boxes and dropped them three times from a 30-foot-high roof. A few tomatoes in those No. 2 cans may have been shaken up a bit, but the cans, themselves, and more importantly, the fiberboard containers had withstood the ordeal.

"International Paper started manufacturing the new boxes in January, 1943. The company made millions, literally millions, of starch-supported boxes. As the war pressed on, servicemen were supplied and nourished by the contents of fiberboard containers carried in on the waves. I thought about it often. Gus Staley had voiced the challenge at that meeting with the foremen, only six weeks after Pearl Harbor. Neither he nor I knew at the time that International Paper plus Staley would be in partnership in the development of a new form of off-shore transportation. Also, we didn't realize that a Staley man would ever be suspected of aiding and abetting an enemy cause. In the final analysis, it was an exhilarating adventure."

But that wasn't all. The fiberboard industry leaned heavily on Staley technology even when the adventures were less adventuresome. Corrugated containers—known as the foundation of the fiberboard industry—also gained from Staley starch despite the fact they never figured in dramatic situations at the seashore. Ranging in size from small to colossal, corrugated containers provided excellent protection for their contents during and following World War II.

In 1981, W. R. Schwandt, Staley vice president, looked back at the fiberboard picture and commented, "During the thirties, the corrugated board manufacturers were using sodium silicate as a bonding agent. The corrugated containers were satisfactory from a strength standpoint, but the silicate was too abrasive. The sandpaperlike binder was not only rough on machinery, but it was uncomfortable and dangerous for people to handle. Then Staley came up with a starch adhesive which was not only strong but easy to use during the process of manufacturing corrugated board. Staley promoted this special starch more aggressively than anyone else in our industry. During and following World War II we had more than 50 percent of the market. We even developed machinery for applying the adhesive. Not only fiberboard companies but brewers and grocery manufacturers turned to Staley for help in furthering the corrugated cause."

In those World War II days, Gus Staley personally controlled almost 70 percent of the corporation's common stock. Paradoxically, the Staley company—like thousands of manufacturing enterprises—was in fact both private and public. Its ownership was "closely held." But it was fundamentally public, and increasingly public, to the extent it operated under public charter, it had almost 3,000 public stockholders, it recruited its employees from the public ranks, it bought its corn and soybeans from the agricultural public, and it sold its products in the public marketplace.

Gus Staley was sensitively aware of the public/private situation. Someday, down the road, he would go all out by "going public" on the New York Stock Exchange. But this was a decision he saved for the early sixties. Thus, in those tempestuous years of World War II, the Staley company remained a family-oriented enterprise. It had certain and obvious advantages in being able to run its own show with minimum intrusion from outsiders—except from the government whose hands were, by World War II, in everyone's pockets, this having been the widely accepted price for achieving the unparalleled accomplishments of a land known as the United States of America.

CHAPTER NINE

STRICTLY BUSINESS

The A. E. Staley Manufacturing Company once had the dubious distinction of fostering an era of "bootlegged coffee."

Even though Gus Staley had nothing against coffee per se, he was dead set against coffee breaks. "When you're at work, you're at work." That was his philosophy. And he wasn't big on work-time intermissions.

Later in life he relented a bit, but during most of the forties and all the fifties virtually no one was ever caught walking through the hallways carrying a hot cup or sitting at a desk nursing the forbidden stimulant. It was against the rules.

Perhaps for the same reason that the Eighteenth Amendment to the U.S. Constitution (Prohibition) failed to achieve widespread compliance, Gus Staley's ban on coffee breaks was less than universally heeded. The ingenuity of employees rose to the occasion. Some workers simply brought powdered instant coffee and paper cups from home and added hot water from the faucets in the men's rooms and ladies' rooms. Others found their own source of supply and, having done so, they would stash the hot brew in the drawers of their desks, furtively taking occasional sips when they felt the coast was clear.

There was a certain moral-victory feeling of accomplishment in the opposition to what some employees regarded as an infringement on personal freedoms.

James H. Beaumont, who was city editor of the *Decatur Herald and Review* for nine years prior to a 23-year career with the Staley company, had both an outside and inside view of the crackdown on coffee breaks under Gus Staley's firm hand. While confirming that games were played during the coffee blackout period and even while citing the fact that a roving sentry was assigned to police the place and to lecture rule-breakers, Beaumont said that, on balance, Gus Staley was simply trying to achieve a working environment in which productivity would predominate over permissiveness. Beaumont also added that "in light of the company's larger priorities, the matter was of minor importance." In other words, a tempest in a coffeepot.

Plainly, Gus Staley didn't like anything that smacked of nonwork frivolity.

In his own personal Spartan regimen, his pace was deliberate and predictable and he didn't like to be rushed into anything. Not until the 1944 Annual Report appeared on March 12, 1945, did he use the two titles "chairman and president" instead of just plain "president," even though he could have—and possibly should have—moved into visible authority and accountability in both positions early in 1941, immediately after his father's death. The plain fact of the matter was that he liked to think things over for a sufficient amount of time. He gave the impression of being a man who never made a snap decision in his life. To the degree that this was a fair appraisal, it was undoubtedly more good than bad.

In caricature, he sat behind closed doors on the eighth floor as an inhibiting force and was sometimes referred to as a "big, fat 'no' " by some of his subordinates. Yet in true character, he simply didn't want to be pressured or rushed. An astute Staley-watcher commented, "Gus was often tarred and feathered by subordinate managers who dodged their own responsibilities for making decisions or who looked for a convenient direction for finger-pointing. Those who did their homework and who approached Gus Staley in the right way, and who didn't become too impatient, found they'd get access, consideration, and a fair hearing upstairs. Granted Gus was demanding. He wanted a comprehensive, well-thought-out plan developed before reacting. Impulsive, hasty, 'quick-and-dirty' propositions got a 'big, fat "no"' every time they went to the eighth floor and that's probably what most such propositions deserved."

In the vernacular of latter-day businessmen, Gus Staley played hardball. Softball was for lesser men, in his view. He may have looked like a gentle patrician, but his armor was always in place. In serving as caretaker and guardian of his late father's affairs, he found no room for idle foolishness, fickle policies, and incomplete plans. He was a strictly business businessman from dawn to dusk. And unstampedable.

Whether or not any of the old-timers would admit it, Gus Staley was, in many ways, a better businessman than his father. This was a hard fact to face in the forties and fifties largely because of the loyalty the founder had engendered at all levels of the company—even out in the factory where the son seldom strolled.

The father—who for sentimental reasons had waited until 1932 to close the unnecessary Baltimore office, where the company was born and bred—left behind a son who was single-mindedly dedicated to fortifying the balance sheet. If the son had ever had the option of closing or continuing an unneeded office in Baltimore or anywhere else, he would have slammed the door with an unsentimental bang.

Yet Gus Staley did, in fact, feel duty-bound to provide generous corporate and personal support to a wide variety of local social, educational, civic, and charitable ventures. "We have a responsibility to provide leadership in United Fund and other such causes," he declared.

On occasions when he was involved in civic philanthropy, his first wife, Lenore Mueller Staley, would tease him about downplaying the fruits of his nobler instincts. Yet she understood he'd feel uncomfortable in seeming to flaunt good deeds of a

140

corporate or personal nature. Not only was he adverse to appearing "soft," but he was also adverse to precipitating someone thinking that "Gus Staley did a noble thing for the purpose of public notice or acclaim."

Lenore Staley was a dutiful mother of three boys, but she was more than that. She was an organizer and hostess, in keeping with Gus's requirements for such assistance, but she was more than that. She was also a constructive "sounding board," anxious to help by exploring with her husband the various options bearing upon his considerations. Gus's 1926 marriage to Lenore Charlotte Mueller, of the prestigious Mueller Company family, had been hailed as a local-level "union of Decatur's Rockefellers and Vanderbilts." Wealth and position notwithstanding, Gus Staley's wife was—and remains—a sparkling and singular personality in her own right. She often provided an extra dimension for her husband's meditation in light of limited feedback at the office.

Roy L. Rollins, who started with the company in 1933 as a millwright's helper and who retired as a vice president and board member in 1970, recently recited a World War II era example of what he called "the real and unappreciated Gus Staley."

Rollins recalled, "I was in the Navy. I was stuck down at a small craft school in Florida in 1944. One day I went over to base headquarters to pick up my mail. It was about mid-December. In the mail was a note from Gus Staley. The note said only, 'Merry Christmas, Roy. We miss you.' Clipped to the note was a check for $1,000—a bonus for being away. It was the most unearned and unexpected $1,000 I ever got in all my life.

"Years later I accidentally learned that Gus knew he was flirting with danger with the U.S. Treasury Department when he went out on a limb and sent me that Christmas bonus. The Treasury Department people maintained I was working for the Navy and not for Staley and therefore a corporate bonus for a nonemployee was not an allowable business expense. Gus was not deterred by such a technicality because he thought he was doing something right. When he helped people he did it quietly.

141

Fanfare would have defeated the purpose. I'm sure he had some pretty big worries on his mind at the end of World War II but he kept his cool."

Rollins was right. Gus Staley did have a few worries at war's end. Example: All that soy flour which the government insisted be manufactured in a hurry was, in fact, overproduced. Earl M. Bailey, who was in export sales for most of his 43 years with Staley, recently recalled that the U.S. government had bought thousands of tons of Staley soy flour for shipment to France, Greece, England, Italy, and the Scandinavian countries—for use in bakery products and prepared meats. "Most of the countries showed little interest in the high-protein flour," Bailey recently commented. "Norway, Sweden and Italy were the only three countries I can think of which indicated they'd try to find a use for the free merchandise from Uncle Sam. And even these countries didn't show much enthusiasm."

Bailey also recalled that "the Staley warehouse at Painesville, Ohio, had stored mountains of soy flour that nobody seemed to want. During a hot, long summer the flour became contaminated by weevils. We found a way to de-weevil the inventory and it was purchased by the U.S. Department of Agriculture for domestic cattle feedstocks."

The unhappy glut of soy flour had a further effect when the Decatur company decided to put its pure, fresh, powdery protein product into several sizes of convenient packages for retail sale. It was trade-named Stoy. Earl Bailey's commentary on this experiment was, "The American housewives were as negative as those overseas. Despite our company's effort to explain the protein plus of the offering, American housewives regarded soy flour as a substitute, an adulterant, an unnecessary evil. Our missionary work fell short. Our soy flour was tan in color and couldn't be used in white bread or plain pancakes. It was appropriate for whole wheat or rye bread and for buckwheat cakes."

In retrospect, retail soy flour was somewhat of a postwar casualty. The experience taught Staley a lot about the way it would market—and not market—the high-protein product in future years.

Unlike many U.S. manufacturing companies that had to retool for peace at war's end, the Staley company was able to avoid the trauma of reconversion. In a statement issued in September of 1945, Gus Staley declared, "We will continue producing the same products we made before and during the war." Then he added that "most authorities do not expect sugar to be in abundant supply until late in 1946 or in 1947," this having been a pivotal consideration in light of the expected drop in corn syrup demand once cane and beet sugar would again be widely available on the peacetime scene. As things turned out, sugar returned in abundance in 1946 and made Staley's sales force fight harder than ever to maintain the favorable profit margins of the wartime era.

Of 3,000 employees, 620 had been called to military duty. And there were 12 who never came home. Returning servicemen were properly reassured when Gus Staley said, "We believe we can reemploy all the servicemen without laying off any of the men who are now with us." And this is exactly what happened.

The postwar skies looked bright. In November of 1946 the company announced a $15 million expansion which would give the corn plant a capacity of 75,000 bushels. But soybeans were far from forgotten. By 1946 soybean meal and oil were manufactured through a new extraction process. In a new $2 million plant with a capacity for handling 550 tons of soybeans a day, the beans were shelled and flaked and then extracted, using a petrochemical solvent called hexane. It represented a major technological advance.

W. Robert Boyer, who monitored the company's finance operations in a variety of positions from 1934 until 1968, recently looked back on the days when the company went to the extraction process. "All of a sudden we began to capture more oil out of the beans," he commented. "Actually, we could have gone to the new process a lot earlier, but Gus Staley was obsessed by the explosive characteristics of hexane. He kept talking, over and over, about a Glidden soybean plant in Chicago which had a hexane explosion in 1935. After we were at a competitive disadvantage for a long time, using an outmoded soybean process, Gus finally said we could go ahead on the new process as long as we'd confine the use of hexane to a location at the outer perimeter of the Decatur plant and as long as he could be assured that every possible safeguard would be installed along with the new machinery."

The old expeller system of crushing soybeans was not immediately eliminated when the new extraction process came on stream, chiefly because all-out production efforts were needed to meet new demands for meal and oil. Yet the days were numbered for the less efficient expeller system which people like Gene Staley and his storied superintendent, George Chamberlain, had developed from 1922 onward. A wag commented, "The expellers are about to be expelled." But they had done their job for more than 20 years. They were simply the remnants of an earlier pioneering period.

And that wasn't all. The company also moved ahead briskly in its product development and marketing operations, allowing that the word "sales" was still being more widely used than "marketing" in the mid and late forties.

On the research and development front there were several notable activities that were born of late-wartime and postwartime needs. The activities included the introduction of corn steep liquor nutrients—made in part from the water used in the corn baths, or steeps—for facilitating the production of those revolutionary antibiotics called penicillin and streptomycin. The activities also included getting into the business of making and selling monosodium glutamate, a flavor enhancer, which had a high-visibility birth and a low-visibility death on the Staley scene.

The nutrients for the so-called wonder drugs brought substantial glory to the Staley cause. Sold to such gilt-edged pharmaceutical houses as Merck, Pfizer, and Squibb, the Staley nutrients helped to establish the Decatur company as a source

144

of sophisticated technology under the aegis of Dr. Wendell W. Moyer, director of research. The pharmaceutical giants, who had been searching for a way to improve their fermentation processes for the effective new drugs, learned straightaway that the Decatur company's capabilities in the laboratory transcended such traditional products as cornstarch, corn syrup, and soybean meal.

The foray into monosodium glutamate was an adventure that soared high and fell fast. Perhaps the product's most unusual accomplishment was that it served as a springboard to emblazon the photo of modest Gus Staley onto the November 13, 1948, front cover of *Business Week* magazine. On page 6, the magazine's story trumpeted the glories of the Staley company's new "flavor fortifier which originated in the Far East," but it said little about the less newsworthy, breadwinning product line whose stability was more in character with Gus Staley's conservative strategy and style. In fact, there was a touch of irony that A. E. Staley, Jr., who didn't court publicity, was a "cover boy" for the first time in his life in connection with an experimental product fated to have a brief fling—a brief fling at Staley, that is.

An additional ironic coincidence was the fact that monosodium glutamate was a product emerging somewhat mysteriously out of the inscrutable Far East, just as soybeans had done in the early, dim past.

The peacetime era following Germany's surrender in May, 1945, and Japan's surrender three months later not only saw the Staley company sticking to essentially the same lines of business, with no major reconversion adjustments, but the era also included what the company called "one of the most chaotic experiences in our history." On October 17, 1946, to the surprise of everyone, the government announced the immediate decontrol of soybeans, soybean meal, and soybean oil. The ceiling price of beans had been $2.30 a bushel. After the government's announcement the price went to $2.85 and then to $3.50. Meal jumped from $59 a ton to $95. Oil went from 13¼ cents a pound to 24 cents. By year's end, the various prices moderated slightly.

A Staley statement for stockholders explained, "With the high prices prevailing for soybeans, our needs for cash mounted rapidly. At the beginning of October 23 we had $15 million on deposit at banks and no notes payable. By October 31 our cash balance dwindled to approximately $6 million and we owed our banks almost $16 million. Notes payable continued to advance through the year until they reached an all-time peak of more than $25 million."

The situation was almost a repetition of some of the founder's crises in earlier days—but, in fact, was limited to the soybean side of the business while, at the same time, the corn refining side of the business was flourishing. Despite the "chaotic" circumstances of October, the year 1946 turned out to be what Gus Staley called "the best in our 40-year corporate history, breaking all records for sales, profits before taxes and net profits." The numbers, respectively, were almost $100 million, $12½ million, and $7½ million.

With corn refining coming heroically to the rescue, it was easy to see—at least for the moment—why Gus Staley was lukewarm on the role of soybeans in his growing corporation.

Spearheading the company's sales growth during the forties was an "around the clock, 7-days-a-week" salesman named Otto D. Sutter, manager of Staley's New York City office. Sutter recently recalled that "during the war years our corn syrup sweeteners—especially Sweetose—made a valuable contribution in light of the scarcity of sugar."

Having joined the company at age 18 in 1922, Sutter gained a reputation in his industry as being Staley's "best foot forward" in the big city. Staley opened its first sales office in 1927 at 25 Church Street in downtown Manhattan and moved to a larger office in the Pershing Square Building 7 years later. But the big move was into the Graybar Building, part of the Grand Central Station complex, in the late thirties and, thus, the company went into an up-front position—adjacent to the head-

146

quarters offices of many of its principal customers—for doing business in the wartime and postwar period.

Sutter said, "Within a few minutes I could walk to the offices of some of our best customers for syrup—including some who also purchased starch. Among the big customers in the Grand Central Station neighborhood were: A&P, Borden, National Biscuit, General Foods, Continental Baking, and Nestle. Also nearby were the offices of some of our starch customers in the paper industry—like Oxford, St. Regis, International, and West Virginia Pulp and Paper.

"Over the years our main assignment was to aid the marketing effort. In addition, we served as a listening post. Also, we represented the company at industry meetings in New York and Washington. And, of course, like all New York offices, we developed an expertise regarding theater tickets, hotels, and restaurants.

"Later on we decentralized some of our responsibilities and moved our office over to New Jersey. It wasn't the same, of course, but I don't think we ever lost our aggressive spirit. But some of the old romance vanished. The big bosses from Decatur used to come in on the Pennsylvania Railroad's Broadway Limited or the New York Central's Twentieth Century Limited, and they relished the excitement of Manhattan.

"Even though 'the old man' always wanted the best in everything, he had a modest taste in selecting New York hotels, but Gus liked the places uptown. Shortly before the founder died, he kidded me one day by asking, 'Ott, why do you put Gus at the Waldorf and deposit me down on Thirty-fourth Street at that fleabag called the Martinique?' He was pulling my leg, of course. He had asked for the Martinique, which was a very comfortable place to live."

Ott (which is what people in the company called him) was in a consultant's role in 1981 while commenting on his "Broadway career." When he officially retired in 1972, he had posted nearly 50 years of service with the company.

Among his most unusual reminiscences concerned the year 1948. This was the time when "young Gus" was really "on top of" the job in Decatur, really running a successful show. In July, the New York office got a message from Decatur that said: (1) Gus is coming to New York and (2) Gus's ultimate destination is Oslo, Norway. Even to the cosmopolitan Ott Sutter, Norway seemed pretty far away for a corn and soybeans fellow from central Illinois.

Norway—contiguous with Sweden, Finland, and the Soviet Union—was invaded and occupied by the Germans during World War II. King Haakon and his cabinet fled the country shortly before the Nazi siege, setting up a government in exile in London. In occupied Norway, a puppet government was established by a Third Reich opportunist with Norwegian roots, Vidkun Quisling, who unsuccessfully attempted to promote collaboration with Berlin. Norway was liberated in May of 1945 and later took leadership in the formation of NATO.

Norway in 1948 was as remote to the interests of the A. E. Staley Manufacturing Company as the Fiji Islands. But here's what had happened on the home front: During World War II, Gus Staley had spent several months in Washington, D.C., serving as a dollar-a-year chief of the Corn Products Section of the War Production Board's Food Supply Branch. In the course of his stay in the nation's capital, Staley developed many contacts in governmental circles. He was sensitive to the cause of patriotism and his new-found friends noticed this.

In July, 1948, the company announced that Gus Staley had been granted a leave of absence by the board of directors in order to accept the appointment as head of the Economic Cooperation Mission (Marshall Plan) to Norway. The announcement explained that "his assignment will involve the stimulation of trade and carrying out of the U.S. $100 million recovery program for Norwegian economic relief. It will be Mr. Staley's job to administer this sum."

The company's announcement also said, "E. K. Scheiter, executive vice president, will be vested with the power and authority of the president in Mr. Staley's absence. Mr. Staley has agreed to stay in Norway a year, if needed. Mrs. Staley and their youngest son, Billy, will join him overseas in the autumn." The announcement added, "Mr. Staley has long felt that the wise administration of the Marshall Plan is the surest way to achieve world peace."

In perspective, Gus Staley's decision to leave the helm was as much of a surprise to employees as his father's decision had been in 1930 when the father unceremoniously announced he was heading for a vacation—his first vacation ever—in Miami.

The younger Staley's stay in Norway lasted until early May of 1949. In the Norwegian government's farewell tribute to the Decatur industrialist, appropriate language was used in describing the manner in which he had achieved success in his mission. The tribute said, "Mr. Staley has a modest and quiet form of manner as a private individual as well as in his official capacity. This form has made it easier for him to offer many a good piece of advice. We have met a businessman quite different from those pictured in American books, not to mention American films."

Gus Staley was honored by the King of Norway before returning to the States. The Norwegian Parliament decorated him with the rank of commander and presented him with a gold medal of the Order of St. Olav.

There is one small and poignant story dealing in part with Gus Staley's Norwegian sabbatical which is not widely known. The story was told in 1981 by former vice president Thornton C. Burwell, perennial traffic manager for the company. Burwell recalled, "On August 7, 1948, I accompanied Gus and his wife, Lenore, to a pier on the Hudson River where the Cunard Liner, *Queen Elizabeth,* was loading passengers for a trip to Cherbourg, Southampton, and Amsterdam. Gus was booked through to Amsterdam, where he'd proceed to Oslo.

"Knowing that Gus was a pretty fair bridge player and knowing he'd have plenty of time aboard ship for reading, I brought along a book on how to become an expert at the game. And I gave it to him just before the ship sailed. As Lenore and Gus and I chatted that morning, in Gus's stateroom, I didn't know I'd never see them together again.

"After the ship departed, I dropped Lenore by her hotel and told her I'd look forward to a reunion once her husband had completed his assignment in Norway."

Burwell had no reason to believe that anything other than a continuation of marital accord would prevail for Gus and Lenore Staley during the subsequent period. To be sure, even the earlier company announcement had stated, "Mrs. Staley and their youngest son, Billy, will join him [Gus] overseas in the autumn."

But that's not the way things worked out. Lenore Mueller Staley and her 5-year-old son never did undertake that 1948 Norwegian journey. After leaving New York, Lenore went directly to Baltimore to hover close to her second son, 16-year-old Henry Mueller Staley, who underwent a serious, complicated spine operation at a Johns Hopkins–affiliated hospital. Knowing her son's recovery period would be tedious and uncomfortable, she rented an apartment in Baltimore in order to stay close to young Henry during his several months of recovery and therapy. During this period a governess at her home in Decatur cared for young Billy. The oldest son, 20-year-old A. E. Staley III, known as Gene, was away at school—at Northwestern.

When Henry's recovery was almost complete, Lenore Staley returned to Decatur. Shortly thereafter, she began consultation with an attorney. She had decided to divorce Gus.

An appraisal of the traumatic period in the life of his mother and father was recently provided by quiet, deliberate, soft-spoken Henry Staley, an inheritor of many of his father's characteristics. (Henry joined the company in 1956 and became the second son of Gus Staley to join the starchmaking ranks. He was elected a corporate officer in 1959 and became a member of the board in 1969.)

Thinking back on the post–World War II period when his father was in Norway, Henry recently commented that "my father's long absence undoubtedly gave my mother time to think about the state of their marriage." After Lenore Staley had been counseled by her lawyer, she established residency in Florida for three months in order to qualify for instituting divorce proceedings on grounds of mental cruelty and incompatibility.

Both Lenore and Gus had established a wide circle of friendships in Decatur in the period between their highly celebrated marriage in 1926 and the divorce action 22 years later. The general reaction to their divorce was subdued, but nonetheless the news of the break was a surprise to all who knew them. However, the many friends of both seemed to want to remain friends of both.

Henry Staley explained further that "my mother moved out of town shortly after the divorce decree was granted. She knew that Decatur would be too small for both of them to live there. She'd inevitably be running into him. She had no feelings against Decatur. That's where she was born. Yet in her heart she was a 'big city' girl. She loved the amenities of an exciting metropolitan area. So she moved to Chicago—and my father stayed in Decatur, running the company, after his return from his mission in Norway."

The forties ended on a high note when the company escaped, almost unscathed, from what could have been a damaging series of lawsuits and a long-term black eye in the soy sauce marketplace. Alumnus William F. Allen, former director of market development for the company, said, "The incident was not without some humorous twists and turns but it didn't seem so funny in the 1947–1949 period. Here's what happened. We always used sodium hydroxide to neutralize the hydrochloric acid required in the process of making a liquid which was the base of that wonderful Oriental condiment called soy sauce. Keep that sodium hydroxide in mind as the story unfolds. A California foods manufacturer was our biggest customer. We'd ship out our basic liquid in 8,000-gallon tank cars and the customer would add additional ingredients. The customer would put its product in bottles and sell them by the millions.

"We also sold five-gallon containers of our basic material to

151

smaller formulators, but the California customer was Number One and we gave it Number One service."

Thomas W. Samuels, veteran Decatur lawyer, recently picked up the story where Bill Allen left off. Said Samuels: "The heaviest concentration of soy sauce consumers was on the West Coast, particularly in California with its large number of Japanese. One day in 1947 the Staley company received a report that all the students in a San Francisco school for girls had become violently ill after using soy sauce at dinner the night before. The Staley people thought that the problem was probably connected with a small, single shipment which may have become contaminated. But when similar reports came into Decatur from other cities in California, the seriousness of the situation and the magnitude of potential liability were immediately recognized. Whole families of soy sauce users were stricken.

"The company ran tests on sample bottles rushed to Decatur —and the tests showed that there was arsenic in the soy sauce! It developed that a few months earlier the company had purchased two tank carloads of sodium hydroxide from a New Jersey company. It was learned that the New Jersey firm had made a shipment in two tank cars which had earlier been used for an insecticide—tank cars which obviously had not been adequately cleaned out before reuse."

Back to Bill Allen: "The Staley company set about to recall every bottle of soy sauce it could locate, reimbursing retailers for every bottle reclaimed. Also the company dumped every ounce of material it had in storage at Decatur. Gus Staley demonstrated conscientious responsibility—in spades. At his instruction a ship was stopped at the Panama Canal where 20 European-bound drums of the Staley product were removed, drums which, alas, turned out to be uncontaminated. But the big concern was out in California. The company's insurance carriers set up a task force on the West Coast for settling all claims. Fortunately, no one died from using the sauce."

Tom Samuels added: "Clearly the Staley company had violated the federal Food and Drug Act. It had sold a contaminated product to its big customer in California. But it had no knowledge it was doing such a thing. Upon learning the full facts of the problem, Staley felt compelled to demand heavy damages from its New Jersey supplier. At the suggestion of our lawyers in Decatur, the matter was referred to an East Coast law firm. I spent several weeks working with a bright and skillful man named Brennan from the law firm. He and I learned that the New Jersey supplier was high class, holding an excellent reputation. But the supplier had limited financial resources and was probably judgment-proof. We finally settled the Staley claim for $50,000. As a result of this recovery and the liability insurance, the company recouped much of its loss."

There were three interesting footnotes to this unusual chapter in the Staley company's annals.

1. Attorney Samuels later said that "the man named Brennan was William J. Brennan. He later served as a judge in New Jersey. I was not surprised when President Dwight D. Eisenhower appointed him to the U.S. Supreme Court in 1956."

2. The recall of soy sauce was the second retail rescue mission for the Staley company within the short span of several years, Stoy soy flour having been called back from retailers when it sat on the shelves and became wormy. The soy sauce incident was a larger crisis by far. The Decatur company, thus, had experience in the unhappy reaching out for unsatisfactory products several decades before consumer activists prompted the federal government to mandate recalls of automobiles and other products. The soy flour and soy sauce recalls represented a bit of Staley pioneering the company wishes had not been necessary, but nonetheless the company moved voluntarily, decisively, and swiftly, in the public interest, in both instances. Ill will with retailers was minimized, if not foreclosed, by Staley's prompt action.

3. Alleged stomachaches and a wide variety of other minor ailments seemed to spread across California like a plague once the news got out that an insurance company wanted to settle soy sauce claims immediately. It was amazing to see how many

soy sauce devotees and recent users materialized overnight. Some of the stomachaches were real. Others seemed to occur magically and simultaneously as a common malady as soon as the news became known in the public press that the gentle condiment, soy sauce, had been identified as a culprit originating with a big company in Decatur, Illinois.

What a decade!

CHAPTER TEN

SMOOTH ROAD AHEAD, EXCEPT FOR THE BUMPS

Whereas the thirties had witnessed the phasing out of Era One, and whereas the forties had witnessed the phasing in of Era Two, the fifties were destined to witness the maturing of Era Two plus a hint of what would be forthcoming in Era Three in the sixties and seventies.

The management development process was evolutionary rather than revolutionary. And it was more orderly than one would normally find in the average American corporation.

When the year 1950 arrived, the founder had been almost 10 years gone but, indeed, not forgotten. One of many reasons why he was remembered concerned his famous 1922 prediction that "our plant will process more soybeans than corn." By 1950 the company bragged, "We are the world's largest in soybeans and second largest [behind Corn Products] in corn," using 50 carloads of beans a day versus 30 carloads of kernels.

Which means: In terms of volume the founder's forecast was correct. But profits were another matter. The kernel was king when judged by earnings. And the bean was often a burr under son Gus's saddle.

James H. Beaumont, who worked closely with Gus Staley for

almost 20 years, recently recalled that many new projects were launched in the fifties, some heroic and some not. In all cases, Gus Staley called the shots, aided by his loyal and outgoing executive officer, E. K. Scheiter, who had the reputation of keeping "the most active bring-up file in the corporation."

Beaumont said, "When Gus studied a project, he really studied it. If we'd ever hear him say something positive like 'the project looks interesting,' that was the signal for a victory whoop. It meant 'damn the torpedoes, full steam ahead.'"

Starting late in 1951, Gus Staley indicated he was leaning affirmatively in the direction of diversifying into mixed feeds, or formula feeds, for livestock and poultry. The occasion was unusual because all of a sudden the tables were turned. This time Gus was accentuating the positive and many of his colleagues were expressing apprehension and dragging their feet.

Up until the early fifties the company had been highly successful as a supplier of soybean meal, corn gluten feed, and corn oil meal for farm and ranch animals. Among its customers were large and small milling companies that made their own blends as well as dealers who sold Staley's basic products and, in addition, sold special mixed feeds for various kinds of livestock and poultry.

"If we go into mixed feeds, we'll be competing with mills and dealers who are our customers," some of Gus's colleagues observed. When they added, "We're not a formulating company," Gus retaliated by saying, "We'll buy a formulating company— or several." Obviously, geographic coverage was an important consideration. The company knew it would have to have formulating plants at multiple locations. Otherwise, freight rates would be crippling.

In sum, Gus Staley was proposing that his company get "one step closer to the farm" by adding hominy, fish meal, meat meal, molasses, minerals, and other ingredients for tailored formula feeds to achieve varying balances of carbohydrate, protein, fat, and fiber for livestock and poultry feed mixtures. Gus Staley reasoned that the introduction of a "value added" line of products would add strength to his balance sheet.

"Look before you leap" was a warning transmitted to Decatur by a distinguished customer and competitor, the Ralston Purina Company of St. Louis, which had staked out a broad franchise in mixed feeds in the major farm communities of the nation, providing what it called "chows" under its famous corporate trademark, the red and white checkerboard. When William H. Danforth, Purina founder, heard a rumor that the Staley company was considering competing head-on with existing manufacturers of mixed feeds, he advised a Staley visitor, "Tell Gus Staley, whom I admire, that we at Purina have already signed up the best dealers."

Gus Staley was aware of Purina's powerful position in the early fifties, but he was not dissuaded. He moved ahead. In 1952, the Staley company introduced mixed feeds for hogs, beef cattle, dairy cattle, turkeys, laying and breeding flocks, and broiler flocks. And it purchased several small milling companies in the Midwest to aid in the formulating effort.

The result? Something less than success.

Problem in competing with customers? No. The Staley effort in formula feeds never became powerful enough to be regarded by customers as serious long-term competition.

The excursion in formula feeds failed largely because the Staley company had only a popgun program competing against the artillery of established companies—such as Purina, Allied Mills, and Central Soya—with vast widespread programs. The Staley mixes were top quality. But so were the mixes from the large established mixers. In an effort to get a foothold in a briskly competitive market, the Decatur company adopted a generous credit policy. By 1954 its accounts receivable were stacked high. Some turkey farmers and others who were fond of the Staley mixtures weren't equally fond of paying their bills. And the Decatur company wound up holding the feed bags, subsequently deciding to tiptoe out of the business and to concentrate on the basic soybean and corn feeds which had long been the backbone of the Decatur enterprise.

Some of the formula feed debts were collected—often at trouble and expense. Others weren't. The mixed feeds "diversification effort" wound up costing the company several million dollars. And Gus Staley, who was normally and instinctively and habitually cautious, became more cautious than ever before.

The year 1952 also brought in a remarkable success story involving a modified starch, involving Staley's Chicago office and involving the manufacture of charcoal briquets by the Kingsford Company of Iron Mountain, Michigan.

The story had actually started in 1951 when a supersalesman named C. C. "Dok" Hollis, manager of the Chicago office, made contact with Kingsford. Hollis promptly learned, during his first trip to the Kingsford location, many details about the 2,000-acre Iron Mountain site that had been initially developed by Henry Ford, who wanted to make charcoal from scraps of maple, beech, and birch left over from the manufacture of structural parts for automobile bodies and station wagon panels (in the era before bodies and panels went completely to metal).

When the Kingsford Company purchased the plant from Ford in 1951, it had the strong belief that the era of the great American cookout was just around the corner. Prior to the fifties, backyard barbecues had still been somewhat of a smoky novelty. In deciding to be the biggest charcoal manufacturer in the world, Kingsford established extremely rigid specifications for its charcoal briquets.

To begin with, the briquets had to be easy starting, long burning, and free of unwanted odors. Also, they had to be strong enough to resist abrasion during shipping and had to be reasonably easy to handle. The need was for a binder better than lignin, which was cheap but pungent, and better than dry-milled corn flour, which was also cheap—and smelled like burning chicken feathers. One more Kingsford specification was that the new stickum had to account for less than 7 percent of the briquets' weight. Quite an order!

Hollis described Kingsford's requirements (and Staley's challenge) to Decatur research and sales personnel. Through a bit of timely serendipity, two Staley chemists, Clifford Smith and a young assistant, James Tipton, recognized that a starch derivative with which they had been working might be the answer. The derivative was sent to Kingsford and it passed all the tests.

Mission accomplished! Henceforth barbecued chicken on a Sunday afternoon smelled like chicken, not like chicken feathers.

Ralph R. Dombroski, who started at Staley in 1948 as a Chicago office salesman, recently commented, "In 1952 we moved in and obtained 100 percent of Kingsford's starch business. Our starch was the binder in untold billions of briquets for 23 years. We held this business until 1975 when, sad to say, we had to discontinue supplying Kingsford because of the relatively low return on that particular formulation of starch."

Lulled not at all by the stability of his balance sheet, Gus Staley, a worrier, worried. He felt he needed a better fix on his company's probable position in that magic land called tomorrow. Also, he was very aware that the so-called art of management was somewhat imprecise and subjective. On the one hand, he valued and trusted the judgments of his colleagues. On the other hand, he fretted about the objectivity and direction of the company's long-term strategies, knowing that in-house judgments inevitably contained a bias here and a bias there—including, of course, a bias or two of his own.

He had the good common sense to realize that outsiders often perceive things that insiders miss. He demonstrated this awareness by summoning to Decatur a prestigious outsider called the Arthur D. Little Company of Boston, a management consultant which would be able to bring an independent viewpoint, an unimpeded perspective, and the "fresh air of objectivity" to deliberations among the corporation's long-term planners.

The Arthur D. Little study, together with its consequential recommendations, made waves. But the exercise—in 1954 and 1955—was eminently worthwhile if for no other reason than it riveted attention on several squeaking wheels where the squeaks were getting louder.

What should be the company's product line 10 years hence and what action should the company take, right away, to move into determined directions? Should the company's growth be internal—lifting itself by its own bootstraps? Or should it be external—via acquisitions? Or both?

Given the proposition that research should be regarded as the lifeblood of a commodities-based company, was the Staley organization devoting sufficient man-hours and dollars to the subject of technology? Or did the company simply have a "what have you done for me lately?" attitude on research?

Perhaps the biggest question of all dealt with whether or not Gus Staley would listen to new—and possibly revolutionary—ideas. Several years earlier he had consulted with the Chicago firm of Booz, Allen and Hamilton concerning his organizational infrastructure and had accepted only portions of the outside experts' recommendations. But this time there was every expectation he would give the "audit" (as it was called) a fair and thorough hearing, for two reasons: (1) It would plumb deeply into R&D, an urgent subject, and (2) it would be geared to the planned achievement of greater earnings down the road, also an urgent subject. Furthermore, the "audit" was his idea and would automatically achieve high-level visibility—and perhaps endorsement—by all top-echelon people.

The Arthur D. Little observations and recommendations were blockbusters. The principal suggestions were:

1. Take technology more seriously and back it up with four times the money and four times the people.
2. Hire the best possible person to come in and oversee the upgrading of basic research, applications research, and process research.
3. Diversify into new high-potential fields.

William F. Allen, who was in a variety of positions with the company from 1942 until 1973, recently recalled the shock waves caused by the Boston consultants' principal recommendations in 1955. Allen remembered that "a three-word slogan was the big thing to emerge from the study. The slogan was 'grow or die.' "

Thomas C. Garren, who was involved in many aspects of the company's technology from 1953 to 1981, remembered that "Lowell O. Gill was technical director at the time of the 'audit.' He had been with the company for almost 40 years. No one was more enthusiastic about the Arthur D. Little recommendations than Lowell Gill who had been a long-time advocate of upgrading the role of technology and who welcomed the validation of such a need as expressed by the outside experts. By the mid fifties Gill's health was failing, but he wanted to leave a legacy of progress in the lab. He was first to volunteer to prepare job specifications for a new overlord to come in and put research on a high plane."

Another outside agency figured prominently in developments that followed, the Heidrich and Struggles executive recruitment organization in Chicago. To Heidrich and Struggles fell the 1956 assignment of ushering into Staley an aggressive vice president and technical director, as urged by Arthur D. Little. Almost simultaneously the Chicago recruiting agency was also asked to usher in the brightest candidate it could find to serve as "house counsel" and to head up a one-man embryo of a Law Department at the Decatur company's headquarters.

The first to be brought in was a man named Dr. Thomas L. Gresham, whose stay was brief.

The second was a man named Donald E. Nordlund, whose stay has been extensive.

Dr. Thomas L. Gresham made a big entrance, riding on the coattails of Arthur D. Little's master plan. His credentials were impressive. He had earlier served as vice president of B. F. Goodrich Company. He was forceful. He was confident. He was anxious to sort things out his own way. Coming on strong from day one and basking in the backing of Gus Staley, Gresham didn't worry too much about the existing relationships and

161

patterns of behavior within the rather conservative—almost staid—halls of management. Among the first to voice negative sentiments was E. K. Scheiter, executive vice president, who was a bit dynamic on his own. Scheiter thought that Gresham's invasion was a bit too blustery for comfort.

From the outset, Gresham trumpeted a loud call for more people—especially more PhD's—and more facilities. Almost immediately he brought in what he called a strong Number Two in the person of Dr. James A. Bralley, formerly with the Rohm and Haas Company, who took the title of director of research.

If Gresham's style was unnerving to some associates, it had the compensating value of being clear and direct. And anyone who didn't perceive his disdain—or mock disdain—for the corn and soybean businesses was simply not paying attention. Occasionally employing small exaggerations to make a point, Gresham cited doomsday forecasts for all commodity businesses, including corn refining and soybean crushing, as a technique to force his fellow-planners to consider the potentials down other paths.

Realizing, as he did, that the Staley company was sophisticated in the handling of a natural polymer called cornstarch and correspondingly sophisticated in a chemical specialty known as polymerization (rearranging molecules to form varying substances), Gresham convinced Gus Staley that the company should move speedily into synthetic polymers and thus position itself firmly along the broad horizons of organic chemistry.

He was a force to deal with. He was a proponent of research plus more research plus more research—in terms of people, funds, and square footage for laboratories. And his clarion cry paid off. Example: In the 1957 Annual Report, the company stated that "the number of people on our research staff is now approximately double what it was two years ago." Such an advance was not only a personal triumph for the new vice presidential high priest of technology, but it served to position the company solidly for its later, greater dependence on broad-

162

based research capability. Example: Shortly afterward, the company advised stockholders that "the Research Division budget represents almost four times the [prior] expenditures."

Gresham was making tracks—fast. He was even envisioning an imposing new $4.2 million research center to be constructed east of the headquarters office building.

And then came the acquisition of U B S (standing for Union Bay State) Chemical Corporation, which marked (1) the fulfillment of the dream of putting Staley on stage in synthetic polymers, and (2) the decline of the Gresham comet. (U B S will be discussed later in this chapter.) In 1960, Dr. Thomas L. Gresham said he felt he could accomplish more elsewhere. So he left the Staley scene, turning over the company's technical establishment to his assistant, Dr. Bralley.

To his credit, Gresham was applauded by Staley-watchers for having provided a dramatic spark to the cause of Staley R&D. Some such observers cited "Gresham's Law," which said, in effect, that "rather than concentrating on cornstarch and soybean oil for edible and certain other traditional purposes, perhaps corn and soybeans should be considered for additional purposes in light of new scarcities, new economics, new markets." Granted, Gresham's late-fifties "Law" didn't specifically mention corn as a raw material for high fructose sweetening agents for soft drinks nor as a source for liquid fuel, but Gresham shook up people's thinking and perhaps he may have ultimately won out—if it had not been for that distracting intrusion called U B S. A case could probably have been made that Gresham was a bit intuitive because, in fact, he championed the cause of using corn for nonfood products long before the Staley company decided to make alcohol for motor fuel and decided, also, to spend big money developing organic chemicals from corn.

Donald E. Nordlund made a less spectacular entrance in 1956, but he was destined to move along, quietly and rapidly, in executive ranks—to the presidency and then all the way up to the role of chief executive officer, and then chairman. He became the chieftain and symbol of Era Three and also became the first non-Staley-family CEO in the corporation's history.

Coming in at $16,000 a year in 1956 at age 34, he almost didn't come in at all. As he recently recalled, "At the suggestion of Heidrich and Struggles, the 'head hunters,' I went down on the train from Chicago to Decatur where I had a meeting with Gus Staley, Ed Scheiter, Tom Samuels, and Carl Miller, Miller having been the company's in-house counsel previously.

"It was a very pleasant introductory session and I was favorably impressed. Yet when I was on the northbound train, returning to Chicago, I had some bothersome apprehensions. So I went to my office and wrote a nice letter to Gus Staley, telling him I felt complimented to have been invited for the interview. I also told him, 'thanks but no thanks.'

"Why? Well, for some reason or another, I had doubts about the scope of authority of the job in Decatur. I wasn't sure I'd have sufficient freedom of action. I should add that I was quite happy being affiliated with an excellent law firm in Chicago. I had practiced law for eight years after leaving the University of Michigan. Things were going well and I didn't want to move into a dead-end position surrounded by corporate constraints.

"As soon as Gus received my negative letter he responded without delay. Expressing regret that the subject of freedom had not been sufficiently explored during my visit, he cleared the air with encouraging assurances. Feeling heartened, I then said okay. Once I joined the company, I learned that Gus's commitment was even greater than he had indicated. In short order, I found myself in attendance at meetings of the Executive Committee and Board of Directors.

"Unsurprisingly, Gus was an exemplary gentleman who was determined to strengthen the company's financial base. He was becoming a strong advocate of research—beyond the momentum which the Arthur D. Little study had accomplished. He felt that R&D motivation over the long haul would have to be internally generated, with strong support from the top. For the first two years, I was the only lawyer in the house. I began to work closely with Gus. We developed a sort of partnership even

164

during those early days, a partnership which lasted for many years."

In 1958, Nordlund was elected a vice president, director, and member of the Executive Committee. Also, he was given responsibility for all the corporation's financial functions—and he invited in another lawyer and began bolstering the company's in-house professional capabilities. In light of his new finance-related responsibilities, he enrolled in accounting courses at Millikin University's night school, even though he had minored in accounting at Midland College in Fremont in his native state of Nebraska.

Also in 1958, the board elected Ed Scheiter as president and chief operating officer, Gus Staley retaining the positions of chairman and CEO. Scheiter was then 56, Gus Staley was 55, and Don Nordlund was an increasingly influential two-year veteran at age 36.

To some degree, the future was thus hazily foreseen as the result of those three management changes in 1958. Among other reasons, Scheiter's age was plainly too close to Gus Staley's for Scheiter to be considered as a candidate to succeed Staley. Astute company-watchers correctly assumed, "It will be someone else, someone younger."

Easily overlooked in the Staley historical archives is a non-business event of October, 1956, which was arranged to help celebrate the fiftieth anniversary of the company's incorporation. The event was an exuberant, carefree, semialcoholic excursion to Chicago not to cheer for the twin causes, corn and soybeans, but to cheer for the Chicago Bears professional football team, which had been created almost 35 years earlier as successor to a 1920–1921 semipro team, the famous Decatur Staleys—sometimes known as the Starchmakers.

James H. Beaumont, director of public relations for the Decatur corporation in 1956, was in charge of organizing the extracurricular activity. Beaumont recently reminisced as follows: "In case anyone had ever forgotten that Gene Staley, our founder, was a pioneer in pro football as well as in starch and soybeans, we had a royal reminder of the past during that holiday in Chicago. The Wabash ran a special train which carried about 500 Staley employees, including our officers. We even hooked on an extra car carrying the University of Illinois marching band.

"On Sunday afternoon at Wrigley Field, George Halas, owner of the Bears, was really caught up in the spirit of the event. The fact that we were observing our fiftieth corporate birthday was only incidental. The big emphasis was placed on saluting the company's involvement with football in the good old days when George Halas, a Staley employee, coached and played for the Decatur Staleys, and when Gene Staley, the proprietor, cheered from the sidelines.

"At halftime at Wrigley Field, many of the old-timers who played for the Decatur Staleys were introduced. George Halas spoke. Gus Staley spoke. And the Illinois band went into a formation spelling out STALEY. Fittingly, the Bears—'our Bears,' we called them—played the Baltimore Colts, keeping in mind our company was located in Baltimore when it was incorporated 50 years earlier. Not quite so fittingly, the Bears lost, 21–20.

"It was the biggest all-out binge in Staley history. George Halas kept saying, 'If it weren't for the Decatur Staleys there never would have been the Chicago Bears.' Nostalgia prevailed. We celebrated going up to Chicago, we celebrated while we were there, and we celebrated coming back. I doubt if any company ever had such an uproarious event for its golden anniversary. It was the talk of the town for a long, long time."

A more meaningful but less exciting scoreboard for 1956 showed corporate sales at $181,040,000 versus $111,618,000 for 1955; earnings of $4,854,000 versus $3,799,000 for 1955; and per-share earnings of $2.61 versus $2.08 for 1955. At casual first glance, those 1956 numbers appeared to be quite a bit better than the respective numbers for 1955.

Yet, as the company's 1956 Annual Report reminded stockholders, the newer numbers were for 12 months of a newly established fiscal year ending September 30, 1956, whereas the

Edwin K. Scheiter, H. P. Dunlap and A. E. Staley Jr., the first three men at the left, took a trip in a Ryan monoplane in 1928. The plane was similar to the one flown to Paris by Charles Lindbergh in 1927.

When completed in 1927, Elevator C had a capacity of more than 5,000,000 bushels of grain.

The founder sits at the winter home which he and his wife occupied in the thirties. The mansion was located alongside Biscayne Bay in Miami. The Decatur industrialist died there the day after Christmas in 1940.

A. E. Staley; Sr., purchased "the home of my dreams" on College Hill in Decatur for $16,500 in January, 1913. The structure is an original Frank Lloyd Wright design.

This is the former Emma Tressler of Bryan, Ohio. She became Mrs. A. E. Staley in 1898, and resided with her husband and children in Baltimore before moving to Decatur in 1912.

A. E. Staley, Jr., took over management of the company following his father's death in 1940.

A. Rollin Staley, the founder's younger son, joined the company in 1931. At the time of his death in 1968 he was a member of the Board of Directors.

Ione Staley was the eldest of the founder's five children, a family which included three girls and two boys.

Mary, the youngest of A. E. Staley, Sr.'s five children, spent much of her adult life in the Chicago area. She died in 1968 in Lake Forest, Illinois.

Ruth Staley left Decatur at an early age, attended schools in the East and settled in Highland Park, Illinois. She lived there for many years before moving to Florida, where she died in 1970.

The company expanded its manufacturing operations beyond Decatur for the first time in 1940 when it acquired this soybean processing plant in Painesville, Ohio. Located near Lake Erie and the St. Lawrence River, it was able to use a nearby harbor which was closer to Europe than some coastal ports.

Herschel Morris, Staley's first starch sales superintendent, is shown in a photo circa 1923.

David P. Langlois joined Staley in 1932 as a research chemist. Co-inventor of Sweetose corn syrup, Dr. Langlois was a successful research leader for the company until his retirement in 1966.

Dr. Julian K. Dale, co-inventor of Sweetose, a proprietary sweetener, was an early member of the firm's research organization. The product was introduced in 1938.

Sweetose corn syrup was sold in large quantities from 1938 on. The product was patented in 1939. It focused national attention on the Staley company's expertise in enzyme technology.

Helen Harder, the first cashier, was the forerunner of many women who contributed to the Staley company's operations.

Lucile May, the company's first nurse, was largely responsible for the construction of a first-aid hospital on the premises of the Decatur plant. A plaque in her memory hangs inside the hospital's main entrance.

Doris Hill Murphy was secretary to E. K. Scheiter from 1923 until his retirement in 1966.

Dr. R. E. Greenfield joined Staley in 1926 as an expert on the company's water supply needs. In later years he was placed in charge of a newly created research engineering division.

Howard File spent most of his adult life heading Staley chemical laboratories and the company's research department. He joined Staley in 1912 when both he and the company were quite young. He retired in 1947 and died in 1951.

During World War II, Staley employees participated in a payroll savings plan with allotments for War Savings Bonds averaging 10 percent of gross payroll. In this photo of ceremonies at the Decatur plant, the 10 percent Treasury Department flag is raised below the American flag.

The "Staley Gardens" were first instituted by the company during the Great Depression as a way to help employees become more self-sufficient. Over the years, employees have continued to till and fertilize the soil and stake out plots each spring.

Clinton P. Anderson, right, Secretary of Agriculture in the Truman administration, was the guest speaker at an Illinois Chamber of Commerce dinner in Decatur in 1945. With him is A. E. Staley, Jr.

Up-to-the-minute market information was kept posted on this "big board" in the grain-buying department. Today's grain buyers utilize individual consoles located on their desks.

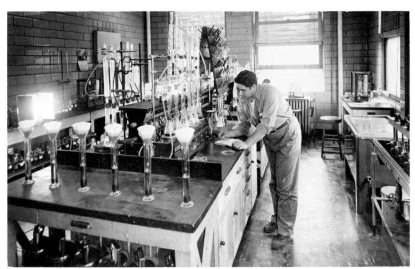

Early research efforts were carried out in laboratories such as this one, forerunner of the company's multi-million-dollar research center.

Otto D. Sutter was named manager of the New York office in 1937. He began his Staley career in 1922.

Transportation of corn and soybeans overland, either by rail or truck, has changed over the years. This early worker in the plant prepares to manually switch rail cars from one track to another.

Early methods of bottling corn syrup made it necessary for workers to "cap" the bottles by hand.

Staley has operated its own fire department at the Decatur plant for a number of years. Working in cooperation with Decatur's city fire department, Staley fire personnel have proved invaluable in a number of emergency situations.

The introduction of "packing lines" included machinery which filled bottles, capped them, and packed them into cartons for shipping.

Horace J. Kapp was elected vice president of the company in 1942. He joined Staley in 1930.

A bagging station in the Staley feed mixing plant of the 1940s could be used simultaneously on different feed formulas.

H. C. Wilber, with supervision over
Elevator C, was division superintendent of the company's terminal elevator division.

John Shyer, the company's first 50-
year veteran.

W. B. Bishop joined Staley in 1927 and
had responsibility for the company's
chemical engineering laboratory for
many years before being made technical superintendent.

1955 numbers covered only nine months of activity. In order to make the Staley fiscal cycle line up more closely with that of the crop year, the company had earlier decided to adopt the new fiscal time period during 1955. And in order to accomplish this, it had to limit its 1955 financial statement to the period between January 1 and September 30. As a consequence, the nine-month "year" during 1955 was not a normal yardstick for measuring relative sales and earnings for the pure and simple reason that they weren't comparable.

Yet, on a 12-month basis, the 1956 fiftieth anniversary sales total of $181,040,000 was a record high for any such period. But earnings were a drag. They failed to match the advance in sales.

Those soybeans. The volatile swings in their prices had always been what Gus Staley called "a cross to bear." Profit margins were seldom as attractive as those for corn. In 1957 the company said tersely, "profit margins disappeared." Even when demand was heavy for meal and oil, Gus Staley simply tolerated the soybean side of the business. Almost as in a simplistic scenario, his subordinates were characterized—or caricatured—as "corn people" or "soybean people." There were more of the former (including Gus, of course) and only a relatively few of the latter, despite the efficiencies of the switchover from the expeller crushing system to the hexane extraction process.

James W. Moore, who joined Staley in 1941 and retired as a vice president of agriproducts in 1977, recently said, "Gus Staley was heavily involved in policy committees in associations representing the corn industry, but I can't recall that he ever attended a meeting of any soybean association. In the fifties, we let the soybean business slip through our fingers."

Sad to say, total soybean sales nationally increased rapidly while Staley's sales remained flat. A few statistics will help tell the story: Staley's percentage of the total national soybean processing dropped from 21 percent in 1940 to 10 percent in 1950, and by 1957 the Staley share dropped to 7 percent. This, by the way, was the year that Cargill, Inc., of Minneapolis—which had diversified beyond its customary grain business into soybeans prior to World War II—went into Number One position in the nation as a soybean processor, a catbird seat that it has never relinquished. (Alas, the Staley position kept slipping after 1957, falling to an ignominious 2.5 percent of the national total in 1973 before rebounding back to a respectable 10 percent in 1981.)

The roller-coaster ride in soybeans, and especially its dips, could be traceable to the understandable disenchantment in the heart and mind of Gus Staley, who had towering respect for his father but who had minimum enthusiasm for the very soybeans that brought his father accolades as a pioneer.

Then into the Staley fold came U B S—of Cambridge, Massachusetts. It was the big news of 1959.

It brought unrealistic expectations to a nice, profitable, conservative corn and soybeans company that wound up going so far as to give birth to an East Coast offspring called Staley Chemical Company!

But mostly the U B S experience showed the pains and perils rather than the potentials and profits of diversification into someone else's game.

The U B S acquisition was a creation of: (1) the Arthur D. Little study, although indirectly, (2) Dr. Thomas L. Gresham, directly, and (3) the company's compelling urge to get into some sort of noncorn, nonsoybean business.

The 1959 Annual Report had an apt sum-up. It said, in part:

"For a considerable length of time, the Company and the management of the U B S Chemical Corporation of Cambridge, Massachusetts, engaged in negotiations looking toward a merger. The negotiations were successful, and the acquisition was completed on June 30, 1959, on a basis which, in effect, resulted in the Company exchanging one share of its common stock for each one and three-quarters shares of the stock of the U B S Chemical Corporation. On the completion of the transaction, U B S became a division of the Staley Company. This

168

acquisition is in line with the Company's stepped-up research and diversification program and is expected to add impetus to the Company's entry into the field of synthetic polymers.

"U B S was originally founded in 1903. It serves industry with a wide variety of chemical products which fall into three general categories: products for use in the shoe industry; polymers for use in the manufacture of wax, paper and paint products and leather finishes; and products used for textile coatings and miscellaneous industrial purposes. In recent years, notable success has been made in the field of polymer chemistry."

The most appropriate comments on the U B S acquisition came in 1981 from Don Nordlund and from a man named Robert M. Powers.

Nordlund said, "U B S did provide an entry into synthetic polymers. It had a floor wax polymer which was extraordinary. However, the acquisition presented our company with many challenges, including the crucial question of who'd have what kind of responsibilities, in Decatur and in Cambridge, for running the show. In light of other priorities, I'm afraid the Staley company allowed U B S to become a bit of a distant orphan. The experiment simply didn't work out."

Powers, who became no less than the Staley company's fifth president late in 1980, also provided his view of the U B S acquisition. A PhD from Emory University, Atlanta, who joined Staley as a research chemist in 1958, Powers has an intense interest in the relationship of technology to profitable operations. In discussing U B S, Powers said, in retrospect, "U B S cost less than $5 million in fact but it cost us more in manpower deployment, executive trauma, and overall distraction. The effort turned out to be diversionary." Powers should know. He was assigned to the task of serving as director of research for the U B S division in 1967 and 1968. "I learned a lot—or, at least, had the opportunity of learning a lot—about people relationships at U B S," he said.

Yet obviously Staley did not acquire U B S for the purpose of setting up a distant orphanage or for providing a clinical opportunity for Bob Powers to learn about people relationships. The U B S detour was, in essence, something less than the Staley company's finest hour. Nearly two decades were needed to absorb and then to cast off the U B S additions to the Staley cause.

Several years after the acquisition had been effected, the NASA space-exploring agency in Washington, D.C., decided it needed the U B S property in Cambridge. Upon departure from the heady environment of Boston-area technology, the U B S operation was downgraded and moved into an industrial area facility in New Jersey, sharing office and manufacturing space with a small leather-finishing subsidiary acquired earlier by the Staley organization.

Ultimately, U B S retreated silently into the wings—as silently as mixed feeds had done earlier. And Staley Chemical Company disappeared from the Yellow Pages.

Yet, in the interim, what was known as "the rest of the company" prospered and set its sights on several realistic goals for the sixties—along more orthodox and traditional paths.

CHAPTER ELEVEN

THE SHOCK WAVES OF THE SIXTIES

The assassination of President John F. Kennedy (1963) . . .

The assassination of his brother, Senator Robert F. Kennedy (1968) . . .

The assassination of Martin Luther King, Jr., (1968) . . .

The frustrations of the war in Viet Nam . . .

The worst race riots in the nation's history (during the long, hot summer of 1967) . . .

Mass demonstrations against the educational system, against the military system, against the business system, against the political system . . .

Protests against nuclear energy . . .

Widespread use of drugs and narcotics . . .

Consumerism . . .

Silent Spring (1962) by Rachel Carson, an antiestablishment indictment of government-sanctioned, industry-conceived pesticides and a plea for a somewhat risk-free environment . . .

Unsafe at Any Speed (1965) by Ralph Nader, an antiestablishment manifesto serving to rally his countrymen against "the lethal design of the Corvair" and against the "entrenched, arrogant, profit-hungry" automobile industry . . .

Advance of the prime rate for borrowing funds from 4 to 4½ percent (1965), the highest in 35 years . . .

These were among the headlines on the pages of U.S. history during the turbulent sixties.

Decatur, Illinois, in the heart of America, was obviously not immune and, indeed, no community and no citizen was unaffected by the shock waves of the sixties. However, Decatur seemed partially shielded by the gentle, swaying cornstalks serving as a buffer zone in all directions. Further protected and isolated by its distance from activists' demonstrations in the big cities, Decatur remained essentially a placid place. O. T. Banton, former local editor and recent author of the history of Macon County, said that students at Millikin University were concerned but were not inflamed into revolt or rock-throwing during the tempestuous era. When in 1967 the students sponsored a "peace vigil," their largest demonstration involved brandishing signs reading, "Draft Beer—Not Students." A stable, stubborn status quo was a harbor and a hallmark in the boondocks—or "boonies"—with advantages outweighing transient disadvantages, Banton suggested. His perceptive point was well expressed—and well taken.

Out at the east end of town in the staunch citadel serving as administrative headquarters of the Staley company, Gus Staley, chairman, had in-house problems of his own. Commenting on corporate performance in his 1960 Annual Report to stockholders, Staley wrote, "Soybean results were the poorest the company has experienced since it pioneered soybean processing in 1922." A "second verse, same as the first" lament, this time the black crepe for soybeans-at-Staley seemed nearby.

Noting, almost with a sigh, that "the company expects to be able to halt the downward trend in earnings," the chairman reported that net profit for fiscal 1960 was $4,520,834 compared with $5,712,982 for the prior year, and that net sales for fiscal 1960 were $155,697,017 compared with $168,704,309 for the prior year.

An unhappy time.

The top four officers in 1960 were Gus Staley, chairman and

chief executive officer; E. K. Scheiter, president; Donald E. Nordlund, vice president, who earlier added international operations to his financial and law portfolio; and Roy L. Rollins, vice president, who was promoted almost dramatically from personnel manager to administrative director of manufacturing, personnel, and purchasing.

Considering that as the decade started Staley and Scheiter were in their late fifties, and also considering that Rollins was only 49 years old, and further considering that 38-year-old Nordlund was a newcomer (1956) compared with Rollins's proud boast of having "started at Staley as a high school boy in the summer of 1925," the big promotion for Rollins, as announced by Gus Staley, was regarded by some insiders as extremely significant in light of possible management succession plans for the near future.

As befits the ancient and traditional grapevine system, gossip among humans on "who's ahead in the high-level sweepstakes?" was commonplace when Staley employees participated in chitchats down by the soft drink vending machine. After all, they reasoned, overseeing the manufacturing and personnel and purchasing functions amounted to a sizable responsibility. Rollins had been on the Staley board since 1954. Was the new up-the-ladder position for Rollins a harbinger of things to come? This was the question. This was the persistent puzzlement in the corridors on east Eldorado Street.

Despite problems, the year 1960 brought several events that signaled stability and growth.

At Decatur, an imposing $4.2 million research center was dedicated on the east end of the property, providing row upon row of modern laboratories that would help attract technical people to the Staley cause, and also providing a theaterlike auditorium for future annual meetings of stockholders and other functions involving assemblies of up to several hundred persons. New ambience. A new plus.

Far away from Decatur another 1960 event took place— quietly—during a European trip that Don Nordlund undertook

173

to investigate investments in chemical manufacturing. The event was a nice, long, relaxed, genial dinner in one of the many superlative restaurants in Brussels, Belgium. His dinner companion was Pierre Callebaut, a principal officer of Glucoseries Reunies, S.A., a corn refining company in Aalst, Belgium, which had achieved solid success in selling starch and syrup on the European continent. Nordlund recently reminisced, "Pierre Callebaut already knew, without my reminding him, that the Staley company had done very little in the way of capital investments outside the United States—surely nothing at all compared with the multinational reach of the Corn Products company.

"I told him I thought the Staley board would consider investing capital in European corn refining if a satisfactory and equitable arrangement could be made. I suggested any deal would have to be reciprocal and would have to provide new opportunities for both parties. I even went so far as to suggest that an interchange of technical information could be mutually advantageous. I also told him perhaps his company could be helpful in licensing some of our research developments around the world."

Things moved fast from there on. By late 1960, the Staley corporation paid $4 million for a 50 percent interest in the Brussels company and for a 25 percent interest in an affiliate of the Brussels company, Tunnel Glucose Refineries, Ltd., of Greenwich, England.

(Subsequently, Pierre Callebaut became chairman and managing director of Glucoseries Reunies and in 1973 he was elected to the Staley board. The 1960 purchase of Belgian and British equities gave the Decatur company its first real foothold abroad and also served to encourage later investments in soybean processing in Spain and in corn refining in Mexico. It also led to corn refining licensing agreements in Argentina, Japan, Korea, and Chile. In the course of assembling equities outside of the United States, the Decatur company targeted toward having its foreign manufacturing interests and licensing contracts account for 10 percent of the corporation's total pretax profits—an objective only sometimes met. Yet, in any case, the international interests amounted to a substantial advance from the initial overseas beachhead that Don Nordlund established in 1960.)

Late in 1962, employees' shop talk in hallways and rest rooms had fresh stimulation when a new, high-level executive known as "the stranger" arrived.

"The stranger" was officially identified to stockholders as "Robert H. Davidson, who joined the company as vice president in charge of marketing and a member of the board. He has extensive experience in the food field and brings to the company a wealth of knowledge and experience."

He was that and more. A 45-year-old aggressive extrovert, "the stranger" was the chairman's protégé. Gus Staley felt his administrative staff would be motivated to higher accomplishment under the rallying magnetism of a man who had gained some fame as a persuasive and dynamic marketing strategist for General Foods. Without delay, the old corporate tom-tom system of internal communications, based on ricocheting rumors and unsupported speculation, surfaced the notion that perhaps Davidson was actually brought aboard as an ultimate replacement for Ed Scheiter, the company's president. As a further consequence, Roy Rollins was perceived to be less of an odds-on favorite in employee rumor-trading concerning the executive suite sweepstakes.

Gus Staley was aware that the new man's entry would make waves. Some internal observers interpreted Bob Davidson's arrival as an indication that the company planned to place more emphasis on consumer goods, considering that Davidson had strong credentials in merchandising consumer products.

Interesting as the guessing games may have been, they didn't last for long. Nor did Bob Davidson. He exited hastily in 1966. If Gus Staley had in fact viewed "the stranger" as a potential crown prince in the high halls of management, he didn't say so. The mere fact that he had reached outside for the creation of a new and prominent upper-echelon position—

and that he did so at a time employees were wondering about long-range plans for top leadership—resulted in what one observer called "small tremors among the loyal and faithful troops."

In sum, morale may have slipped a bit, but it didn't slump seriously. After all, Gus Staley was the boss and was far-and-away the principal stockholder. He not only had every right to "try something new," but he also had an opportunity to demonstrate to his colleagues that he was indeed willing to "try something new."

The business of being far-and-away the principal stockholder didn't necessarily bother Gus Staley—and in 1963 he had effective control of more than 45 percent of the company's shares —but he was bothered by the fact that Staley stock moved extremely slowly on the over-the-counter market, even in Decatur. On many days Decatur brokers were able to inform Gus, "Zero Staley shares moved yesterday." This was disconcerting. And the situation failed to promote a healthy, active national market for Staley shares. Particularly if a broader identity on the business scene was to be viewed as an asset, rather than the company being positioned as a secret in the cornfields, there would seem to be some advantage in having Staley shares listed on the New York Stock Exchange. Visibility—the name of the game—would obviously be enhanced. The company knew it met all NYSE requirements.

In point of fact, Gus Staley had brooded about the situation for several years. He had talked to investment bankers. He had talked to businessmen in blue chip industries who gave him their opinions on the advantages of being "listed" on "the big board." He had discussed the situation with his own directors, of course.

And then, all of a sudden, in 1963 he was ready to go. An associate who worked closely with the Staley chairman at the time said, "He dragged his feet and dragged his feet and then out of the blue he appeared with an urgent order to start yesterday if possible but tomorrow at the latest."

On May 10, 1963, the company issued a news release saying

that its chairman, A. E. Staley, Jr., appearing that day before the New York Society of Security Analysts, had said:

1. The company would list more than 2¼ million shares of common stock on the New York Stock Exchange on May 29.
2. "Continued growth" would likely occur in the company's "corn refining, consumer products, chemical, and overseas operations." (Soybean operations were not mentioned up front in the rundown of principal operations, but such marginal matters as consumer products, chemical, and overseas operations were listed in the first paragraph of the company-written news release.)

With Ed Scheiter and Don Nordlund sharing head-table prominence at the security analysts' luncheon meeting in downtown New York, Gus Staley summarized his viewpoint in four words: "We are growing up."

His speech was informative, factual, and straightforward. James H. Beaumont, who had public relations and then marketing responsibilities for the Decatur company from 1955 to 1978, recently recalled, "I worked closely with Gus in the preparation of that 1963 speech in New York but he actually hooked all the information together himself. He realized that his appearance on Wall Street represented a significant outing for his company. He did his usual thorough, diligent, responsible job. He showed his stature, his integrity, his familiarity with all aspects of the business."

During the course of his New York remarks, Gus Staley mentioned there were "ten other corn refiners" and "scores of soybean processors." He stressed that 60 percent of the Decatur company's fixed assets were in corn refining, "which ranks first in profit contributions."

He added that the product group ranking second in profitability was grocery products. "We want to do much more in the consumer field," he stressed. Then in third place came soybeans, sad in tone. He explained that "margins are low" in soybeans; that no soybean expansions were being planned because "we feel that other pastures are greener"; and then he added, somewhat condescendingly, that soybean operations, often showing an operating loss, "have absorbed overhead costs which would otherwise have to be charged to other activities." If his audience concluded that soybeans were bad baggage and a drag on company earnings, the audience was very much correct.

Gus Staley concluded his remarks by saying, "More than 360 patents mark the progress of Staley research." Then he mentioned, "There are 2,273,348 shares of Staley stock outstanding, almost half of which is held by nonfamily interests. We have some 5,300 holders of common stock. We feel we have reached a point where a good market can be maintained on the New York Stock Exchange."

If it is true that being listed on the New York Stock Exchange is like a singer finally making it at the Metropolitan Opera, then it can also be said that Gus Staley contributed a professional, competent, soft-spoken solo in his May 10 prologue before the listing of his company's stock. Although there were no "bravo!" calls following his luncheon address, there were appropriate congratulations for the Decatur company's impending "arrival" on Wall Street. From a low of $34½ per share in 1963, Staley stock went to a high of $46 in 1966 and to $50-plus in 1969, with occasional dips down almost as low as $30 per share in the volatile world of stock transactions during the company's first six years on "the big board."

A few business analysts were not bullish on the company's prospects following that coming-out party in 1963. *Forbes* magazine, famed for its own flair in "interpretive journalism" and noted for needling those corporations not meriting its favor, came out with a rather negative appraisal of the Decatur company in its issue of October 1, 1963.

Commenting on the Staley company's plans for a $10 million expansion of Decatur production facilities, *Forbes* used "Reluctant Expansion" as its headline. *Forbes* added, "The company is 40 years behind Corn Products in making a big push overseas." *Forbes* then added, "Staley is paying for being ultraconservative in an expansionist era." Then, as the coup de grace, *Forbes* used a boldface subhead near the end of the Staley story that read, "Aiming Low," and it quoted Gus Staley as having commented, "Other [more successful] companies would not have grown any faster than we did if it had not been for their acquisitions. We haven't been as aggressive as good judgment indicated."

Apart from the nonreportorial, subjective, negative tone of that story—merited or unmerited notwithstanding—the *Forbes* piece was regarded as a low blow in the judgment of the magazine's readers in Decatur, Illinois, especially considering that the story appeared at a time when the Staley company was on an upbeat, semientrepreneurial course and needed all the encouragement it could get for its preliminary steps away from —at least in this one instance—its ultraconservative ways.

Roy L. Rollins, who retired in 1970, recently remembered "that 1963 *Forbes* insult, " as he called it. He recalled, "For some reason or the other, I was probably the first person in the office to have the *Forbes* article land on my desk. Because a lot of our executives happened to be out of town that day, I had the distinction of taking *Forbes* magazine upstairs to show it to Gus Staley. I didn't want him to hear about the story from a customer or from the competition so I felt it was my responsibility to show him the bad news promptly."

Poor Rollins. Knowing, no doubt, that since all the way back in ancient literature messengers bearing bad news for the king have been traditionally and summarily beheaded, Rollins was told by Gus Staley, "Roy, sit down until I read the article."

So . . . Rollins sat down.

Did Gus Staley say, "Roy, how do you want your coffee? With cream or black?" No.

Was Gus Staley angry when he read the *Forbes* piece? Yes.

Rollins recalled, "Gus kept using the same word—'unfair.' That was the right word. The story was not inaccurate but it was unfair. It strained to reach negative conclusions despite its mention of our big expansion and forward plans. Gus's early reaction was, 'I think I'll write the *Forbes* editors and give them a piece of my mind.' I said something like, 'What good will that do, Gus?' Then, after a long period of silent thought, he called in his secretary, Estella Launtz, and he quietly, deliberately dictated a letter to *Forbes*. The letter said, 'I have been a faithful servant of my father's affairs.' Then Miss Launtz asked, 'Is that all you want to say?' Gus replied, 'Yes.' And then she and I were dismissed."

It should be explained that the "expansion" referred to in *Forbes* magazine dealt with the Staley company's 1963 decision to construct a $10 million plant in Decatur to produce 100 million pounds a year of crystalline dextrose, a sweetening agent 80 percent as sweet as sugar—by a revolutionary process. When the company made its first announcement on August 30, 1963, the *Decatur Herald* understandably played the story along positive and parochial lines. With the Staley company's employment to be increased by 70 to 100 jobs as a result of the dextrose operation and with 200 building trades workers to be needed for construction, the local paper heralded an appropriate huzzah for the project, using an eight-column headline on page one plus a photo of Gus Staley. Mayor Ellis B. Arnold was quoted as saying that the implications of the Staley program were bigger than the expansion itself.

Yet neither *Forbes* nor the *Decatur Herald* had the dextrose story in full perspective. An unbiased, independent version of the Staley expansion into dextrose was recently provided by Dr. Brian W. Peckham, assistant professor of economics at the University of Utah, Salt Lake City, whose 1979 doctoral dissertation at the University of Wisconsin, Madison, was entitled "Economics and Invention: A Technological History of the Corn Refining Industry of the United States." (Excerpts from Dr. Peckham's exhaustive, 680-page treatise are used herein with his permission and encouragement.)

Dr. Peckham has reported:

In the early 1950s the Staley management, despite favorable results in pilot plant experiments, decided against putting the company into manufacturing crystalline dextrose. There were perhaps several reasons why A. E. Staley, Jr., was reluctant. Surely the most important reason was his apprehension about investing the necessary $10 million just after the firm had finished spending almost $37 million to expand and modernize both its wet milling and its soybean processing operations and to put up a monosodium glutamate plant that technical change had rendered obsolete only a few years after it was built. In addition he was perhaps also apprehensive of entering into competition with Corn Products which had . . . decades of experience developing and marketing crystalline dextrose and which at the time probably accounted for about 90 percent of U.S. output of this commodity.

Wishing to realize a return on the company's research investments, the Staley management chose to try to sell its glucoamylase process to Corn Products. . . . In 1953, Dr. David P. Langlois and Dr. A. Willard Turner of Staley provided Corn Products with copies of reports on their fermentation research. The older company [Corn Products] was still relying exclusively on the conventional acid process to manufacture starch sugar.

About 1951 or 1952 a few scientists at Argo, Illinois, had begun investigation into new enzymatic methods. But the managers at Corn Products showed little enthusiasm for the early research on glucoamylase. It is therefore not surprising that they also showed little enthusiasm for the products of similar research done earlier at Decatur and now being offered to them in the form of a license to use Staley "know-how." [Author's insert: Staley had put a price tag of $250,000 on its "know-how."]

By May, 1954, the Staley firm was ready to proceed with patent applications. In the late fifties scientists at Argo made progress developing their own glucoamylase process. To determine the feasibility of operating the process on a commercial scale, Corn Products set up a special pilot plant in an old factory building near Krefeld-Uerdingen on the Rhine River in Germany. Testing began there in mid-1957.

When news of the pilot plant operations in Krefeld reached Decatur, suspicions arose that Corn Products might, after all, be making use of Staley technology which earlier Corn Products had reviewed and then declined to purchase. As a consequence, Staley officials requested a meeting with Corn Products to seek information on the Krefeld process and to determine if grounds existed for a suit to recover damages for patent infringement.

Sources within the Staley company declared that two Corn Products representatives conceded that the fermentation process used at Krefeld was the one they had learned about from study of the Staley reports several years before. However, [other] sources within Corn Products insisted the mold culture used at Krefeld was distinct from the culture developed by Langlois and Turner at Staley.

Whatever the course of the discussions, their outcome was a cross-licensing agreement between the two companies under which Corn Products assumed an obligation to make payments to Staley over a period of two to three years beginning about 1961. Sources within Corn Products asserted that their company's acceptance of these terms reflected only its desire to avoid the expense and risks of possible litigation and not its assent to the Staley claims. The best evidence, however, is that the payments called for under the agreement were far from nominal and amounted perhaps to $2 million.

The disagreement between Staley and Corn Products apparently generated no deep antagonism and was soon followed by the restoration of completely amicable relations between the two companies.

That, then, is Dr. Brian Peckham's background of the Staley company's role in the development of a sophisticated process for the manufacture of crystalline dextrose—tracing back to 1954. To the degree that *Forbes* magazine indicated that Gus Staley was "ultraconservative in an expansionist era," *Forbes* was on target as demonstrated by the fact that the Decatur company did not decide to build a dextrose plant until 1963 and did not begin production until 1965. Procrastination, to be sure.

Robert M. Powers, former director of research who became Staley's fifth president late in 1980, recently said, "We had the technological base to get into dextrose earlier and to capitalize on our early discoveries for making a product which would lead us into other lines of business (such as high fructose corn syrup), but we simply didn't have the courage to back up our technology with dollars."

In 1965, Donald E. Nordlund, a 43-year-old lawyer, became the fourth president in the company's history in a move that finally put a damper on employees' curiosity about Gus Staley's plans for the management succession process up in the rarified atmosphere of the eighth floor of the headquarters office building. Even though the 1965 announcement about Nordlund's selection for the Number Two job didn't specifically say Nordlund was the heir apparent to the top position of chairman and chief executive officer, the future was plainly forecast by his elevation to the presidential position.

Gus Staley remained chairman and Ed Scheiter, who had been president since 1958, became vice chairman of the board with a plan to retire from active duty in 1966 but to remain on the board.

The background on that 1965 development was recently recounted by Nordlund himself:

"In the prior year, 1964, Gus Staley called me up to his office. He explained that for a long time he had been thinking about the future course of the company and about the kind of leadership which would be required to guide the company's efforts— down the road.

"And then he told me something which was a rather private secret, probably known only to his secretary, Estella Launtz. 'Every year,' Gus explained, 'I've been writing a memorandum, one copy of which is safeguarded here in Decatur and another copy of which has been locked up at the Baltimore Safe Deposit and Trust Company.' Then Gus added, 'Your name is on that memo.' That's how I found out Gus wanted me to be president and to succeed him, later on, as chairman. He added that he had reviewed the matter with his outside board members and that they were in unanimous agreement.

"Gus had explained in 1964 that he didn't want to make any announcement until November of 1965, which meant that it would be necessary for me to help keep the information secure for more than a year.

"When Gus further explained that he felt a sense of relief in informing me and that he had deliberated long and intensely on the subject of management continuity, I surely wasn't surprised on that score. I needed no reassurance that he had not made a hasty decision. I knew him well enough to appreciate that impulsive decisions were not part of his management style or character.

"Then he added, 'I intend to begin phasing myself out of the picture, too.' He was still in pretty fair health in 1964; he was 61 years old. He said, 'Nothing would make me happier than to free up a little personal time so that I can travel with Eva [his second wife] who means so very much to me. I owe it to her and maybe I even owe it to myself.' "

Sawdust is, as any schoolchild knows, an accumulation of small particles of wood resulting from various manual and mechanical cutting and trimming operations in the lumber industry and allied businesses. No throwaway by-product, sawdust is sold for many purposes, not the least of these being that it would be a monstrous nuisance to store or to dispose of in an ecologically sensitive society concerned about all forms of waste disposal, with the Environmental Protection Agency in Washington serving as a "big brother" monitoring the overall situation.

But how about small particles of potatoes—yes, potatoes—which remain after potato chips and frozen French fries are processed? Schoolchildren may or may not know that millions

184

of pounds of bits and pieces of potatoes accumulate every year —to be casually discarded or deliberately salvaged.

The Staley company became seriously interested in bits and pieces of potatoes in 1966 when it purchased starch-recovery operations from the Morningstar Division of International Latex and Chemical Corporation. The principal plant sites were at Monte Vista, Colorado, in the Rocky Mountains, and at Houlton, Maine, near the Canadian border.

It should be explained that in earlier years, the starch-from-potatoes industry thrived in Colorado, Maine, Idaho, and other "potato states," using culls (small, poorly formed, or damaged potatoes) as the raw material for making starches for paper manufacturing and other industries. Then two things happened: (1) Federal regulations clamped down on water pollution caused by potato residues, and (2) the dehydration industry began to compete for purchase of those "ugly spuds," sending their prices upward and limiting sources for starchmakers.

Staley's initial interest was in making potato starch but, thanks largely to a man named Paul Neumann, the Decatur company later broadened its interest to include a recovery process in Colorado which turned a waste-disposal problem into a profit.

Neumann and his assistant plant manager at Monte Vista, Stephen Tyler, are given principal credit for developing dryers and filters which have enabled Staley and other potato processors to entrap tiny scraps and to turn the recovered bits and pieces into a productive resource in the manufacture of specialty starches. Of equal or perhaps greater importance, such a recovery system enables "chip and fry" manufacturers and other potato handlers to stay on a friendly basis with the EPA.

Considering that most Colorado potatoes are grown in gravelly soil, easily picked up with the vegetables at harvest time, Neumann also designed a "de-rocker" which separates rocks from potatoes. All the machinery used in the handling and recovery process is a proprietary asset of the Staley company which licenses its hardware and its know-how widely in the potato processing industry.

Neumann, who recently retired, explained, "About 30 million pounds of bits and pieces are captured every year by companies using the Staley recovery system. This recovered scrap represents starch material that used to be thrown away."

Neumann noted that potatoes are Number Two to corn (and tapioca is Number Three) in providing a source for starches and that Staley is still grinding nine tons of potato culls an hour at Monte Vista. He explained that potato starch has some unique qualities and then he added, "our own starch helps make the paper and the paper coating for the high-quality pages used in *National Geographic* and other magazines."

And if people thought Neumann was ingenious in his starch-recovery days at Staley, wait until they hear this: He has retired to Arizona where he intends to try out a "dry sluicer" of his own invention—a device that uses air instead of water and which, he hopes, will capture gold dust from the sands of the desert.

Two deaths clouded the Staley horizon in the late sixties.

On February 25, 1967, Mrs. Emma Tressler Staley, widow of the founder, died at age 92 in Miami. She had married A. E. Staley, Sr., in 1898 when she was 23 years old and he was a 31-year-old salesman peddling packaged Cream starch, operating out of Baltimore. Balancing her husband's aggressive and dominant manner with sensitivity and shy behavior, Emma Staley was a talented pianist and author of poems who stayed supportively in the background and who was credited by her husband as having been the most beneficial and ennobling influence in his lifetime.

Following her husband's death in 1940, Emma Staley decided that the big house on College Hill—which Gene Staley had called "the house of my dreams"—was too much to care for. Without delay she moved to Florida, to remain for the rest of her life. Subsequently she donated the 30-room Decatur house and its furnishings to the YMCA.

Newspapers listed Emma Staley's estate at $750,000, but people who knew her realized that this was only a fraction of her wealth. Under terms of her will, the holdings were divided equally among her three daughters and two sons, except for bequests to the First Presbyterian Church in Decatur and to the Decatur and Macon County Hospital.

The second death, occurring February 2, 1969, had a more direct and immediate bearing on the affairs of the company in terms of Gus Staley's desire to stay on the job. On that day in 1969, Eva Coddington Staley, Gus's second wife, died in Decatur at 46 years of age. Since Gus's remarriage in 1951, Eva Staley had become known as one of the most gracious hostesses and homemakers in Decatur. Strikingly beautiful, she "made me proud to be her husband," Gus had remarked.

In 1952, Eva and Gus had a birth in the family, a boy—Gus's fourth offspring and Eva's first. They named him Robert Coddington Staley and expressed the hope that someday he'd go to work for "the company." (He did—and does.)

Eva Staley's death was traumatic to those closest to her. Early in 1968 she had learned she was the victim of terminal cancer—in an advanced stage. Gus's second son, Henry, recently recalled, "Eva's illness was prolonged—a real tragedy. She never discussed her plight with anyone. Even when she went to New York for radiation treatments and even after she underwent surgery, she never showed any signs of despair even though she knew the cancer would be fatal.

"She always looked radiant. Actually, shortly before her death she was so positive and hopeful—at least in her behavior and attitude—that I actually believed she was making progress. Yet, shortly after Christmas of 1968 she began to weaken and six weeks later she was gone."

Intimate friends of Gus have observed that "he never really recovered. He loved Eva beyond description." After her death he found his home at 5 Montgomery Place a lonely place.

Don Nordlund recalled that "in the springtime of 1969, Gus Staley came into my office and said he'd like to amend something he had told me in 1964. He reminded me that five years earlier he had voiced the wish he could gradually phase out of responsibilities at the company and begin to spend more time with Eva and to do more traveling with her.

"Happily, he was able to accomplish some small part of his

objective in the interim. But after he sat down in my office, he said, 'Now that Eva is gone, the company is the only thing I have to live for. There'll be no interruption in the plans for you to take on more responsibilities but I'm afraid you'll be seeing more of me around here than you and I had counted on. With Eva gone, the office is my only home.' "

Unknown to both Don Nordlund and Gus Staley at the time, Gus would shortly wed again, to Catherine Robinson Hull. The union ended in divorce in 1974.

Also unknown to both Don Nordlund and Gus Staley at the time, Gus would enter the new decade of the seventies in rather robust health only to learn that he, too, would fall victim to a succession of health problems. These ailments would gradually become incapacitating and would, in turn, make him happy he had "contingency plans" for turning over leadership to the first non-Staley chief executive officer in the history of a company founded by his father in the dawning days of the century.

Above all, Gus had all along felt obliged to serve as the steward and custodian of the legacy passed on to him by his father. Despite *Forbes* magazine, despite those pestiferous soybeans, despite the "lonesomeness of the high command," his loyalty to, and respect for, his father had never ebbed as time ticked by.

Anyone wanting to wrap up the Staley story of the sixties without including "the saga of air conditioning" would be overlooking one of the most refreshing episodes in the company's history. Granted, the story may not have been the most important, but it was, beyond doubt, a special breath of fresh, cool air.

The story started on May 13, 1969, when the board of directors approved an initial sum of $1,340,000 for installing air conditioning in Staley's main office at 2200 Eldorado Street.

In order to appreciate this revolutionary development, a bit of background information is necessary.

When "The Castle in the Cornfields" was built—without refrigerated air—40 years earlier, some wistful and optimistic planners had proclaimed that the administration building's ventilating system would keep offices and corridors comfortable during the long, hot summers of the midwestern Corn Belt region. Or, at least, that was the theory used by wistful construction engineers. However, the fact of the matter was that the thick-walled Staley administration building became a superheated oven during the summer months. Employees—weary, wilted, and worn by entrapment in muggy confinement—were finding it difficult to be their productive and creative best under circumstances of oppressive heat and humidity. And there seemed to be no prospect for improvement.

Why no prospect for improvement? The answer was simple. Gus Staley simply didn't believe in air conditioning. "It would be a frivolous cost burden," he said. And he added, "The workers in the plant don't have it."

Through the fifties and sixties when other office buildings in Decatur were being mechanically cooled to facilitate summertime comfort, and when restaurants and hotels and residences were being similarly equipped, Gus Staley had remained adamant. Regardless of the high temperature in his own office or in the boardroom or wherever, he had remained a stubborn stoic. He had never complained. Always bedecked in a woolen suit—along with an always freshly starched shirt and conservative necktie—Gus Staley would have been disloyal to his own convictions if he had ever let slip a mere "Warm, isn't it?" An oscillating fan in his stuffy office also would have been an admission of personal discomfort. So—no fan. Working in shirtsleeves would also have been a betrayal to his cause. So—no shirtsleeves.

If the *Guinness Book of Records* had investigated the subject of air conditioning in American office buildings in the late sixties, the odds would have been heavy that the Staley administration building would have been duly listed as "the last holdout" and as a nostalgic relic of early Americana.

A longtime member of the Staley staff named M. Ray York recently commented on the discomfort factor during the "good old days" when the "castle" was a kiln. York, longtime building superintendent at Decatur, remembered that "during the days before air conditioning we had to have a crew clean the office building thoroughly every night. With trucks in constant parade, churning up dust on the adjacent plant property, the office became the favorite landing place for airborne debris. It was necessary to keep the windows open during the daytime, but we'd shut every window at 5:30 in the afternoon. People in the Personnel Department were telling me that some job applicants, who would visit our office for interviews, decided 'no thanks' after experiencing brief periods of discomfort during a visit to our hotbox."

Ray York may or may not have been advised, but early in 1969 Don Nordlund and other executives came to the conclusion that the company should join the human race and invest in air conditioning in order to improve employee productivity and morale. By this time the executives had endured enough bad jokes such as "I hear it's cooler next to the boilers in the plant" and "I think I'll become a chemist so I can bask in the blissful hideaways of the air-cooled Research Center."

The strategy mounted by Gus Staley's principal lieutenants was simple. They said, in effect, "If we can confront Gus with a well-thought-out plan, he'll buy it—and the board of directors will go along." And that is precisely what happened. Gus Staley, board chairman and CEO as well as principal stockholder, could have thwarted the plot—beg pardon, the plan—once it was finalized for board presentation. But he didn't. With an understandable reluctance born of a longtime, firm, adamant, and entrenched position, he finally capitulated to the viewpoint of his colleagues.

Ray York said he well remembered "the day in 1969 when my boss, Don Rogers, received a phone call from Ed Freyfogle, head of the Engineering Department, advising that the board had acted and that we'd all be going full tilt ahead on the installation of air conditioning. The news was so good that I almost didn't believe it."

No longer would York have to hear good-humored and not so good-humored complaints and occasional exaggerations such as "Ray, it's 113 degrees in my office" and "My telephone earpiece is so hot it burned my ear." But York knew the new job ahead would involve a massive renovation to accommodate air conditioning in a thick-walled structure without ductwork.

The renovation wound up costing a total of $2.5 million—far above the actual $1.7 million needed 40 years earlier to build and equip the whole building. The J. L. Simmons Company returned as general contractor, bringing in sheet metal workers, electricians, plumbers, painters, carpenters, and other craft workers—all heroes as far as sweltering employees were concerned.

"Putting ductwork in a fortress was a very large job," York explained. "We had 160,000 square feet of office space to cool. We needed 700 tons of air conditioning. Ceilings had to be lowered everywhere—to provide space for ductwork—except in the lobby, rest rooms, executive dining room, basement, and the eleventh floor." The east half of the building received the first delightful wafts of cool air in the summer of 1970 and occupants in the rest of the building joined the human race in 1971.

The company was able to move into the new, air-cooled era of modern business without sacrificing the grandeur of its ornate lobby and without detracting from the overall ambience of the original internal layout. The "showplace" which was founder Gene Staley's pride and joy remained a "showplace." The board's favorable nod in 1969 thus became one of the most memorable decisions of the sixties, assuring that in future years office inhabitants would find summertime comfort in their towering edifice at the east end of town.

Time—as it always does—marched on.

CHAPTER TWELVE

THAT SHANGRI-LA CALLED RETAIL

The Staley company "went retail," as the saying goes, from the day of its birth near the turn of the century. Cream starch for the kitchen and Cameo starch for the laundry were early products on grocers' shelves. Later on, syrups for pancakes and waffles became popular retail items, carrying the Staley label.

Yet, as the company grew, it veered away from retail and concentrated on becoming a supplier to industrial processors. Carload shipments became a specialty. Emphasis was placed on debottlenecking old plants, on reducing unit costs through economies of scale, on technological upgrading, and on expanding production capacities. Slowly but surely, productivity was drastically improved.

In the forties and fifties—especially the fifties—when the gospel of diversification reverberated through the Decatur hallways, no one wanted to abandon the corporation's industrial ramparts, but hardly a day passed when someone didn't dream out loud about the glories at the end of the retail rainbow.

Yet, how does a company acquire a franchise and a presence in the consumer goods marketplace? How does a company emerge with the right new product at the right time at the

192

right price in the right place—in partnership with Lady Luck of course? Does a company simply invent a product or process in-house and send it into a waiting world where some real or imaginary consumer need, hitherto unmet, cries for a solution, a remedy, a quick fix? Or does a company launch a trendy, "me, too" product to ride the coattails of some other firm's winner?

Or does one obtain a franchise in the consumer goods marketplace via the shortcut expediency of simply going out and buying an existing franchise on Main Street, USA?

The traditional dream, of course, is to invent and patent a proprietary product that will reap resounding rewards overnight. Peter Drucker, latter-day business scholar and author, has called such an accomplishment "possible but not probable in the turbulent world of consumer goods but, in any case, the neatest trick of the week."

The plain fact of the matter at the Staley company was that some of Gus Staley's lieutenants had a hankering to journey onto retail roads, high risks notwithstanding. And Gus wasn't big on high risks. The dilemma, therefore, was simple: A non-chancy chief executive officer wasn't too eager to become heavily involved in chancy forays into the wondrous and worrisome realm of retail merchandising, considering that his company had a heavy-volume, big-bulk, industrial sort of power and personality.

Particularly in the forties, when war-related problems proliferated, the company was tucked cozily into a security blanket of doing what came naturally; namely, moving massive shipments of corn and soybean products to processors in such industries as paper, leather, packaging, textiles, animal feeds, and, of course, food. In such a lifestyle the company's comfort factor reposed. The corporation had grown accustomed to thinking in terms of trainloads—ton upon ton upon ton. (And that's where approximately 95 percent of the cumulative earnings have been generated over the total period from 1906 to 1981.)

Yet, that Shangri-la called retail has always beckoned and the Staley company has not been immune, over the years, to various flirtations—involving both internal (homemade) and external (purchased) products.

That the record has been spotty is understandable. "Every try a triumph" has not been the track record at Staley or anywhere else. The American business system is not simply the "profit system." It's the "profit and loss system," based on risks and rewards. Gus Staley knew this all along. In agreeing occasionally to venture down retail paths he simply hoped to have more winners than losers and to have the performance of the former more than compensate for the disappointments of the latter.

The "mixed bag"—beyond the early starch and syrup products for retail—began to materialize in the forties when a loser, a semiwinner, and a real, honest-to-goodness winner came onto the public scene.

To appraise the loser expeditiously let it simply be said that Stoy soy flour represented a noble effort to reduce a bothersome inventory brought about by the government's demand for increased wartime production of soy protein. Shoppers didn't have soy flour at the top of their lists. The product just sat quietly on grocers' shelves. Ultimately, the product was recalled. Happily, its distribution had not been widespread and the dollar loss to Staley was minimum. Yet the black eye in the grocery trade was surely not a plus.

Ironically, soy flour was (and is) a highly meritorious product. Used as a binder and supplement in prepared meat products and also used in certain bakery items, soy flour has been cheered as a superior source of protein. When the epitaph, R.I.P., was inscribed for Stoy, there was general agreement that the company's introductory merchandising effort was largely at fault—not the quality of the product itself.

The second retail entry, the postwar-era winner, was Sta-Flo. Not surprisingly it was—and is—starch. Liquid laundry starch. Up until its appearance on the market, no company had been able to keep starch in suspension in a liquid. However, the problem was solved in the Staley company's laboratory—not too unlike homogenizing milk.

Being first on the market with a ready-to-use liquid starch, the Decatur corporation was anxious to achieve national distribution. Some delays occurred in obtaining a sufficient supply of bottles, but this difficulty was overcome. Sta-Flo became a success at retail outlets coast to coast. An "unbelievable" (Gus Staley's adjective) $3 million was spent for Sta-Flo advertising in 1947. Retail price: 26 cents a quart.

And then there was a third adventure—with retail overtones. It involved a flavor enhancer, monosodium glutamate, called Zest (a trade name Staley was able to register within the confines of food additives despite the ownership of the same word by Procter and Gamble for soaps).

The initial markets for Zest monosodium glutamate in 1948 were the food processing industry, which purchased 50- and 100-pound drums, and restaurants and hotels, which purchased 10-pound and 1-pound containers. By the time the product was readied for retail, it was in 4-ounce containers.

Zest came on like a winner. The result of what the company's Annual Report called "17 years of effort in research and in the pilot plant," the product seemed destined to stimulate the taste buds of millions of Americans just as the same generic product had gained widespread acceptance in the Orient where bland foods seemed to need a flavor boost.

But just when things looked bright, a cloud appeared. Whereas Staley used corn gluten as the principal raw material for its flavor-enhancing crystalline powder, a competitor came up with a process involving the use of beet sugar waste—at half the cost. For a while, Staley turned its back on its own technology and purchased bulk quantities of its competitor's economical product, for packaging at Decatur. But finally, Zest joined Stoy in the graveyard of well-intentioned experiments in the marketplace. Meantime, on shelves everywhere, shoppers began reaching for the competitor's monosodium glutamate, called Accent, a product that has since been dominant at the corner store.

While Gus Staley's not-to-be-discouraged colleagues kept looking for "something new," Gus kept repeating, "There's not much new under the sun."

Then came the good news—in 1954. That's when the company fortuitously encountered a completely new product called Fluff-It.

Henry Volle, who was active in marketing Staley consumer products from 1946 until 1969, recently commented on Fluff-It, saying, "I'd call it the most successful grocery product in the company's history."

Volle explained, "Early in 1954, a Staley salesman told his superiors at Decatur they ought to visit a Cleveland, Ohio, dentist named Dr. Charles Robinson, who had grown tired of having his neck scraped by the abrasive texture of his white cotton jacket. Even when the jacket was unstarched, it was uncomfortably rough rubbing against the dentist's sensitive skin.

"The word reaching Decatur was that Dr. Robinson had talked to some other dentists and learned that they, too, had been bothered by the sandpaper characteristics of freshly laundered jackets. Dr. Robinson checked into the problem and learned that since the introduction of Tide and other synthetic detergents, the natural oil residues in fabrics were being removed and the fabrics were becoming more abrasive. So the good doctor did something about it. In his spare time, he set up some equipment in his garage and made small batches of a fabric softener. He put it in bottles and sold it through a local distributor. And he called it Fluff-It. The product was not only an effective softener but it also reduced static electricity in fabrics.

"When we sent several technical people to Cleveland to check on the liquid product made in the dentist's garage, Dr. Robinson agreed to sell his backyard business to Staley on the condition that he'd keep all rights for the state of Ohio. Staley not only took over the product and promoted it heavily but it changed the trade name to Sta-Puf rinse, mainly because our company was fascinated by the idea of having its product names begin with the syllable 'Sta.' "

The story of Sta-Puf was recently embellished by John A. Dellert, who in early 1981 was director of marketing for the

Staley Consumer Products Group in Oak Brook, Illinois, a suburb of Chicago. Dellert related, "Sta-Puf was an innovator in the fabric softener field, which has since become a half-billion-dollar business for the varous companies in it. The Staley company had the good judgment, early on, to go national. No one realized at the time that Sta-Puf rinse was simply the first generation of a product line and that two additional generations of development were down the road.

"Procter and Gamble accounted for the advent of the second generation when it came out with a concentrated fabric softener called Downy in the late fifties. We at Staley kept selling our single strength Sta-Puf despite Procter and Gamble's new entry, but ultimately we added a concentrated formulation to our line. More recently, the industry has introduced the third generation in what we call in-dryer sheets.

"But the liquids are still used. Some people prefer them even though they require the user to make a return trip to the washing machine during the rinse cycle—unless the washer is equipped with an automatic dispenser. But the in-dryer sheets represent the real growth segment of the market. Staley introduced Sta-Puf sheets in 1979."

Hip-o-Lite Marshmallow Creme, a 1958 addition to the Staley grocery products array, was an indisputably legitimate innovation. It was destined to remain in the Staley catalog for 15 years.

Invented in 1905 by a Greek-born St. Louis candy maker named Walter H. Hipolite, the product was initially manufactured in small batches using corn syrup and egg albumen as its basic ingredients. After thriving under several owners in the St. Louis area, it was sold to the Staley company under the rationale "What could be better than an exclusive specialty product using a corn refinery's own corn syrup?" It was a "natural," a "given," a gooey white hope for success under the Staley retail products banner.

Henry Volle recalled, "Hip-o-Lite had earlier been made in 200-gallon batches. We at Staley tried to make it in 2,000-gallon batches. But the syrup kept going to the bottom and the albumen kept coming to the top. We finally perfected a continuous process and sold the product successfully on a regional basis. It was a big seller around the Thanksgiving and Christmas holidays. Actually, the product was so good that Kraft Foods decided to get into the business in the sixties. When Kraft Marshmallow Creme came onto the market on a national basis at low introductory prices, we suspected the lifespan for Hip-o-Lite would be threatened, keeping in mind that Kraft is a fine company with a broad franchise in retail food products.

"But Hip-o-Lite was an exciting product—and it made fantastic fudge."

Fudge—that creamy, chocolate-flavored, high-caloric delicacy whipped up in the kitchen on a lazy Sunday afternoon—can obviously be made from a variety of recipes, but Hip-o-Lite promised what was known simply as "the world's best fudge." An enticing substance in a glass jar, Hip-o-Lite was also used judiciously in sweet potato casseroles. And on ice cream. It was the base for cake frosting. It even transformed the lowly graham cracker into a culinary feast.

It was occasionally profitable while it lasted—and it lasted until 1973. P.S.—Kraft Marshmallow Creme survived. It is also good for fudge. And it contains corn syrup supplied by the A. E. Staley Manufacturing Company of Decatur, Illinois.

The sixties brought some additional specialty products into Staley's retail camp, all by acquisition.

Sno-Bol (1962) is not exactly the kind of retail product appropriate for extended discussions at the dinner table or at the country club. Sno-Bol is a toilet bowl cleaner. It was recently ranked best of its class by *Consumer Reports* magazine. In 1981, it sold just behind nationally distributed Lysol, even though Sno-Bol had only regional distribution. Importantly, this unglamourous, highly efficient product achieved commendable profitability.

Rain-Drops (1967) was a water softener. It has been marketed in respectable quantity in such hard-water states as North

In August, 1948, A. E. Staley, Jr., company president, left New York harbor on the Cunard liner *Queen Elizabeth,* bound for England en route to Norway. In the bon voyage party before the ship sailed were his mother, the founder's widow, Mrs. Emma Tressler Staley, and his wife, Mrs. Lenore Mueller Staley.

A. E. Staley, Jr., addressed the Senate Foreign Affairs Committee in 1949 following a year-long assignment as director of the Economic Cooperation Mission (Marshall Plan) in Norway.

This medal is the "Commander with Star of the Order of St. Olav," presented to A. E. Staley, Jr., for his service to Norway.

One of Staley's first chemists, Lowell Gill, joined the company in 1915 and stayed on to make contributions in major areas of R & D.

Technical Director Dr. Thomas L. Gresham, with the company only a short time, conceived the present Staley Research Center.

A. E. Staley, Jr., is shown with Edwin K. Scheiter. The former was the founder's older son, who joined the company at an early age and went on to become president and chairman. Scheiter started in 1918 and became the company's third president.

A. E. Staley, Jr., cut the ceremonial birthday cake during festivities marking the 50th anniversary of the company in 1956. Looking on are, from left, Decatur Mayor Clarence Sablotny; Decatur Chamber of Commerce President E. Wayne Schroeder, and Frank M. Lindsay, owner and publisher of Lindsay-Schaub Newspapers, Inc.

A. E. Staley, Jr., center, and his younger brother, Rollin, are shown with George Halas, owner of the Chicago Bears, at Wrigley Field in 1956, the company's 50th year. Halftime ceremonies were devoted to the Staley organization, which sponsored the Bears' predecessor team, the Decatur Staleys, starting in 1920.

W. R. Boyer was elected director and treasurer of the company in 1955.

A. E. "Gene" Staley III, son of Gus Staley and grandson and namesake of the founder, joined the company in 1952 and left several years later to go into business for himself in Chicago, where he now resides.

Ruth Cade, for many years editor of *The Staley Journal,* used the in-house publication to inform employees and retirees of company goings-on. Established in 1917, *The Staley Journal* was one of the first magazines of its kind in the United States.

Eva Coddington became Gus Staley's second wife in 1951. A native of Chicago, she was very active in Decatur civic affairs prior to her death in 1969.

Garry Moore, left, advertised "Sta-Flo" starch on his morning network television show. With him are Denise Lor, a singer on the program, and Durward Kirby, the show's announcer.

Radio and television personality "Smiley" Burnette made personal appearances during the fifties to promote Staley consumer products. Also identifiable in the photo are, left, Joe Schultz, and right, Henry Volle, former Staley employees. Rol Staley is driving the automobile.

Staley consumer brands included popular laundry and home care products.

Mary Mathews (a pseudonym) was popular with homemakers of the period, giving advice on the use of Staley's various home care products. Mary Mathews' famous recipes featuring Staley products as ingredients were also popular items.

Staley made several important acquisitions in the 1960s, including that of Wagner Products in 1968. Wagner, of Cicero, Illinois, was a producer of fruit-flavored beverages.

Here is an array of Staley consumer products. The company disposed of most of its retail products line in 1981.

Dakota, South Dakota, Minnesota, Wisconsin, and Michigan. In early 1981, Rain-Drops powder, in boxes, was alive but not thriving in Staley's retail array.

Diaper Sweet (1967) was an especially unglamorous addition to the retail line. It was a scented powder for use in presoaking babies' diapers. The surging popularity of disposable diapers from Procter and Gamble and other national companies has tended to worsen the odds for long-term growth in profits for Diaper Sweet.

Lightning White (1967) had only a brief appearance on retailer shelves. It was a nonbleach laundry whitener, developed especially for wash-and-wear fabrics. It was headed for national distribution in 1968 and seemed to be a promising entry in the retail field. Then the big "soapers" came out with a competing product, based on new enzyme technology, and Staley's bolt of lightning promptly disappeared.

Wagner fruit-flavored drinks (1968) represented a more ambitious undertaking on Staley's part. Purchased from Wagner Industries, Inc., of Chicago, the Wagner line was marketed nationally, with marginal success. Appearing in such flavors as orange, grapefruit, grape, peach, apple, and tropical punch, using corn sweeteners or saccharin for sweetening agents, the Wagner drinks encountered price pressures and heavy competition on grocers' shelves. In the late seventies, prices plummeted for concentrated juices (versus Wagner's 10 percent natural flavor and 90 percent dilution). Also competing in such a product area were Tang–type and Kool Aid–type powders plus a wide variety of other uncarbonated refreshments such as Hi C and Hawaiian Punch.

In the more recent era, the Staley company continued to expand its grocery products line for retail sale and also for nonretail sale. Examples include: (1) the acquisition of Gregg Foods Company (1976) of Portland, Oregon, which had the leading retail tub margarine in the Northwest and which marketed salad dressing and other food products up and down the West Coast; (2) Re-Mi Foods, Inc., (1980) of Elk Grove Village, Illinois, which specialized in products for the institutional food service field. (In 1981, Americans consumed as much food through restaurants, hotels, fast-food takeouts, and institutions as that which was prepared at home, which means that if such a trend is maintained, the food service field seems to hold promise.)

Question: In a world where Procter and Gamble spends a fortune on advertising (more than $600 million in the year 1981), what were the chances for an essentially industrial company, such as Staley, in the field of consumer products?

Answer: Its been an up and down experience, but during many years Staley did well. There were even a few times when grocery products represented the second most profitable group in the company, far behind corn products but slightly ahead of soybeans.

During the period when Gus Staley sat sternly at the command post, his rule-of-thumb was to spend no more than $3 million for any single acquisition. In the case of Rain Drops and Diaper Sweet, he insisted on a trial period of being a licensee before "taking the plunge" into actually purchasing the rather modest properties. In the case of the Wagner line of fruit-flavored drinks, Gus Staley broke all rules by going to $15 million as the acquisition price. In perspective, $15 million was a lot more than the $3 million rule-of-thumb, but it was petty cash in the big leagues of national consumer marketing.

In fairness, mention should be made that changes in the marketplace, beyond the Staley company's control, impacted the fate of some of its consumer products. Cream starch for the kitchen—which sold at retail for 10 cents for a 1-pound package 80 years ago and which sold for 70–80 cents in 1981—has been a declining item. Store-bought pies, puddings, and gravies have tended to minimize the preparation of homemade delights requiring cornstarch. Similarly, Sta-Flo laundry starch was negatively affected by the emergence of drip-dry, wash-and-wear apparel needing no stiffening to survive and flourish in a more casual, more informal, less starchy, less rigid, new American era.

Inevitably, some Staley watchers point out that Gus Staley

—during his more than 30-year period of leadership—should be given credit for some of the retail businesses he *didn't* get into. Example: He once almost made a substantial capital investment in an attempt to obtain a national franchise in pet foods after having acquired a small company making Vitality brand dog and cat foods. Would he have competed in an all-out way against Purina's Dog Chow and other nationally advertised products or would he have tiptoed timidly into a major-league, multibillion-dollar market with a modest, minor-league effort? One will never know. Suffice to say he looked, listened—and stopped, perhaps judiciously in light of other faint feints.

Observers have pointed out that the Decatur company has been able to dabble in consumer product ventures—ranging from test-marketing to full-scale, coast-to-coast distribution— because of its staunch financial base, thus leading to an accumulation of important experience in, and a sense of familiarity with, the ebb and flow of events in the Shangri-la of consumerism.

Perhaps so. And the company's consumer products ventures also contributed one additional sidelight, by virtue of bringing one extra member of the Staley family into the firm—Augustus Eugene Staley III, grandson of the founder and eldest son of Gus. "Young Gene," born in 1928, was employed by the Decatur company from 1952 until 1958, heading up advertising efforts for grocery products—and also for soybeans. After leaving the company, "young Gene" moved to Chicago to pursue an ad agency career.

The big news came on July 24, 1981, when the Staley company announced it had agreed to sell its Consumer Products Group to Purex Corporation of Lakewood, California. The agreement called for Purex to purchase the assets of the Decatur company's household products and retail food products, excluding Wagner fruit-flavored drinks and Gregg's margarine and salad oils, for an undisclosed amount of cash (later to be revealed as approximately $10 million).

Two weeks later, an additional announcement disclosed that

201

Staley had agreed to sell its line of Wagner fruit-flavored beverages to Westin, Inc., a diversified food company headquartered in Omaha, Nebraska. "Several million dollars" was the price Westin paid.

The second announcement added, "This completes the company's plan for divesting its consumer products business. However, Staley will continue to remain active in the food service field through its Gregg and Re-Mi operations."

Subsequently, chairman Nordlund explained, "We had actually decided early in 1981 to put our consumer products up for sale. And, believe me, that was a rough decision.

"Over the last several decades, our retail products did amazingly well, considering they were always an adjunct to our main lines of business. In more years than not, they added to our profitability. Many were highly innovative. Many helped increase public recognition of the name Staley. In the sixties and seventies, the Consumer Products Group experienced real growth. But the growth was not quite up to company expectations.

"As many businessmen have discovered, it's not only important to know when to get into a new activity but it's also important to exit when evidence suggests continuation would not be compatible with company aspirations down the road. We owe it to our stockholders to deploy our capital, our energies, and our strategies in those fields which promise the greatest long-term rewards. As conditions change in the marketplace, a company has to be sufficiently mobile and flexible to enable it to capitalize on its biggest opportunities.

"It would be my judgment that in the forseeable future Staley will concentrate on doing the things it knows best—playing from strength, so to speak. This doesn't mean we'll not continue to invent new products. It doesn't mean we won't continue to apply our storehouse of technology to filling human needs. But it does mean we'll zero in with greater intensity in providing corn and soybean products to those industries and businesses which rely on our expertise to enable them to serve the consumer.

"We'll continue to be on Main Street, USA, and in fact we'll increase our presence there. But probably not under the Staley retail label. We'll often be the special ingredient in someone else's product. There are rich rewards awaiting down that road."

CHAPTER THIRTEEN

THE SWEETEST STORY EVER TOLD

Not that anyone would want to but . . .

If a person would crush a well-soaked kernel of hybrid corn between his or her molars, there would be no taste of sweetness. Yet when starch from a kernel is subjected to the wonders of science, a metamorphosis occurs and, *voilà*, America's leading grain crop—corn—becomes the strongest competitor to the world supply of cane and beet sugar.

It's all as simple as that.

Or, well, almost as simple as that.

There have actually been four milestones in Staley's development of corn-based nutritive sweeteners (in contrast with nonnutritive, noncaloric synthetic sweeteners such as saccharin):

1. After World War I, when sugar remained in short supply, the Staley company made a corn syrup that was about 40 percent as sweet as sugar. It was referred to as CSU—corn syrup unmixed. It was a generic product that ran deep into history, having originated in Russia in 1811 and then later been popularized in Germany and France. Manufactured at Decatur in a process called acid hydrolysis, the company's initial corn syrup

had limited use—okay for giving a glistening sheen to hard candies; okay for mixing with sugar or molasses in a pancake syrup; okay for relieving some, but not much, of the demand for sugar in a wide array of end products; okay for helping customers cut their costs.

The company's founder, Gene Staley, was not particularly worried by the limitations of his not-so-sweet corn syrup. In fact, he was so entranced by the product's potential that he had a 24-inch conduit established between his plant and the Sangamon River in order to pump in sufficient water to sustain the operation of what was called "the glucose factory"—a turn of events that ultimately led to the creation of 3,300-acre Lake Decatur.

2. Immediately prior to World War II, Staley scientists introduced an enzyme-made syrup called Sweetose when once again the world was running short on sugar. Sweetose came onto the market with the proud boast that it was approximately 60 percent as sweet as sugar and half again as sweet as regular corn syrup. Both the degree of sweetness of Sweetose and the proprietary, patented enzyme technology were hailed as firsts. (It may be worth recounting that enzymes are natural, organic catalysts capable of causing chemical reactions.)

3. In the mid sixties, after a long period of hemming and hawing, a more sophisticated enzyme process was introduced to bring about the high-volume production of crystalline dextrose. At this third major milestone, Staley was able to say its dextrose product was approximately 80 percent as sweet as sugar and twice as sweet as conventional corn syrup.

4. And in the seventies came the IsoSweet line of high fructose corn syrups, some of which could properly be called as sweet as sugar—or more so. Benefiting from the use of a third enzyme in addition to the two enzymes required for dextrose, the new sweetener was destined to give the Decatur company the opportunity of becoming "Number One in the world" in an exciting new era of corn-based sweetening agents which would, for example, replace billions of pounds of sugar in most of America's major soft drinks.

From 40 percent as sweet to 60 percent to 80 percent to bingo. That, in brief, is the four-part sweetener story.

The Orient has cast its shadow on Staley people more than once.

Over a hundred years ago, in 1880, when the company's founder, Gene Staley, was a barefoot boy living on his father's farm in North Carolina, a Methodist missionary freshly back from China pulled out a handful of soybeans, sparking the interest of a young lad who much later would establish the first commercial soybean-crushing plant in the United States—in 1922.

As late as 1940, Manchurian soybeans continued to pour into the United States in high volume—competing against Gene Staley's domestic suppliers of beans—until Pacific Ocean shipping lanes were cut off by the war which followed the Japanese attack on Pearl Harbor.

A rather recent technological breakthrough in Tokyo particularly merits mention among the Oriental influences that subsequently reached as far as Decatur, Illinois.

Normally given broad recognition for their innovations in electronics, cameras, and automobiles—innovations launched in less than two decades after V-J Day—the Japanese also lost no time in achieving world leadership in the development of many new strains of industrial enzymes and other intermediates produced by fermentation.

Japanese superiority in developing new enzymes for sweeteners was recognized in the early sixties by the scientists at the Staley company, but it was not until 1965 that a Decatur representative met face-to-face with Japanese scientists in a friendly confrontation prompted by the Staley company's interest in high fructose corn syrup. This syrup was manufactured in Japan in the first commercially feasible process using enzymes —in very modest quantities.

The story of that 1965 confrontation, and of subsequent developments leading to Staley becoming preeminent in high fructose corn syrup, provides one of the most intriguing examples in twentieth-century scientific literature. Not as exciting, of course, as moon shots and satellite signals, the intense struggle to win the "sweetness war" was—and is—perhaps the most suspenseful chapter in the annals of the corn refining industry.

There is one big problem with scientific adventures. Cloaked in the closets of proprietary data and security; couched in the foreign languages of chemistry, biology, bacteriology, enzymology, or whatever; obscured by the "tech talk" of engineering, industrial scientific adventures are often understood and appreciated only by those relatively few intellectuals who are fluent in the complicated jargon of scientific specialties. Translations into popular idioms have made slow headway over the years, especially in product development not directly related to consumer concerns or to public projects.

Yet the excitement in science—though often hidden—is immense. Much of the excitement is traceable to extremely brisk competition among scientists—country versus country, company versus company, laboratory versus laboratory. In some countries (Japan, for example) governments throw their weight behind their scientists engaging in competitive assaults, feeling that national survival—no less—is at stake.

In sports, competition is easily recognized and appreciated because of the easy identification of the efforts made by winners, near-winners, and also-rans. Sports are an open book. "Trade secrets" are virtually nonexistent. Inevitably the element of competition is the carrot and the stick—the spark that prompts humans to run faster, jump higher, and become champions.

The scientific race among competing technology-based companies is often no less intense. Yet in keeping watch on technology-based companies, it is not always easy to identify the principal players by their numbers. Scientific adventures are frequently obscured by a traditional scrim of secrecy and blurred by the complexities of technological specialties in which PhD's—even the best PhD's—sometimes find difficulty in communicating with each other. Sitting on the other side of

207

the fence, the general public normally doesn't even try to understand the mysteries and mystique enshrouding the remote and presumably dull labyrinths of science.

The story of the development of high fructose corn syrup has been recorded appropriately in scientific and trade journals, but it has had limited exposure in the popular press. The Staley part of that story is especially intriguing considering that Staley's start-up was a bit late and that the company's first-place finish was spectacular (allowing that the word "finish" is never a permanent prize in the ongoing activity of business where nothing is ever really finished).

The Staley investigation, specifically into the technical details of the high fructose material, occurred in 1965 when Dr. Hans Wolff, one of four research directors at Decatur, went to Tokyo to learn about enzymes destined to revolutionize the business of amplifying the sweetness of corn syrups. During the prior year, Don Nordlund, who was vice president with international (among other) responsibilities, and William B. Bishop, director of facilities planning, had been in Tokyo for meetings with a Staley soy oil licensee, Hohnen Oil Company, Ltd., which was considering going into corn refining. On that 1964 visit, Nordlund and Bishop had a meeting with officials of the Japanese Fermentation Institute during which enzymes-for-sweeteners were discussed, but at that time no licensing of Japanese enzyme technology was available.

But when Dr. Wolff got to Tokyo a year later, he learned that another American company had recently arrived at the Otani Hotel and seemed to have gained an inside track. Dr. Wolff discovered that visitors from the Clinton (Iowa) Corn Refining Company Division of Standard Brands, Inc., had already been invited to undertake investigations at Japanese laboratories where important advances had been made in enzyme technology.

But Staley was not the only Johnny-come-lately on the Japanese scene. Corn Products Company and Union Starch Company were fellow also-rans. The tardy arrival of Corn Products was somewhat ironic considering that at this company's laboratories at Argo, Illinois, much successful work had been done in the fifties converting glucose to fructose enzymatically —that is, through the use of enzymes.

An insight into the 1965 goings-on in Tokyo has been uniquely provided by Dr. Brian W. Peckham, whose 1979 doctoral dissertation at the Graduate School of the University of Wisconsin, Madison, covered the history of the U.S. corn refining industry.

Dr. Peckham reported that the initial proposal made in Tokyo by the Clinton Division of Standard Brands was unacceptable to the Japanese, who were highly aware of the value of what was known as the Takasaki-Tanabe enzyme process. Dr. Peckham explained, "In an effort to expedite the discussions, Clinton engaged the services of a Japanese lawyer who, raised in New Jersey, had an excellent command of English and was able to speed up communication across the large table which separated the two parties to the negotiations."

Peckham continued, "After almost a month of discussions, the Japanese Ministry of International Trade and Industry accepted terms of a contract under which it granted Clinton exclusive U.S. rights, including the right to sublicense, to the Takasaki-Tanabe process. Thus when representatives of Corn Products, Staley, and Union Starch visited Japan and failed to secure legal access to the Takasaki-Tanabe technology, they left their companies with the alternatives of either developing their own distinctive enzymes and processes or trying to obtain from Clinton a U.S. sublicense."

Dr. Hans Wolff returned to Decatur empty-handed, but his journey was not without consequence. Based on the knowledge he had gained in Tokyo, he was convinced that his employer should try to find a way to participate in what he sensed to be the high promise of high fructose corn syrup. During 1966 and 1967, Dr. Wolff was active at Decatur in spirited discussions regarding the best way for Staley to plan its strategy. He found chairman Gus Staley only moderately interested; he found his scientific colleagues rather intensely interested; he found the Staley marketing people sparked by the potential challenge of

209

developing from scratch various sales strategies for various markets for the potential new product—if it ever evolved.

The company's "should we?" or "should we not?" dilemma was exacerbated when Clinton sent a scouting expedition to Staley and to other corn refiners, offering to sell Japanese-developed enzymes and knowledge. Dr. Peckham has reported that Clinton's anxiety to share with others was prompted by "possible commercial and antitrust problems." Plainly and in particular, Clinton was anxious to win over Staley as a sublicensee under a contract that would provide (1) enzymes, (2) a license to manufacture and market high fructose corn syrup, and (3) a general "know how" agreement to last over a 10-year period. A schedule for Staley's payment of royalties was the crucial and continuing part of the package. In 1968, the pact was signed, involving an up-front payment to Clinton of $1 million. Clinton expressed satisfaction that Staley's entry into the high fructose business would provide a second reputable manufacturer, an important plus considering that many, if not most, sweetener customers were apprehensive about aligning themselves "at the mercy of" a single supplier.

Shortly thereafter—in the spring of 1969—the Staley company boldly announced to the world it would use the Japanese technology (via Clinton) at a modern, new, $35 million plant to be established at Morrisville, Pennsylvania, near Philadelphia.

Principal dates in this saga were:

February, 1967—Clinton made its first shipment of high fructose corn syrup, two years prior to getting into full commercial volume.

February, 1971—Staley began shipping quantities of high fructose corn syrup, which it had obtained from Clinton, to "seed the market" among "test customers" in new territories.

April, 1972—Staley's commercial-scale plant in Pennsylvania came on stream, using Clinton enzymes.

As luck would have it, refined sugar prices plummeted in 1972. Falling to an attractive low of 12 cents a pound, sugar found only modest competition from high fructose syrup selling at 10 cents a pound (on a dry substance basis). But this uncomfortable and unprofitable position for Staley's IsoSweet high fructose syrup was not to last for long.

Knowing it was better to be Number Two than Number Nothing, the Staley organization found its spirits buoyed by the opportunity to move into a new product group with strong purpose rather than with timid pussyfooting. Don Nordlund, then president, who in 1971 began to take over the company's management reins in light of Gus Staley's declining health, promulgated a two-tier policy that embraced: (1) an all-out sales effort capitalizing on the geographic advantages of the Morrisville plant in the busy, bustling eastern region of the country which was alive with big bakers and independent soft drink bottlers who'd be potential customers for the new syrup, and (2) a vigorous research effort moving ahead without delay toward achieving a sense of independence in enzymes. Indeed, the goal involved finding a better-than-ever enzyme, keeping in mind that the corporation's R&D people had developed—over 30 years—more than a casual acquaintance with enzyme technology.

The company insisted, however, that it didn't want to get into the business of making its own enzymes—a specialty that had always been farmed out to enzymologists.

Happily, the price of sugar didn't stay suppressed. As wholesale prices of refined sugar quadrupled from late 1973 to late 1974, food processors greatly increased their consumption of IsoSweet and the price of high fructose corn syrup escalated correspondingly. Importantly, a subliminal goal was achieved during this tumultuous period, namely, food processors became familiar with the new syrup and no longer felt that expensive sugar would have to be an eternal rope and boulder around their necks.

But it was not all sweetness and spice for the Staley starchmakers. While gaining valuable lead time through their affiliation and royalty arrangement with Clinton, they felt hampered by being tied to Clinton's position as enzyme supplier and felt, also, that a more efficient process of manufacturing was achievable.

L. E. Doxsie, who retired as executive vice president in 1973 after more than 40 years of service, expressed an attitude of impatience a few years ago when he was reminded that some observers viewed Staley's "capitulation" to Clinton as the desperate act of an also-ran. "Even though we wound up as a direct competitor of Clinton in the marketplace, disadvantaged by the premium we paid as sublicensee, the arrangement was helpful to both parties," Doxsie stated. "In no way were we foreclosed against pressing our own investigations into enzymes made elsewhere to our specifications and in no way were we inhibited in our search for a better process to give us better profits. On balance, I'd say the Clinton contract served to give us momentum when momentum was precisely what we needed."

In *Business Week* magazine, Don Nordlund commented that food processors "did not rush to accept high fructose corn syrup. It didn't sell itself. Food and beverage processors do not readily change formulas to accommodate an unproven ingredient." Freely translated, this meant there was a mountainous amount of spadework to be done by marketing personnel.

Robert E. Smith, director of sweetener sales for Staley, recently reminisced on the trials and tensions of the period when Staley was pressing its high fructose homework night and day.

Involved directly with the challenge of developing new markets for the Morrisville output in 1972 and thereafter, Smith said, "Nordlund was right when he said there was no line of customers waiting impatiently outside our doors. We were flying blind with precious few built-in, automatic customers. We had a new product which we knew had a fantastic potential, but we didn't have a sufficiently cost-efficient process and we didn't have an avenue, yet, to the soft drink industry which we knew was the nation's largest user of sugar.

212

"Obviously our stake in high fructose corn syrup was influenced by the ups and downs of sugar prices, but we couldn't sit back and wait for the peaks to occur in sugar. We had to go through the painstaking effort of formulating our own marketing plan, regardless of where the enzymes were coming from, regardless of royalties, regardless of the pace of progress toward becoming self-sustaining.

"We had to go to customers' labs and plants to help them adapt their processes to our new syrup. Our progress may have been slow but it was steady. We knew we were at the leading edge of new technology. We were an advance guard, alerting customers to the benefits of a new era."

In perspective, the year 1974 was crucially important on the high fructose syrup front. Don Nordlund was still president, the Number Two position in formality. But he was briskly Number One in fact. Nat Kessler was technical vice president. Robert M. Powers was vice president in charge of research.

Bob Smith, the new syrup's sales planner, recently explained, "Our juggling act required a lot of dexterity. On the one hand we had to squeeze every ounce of gain out of our arrangement with Clinton and we had to plan our marketing as though our life depended on capitalizing on what we had. On the other hand, our company was reaching toward better processes to result in lower production costs based on our own engineering and our own private enzyme sources. We were living in the present and the future simultaneously.

"Nat Kessler and Bob Powers were out of town a lot. I'll let you know where they were. They were on trips to Copenhagen, Denmark, where they spearheaded many discussions with a company called Novo Industries S/A. Novo was—and is—one of the world's leaders in the development and manufacture of enzymes. Kessler and Powers and their colleagues kept informing Novo of our needs and supervised testing Novo enzyme samples in our Decatur labs.

"The big push was to put our second production unit on stream for IsoSweet high fructose syrup—at Decatur. People

213

worked heroically to pull it off—in 1975. Engineering and construction teams showed they could accomplish the impossible. This was one of the most gratifying accomplishments in Staley history."

Kessler recently added, "As early as 1975, when we began to capitalize on our own new know-how, we began to use some enzymes made by Novo. We phased out of the Clinton agreement by degrees and became totally independent by early 1978, ten years after signing the sublicensee contract."

Thus . . .

Jockeying between "hanging in there" during Phase One and creating the conditions for liberation from Clinton bondage in Phase Two, one might wonder, "When and how did Staley take a front position while uncomfortably carrying two kinds of baggage?"

The "when?" was actually in 1976. That's when Staley overtook Clinton and went into first place. The "how?" involved moving IsoSweet production into a third plant—a highly computerized $115 million unit at Lafayette, Indiana.

That leads to the big question: "What was the cause for the transformation from being 'staid, old Staley,' which was once a too-frequent saying in the industry, to an aggressive corporation hell-bent on outrivaling, outproducing, and outselling everyone else on the high fructose front?"

Answers to this question from many knowledgeable people in and out of the company are in many forms, but when the various answers are distilled into salient shorthand, they're all the same. In consensus, the "cause" is summed up in a two-word explanation. The first word is "Don" and the second word is "Nordlund."

Several people used the same offbeat comment that no doubt could be traced back to some perceptive observer given to picturesque speech: "Nordlund bet the whole box of jewels when he decided to build the Lafayette plant." Bob Smith had a special insight. He added: "I'll never forget how the period of Nordlund's aggressiveness and his will-to-win spirit began to take hold within the company. He didn't like playing second fiddle in the world of syrup. He changed our outlook. He made all of us at Staley feel like winners."

Up until the early fifties, the Coca-Cola company in Atlanta was so particular about the ingredients used in Coke that it had not permitted beet sugar to be used as a sweetening agent in what was then called "the pause that refreshes." Guarding its secret formula as if it were gold at Fort Knox, Coca-Cola had earlier permitted cane sugar—and cane sugar only—to be the sweetening base of its bottled product and its fountain concentrate.

The attitude implicit in that example typifies the way each leading manufacturer of soft drinks has always hovered over its proprietary formulas. Trademarks and manufacturing processes have always been regarded—and will always be regarded—as priceless assets of the major soft drink companies, and as an important part of stockholders' equities.

A larger user of corn and beet sugar than any other industry in the nation, the soft drink industry was concerned about sugar prices long before the early seventies when high fructose corn syrup began to appear seriously on the U.S. scene. With the old 5-cent bottle of a soft drink having gone up and up and up and up; with labor and distributing costs skyrocketing, what good news could the leading soft drink manufacturers and licensees and bottlers find to keep costs somewhat in check while at the same time maintaining product quality and uniformity in their refreshments?

High fructose corn syrup was not only a solution, in part, to the beverage industry's cost problem, but for the first time it opened the soft drink industry's doors to the corn refiners who heretofore had never been able to get past the receptionists' desks. Staley salesmen, with several corn syrups and dextrose in their line, had never been welcomed at Coca-Cola, PepsiCo, Seven-Up or any other principal soft drink establishment.

The soft drink companies' cost-price squeeze and the emergence of high fructose syrup just happened to juxtapose, to the delight of everyone except those at sugar plantations and refineries around the world.

Never self-sufficient in sugar, the United States in the early seventies was finding imported sugar—accounting for almost 60 percent of the nation's requirements—was adding to the country's deteriorating balance-of-payments situation and posing a threat of inflation (then still only a small national concern).

"Buy American!" was a slogan finding strong agreement at Decatur, Illinois, where the heaviest capital investments in the Staley company's history were called for as a price for staking a solid claim for IsoSweet. Staley was competing with Clinton and several other American corn refiners which had also gone beyond the "point of no return" in quest of the pot of gold at the end of the high fructose rainbow. (And an aggressive rival company also headquartered in Decatur, Archer Daniels Midland Company, was prominent among Staley's fast-moving competitors which were aiming their sights on the soft drink industry as the most tantalizing target of all.)

With the first formulation of IsoSweet selling 10 to 15 percent below the cost of "medium invert" sugar used by soft drink manufacturers, the Staley company felt it could make not only a temporary inroad in a tempting new market but that it could gain a permanent foothold long-term. This assumed that it could establish beachheads at Coca-Cola and elsewhere and could thus become familiar with the soft drink industry's stringent quality requirements and effectively respond to those requirements.

When IsoSweet initially came onto the market, it contained "42 percent fructose." This was a liquid approximately 92 percent as sweet as sugar. At the time, it was the only high fructose syrup technically feasible and the only one the Staley company could provide soft drink manufacturers for testing.

"A syrup 92 percent as sweet as sugar simply isn't sweet enough for all our needs," the soft drink people said. It was, however, sweet enough for some purposes and several soft drink companies decided to begin using the initial fructose product—in what the beverage trade calls "flavors," such as orange, grape, and cherry. These soft drink companies had two objectives: (1) to trim costs and (2) to familiarize themselves with the new liquid sweetener.

The shot heard around the world of soft drinks and the world of corn refining came in 1974 when the Coca-Cola company decided to use Staley's "42 percent fructose" (92 percent as sweet as sugar) in its "allied flavors"—principally the Fanta brand fruit-flavored drinks. Coca-Cola specified that IsoSweet would be used to replace 25 percent of the sugar. In other words, the sweetening for the Fanta drinks would be 75 percent sugar and 25 percent high fructose corn syrup, with IsoSweet actually accenting the flavors in noncola beverages.

A small beginning—but a beginning. An upstart product had gained acceptance in the hallowed halls where only sugar had been permitted entry since the dawn of time in soft drink history. Coca-Cola's cola brands were not involved, but the folks at Staley said to themselves, "Be patient."

Then came Squirt and Orange Crush, and Dr Pepper—each soft drink to use IsoSweet as a 25 percent sugar replacement. PepsiCo's Patio and Teem brands were the next to come in as IsoSweet users, and—encouragingly—on the basis of 50 percent corn syrup and 50 percent sugar.

Nehi, Royal Crown Cola, and Seven-Up were also among 1974 switchovers to IsoSweet—at the 25 percent level, and in 1975 Dr Pepper went from 25 percent to 50 percent.

Then came a three-year pause during which the 1974 and 1975 "testers" in soft drinks continued to use IsoSweet and during which, alas, the rest of the vast market, approximating 90 percent, decided to continue to maintain a status quo position with sugar sweeteners.

"It may have been status quo in terms of new contracts, but it wasn't status quo in terms of activity at Decatur," said Bob Smith, remembering the tempo. "Leading companies in the soft drink industry had told us very plainly we needed a sweeter syrup—fast. So we went all out in that direction—fast.

"I've never seen Staley people more determined. Tom

Fischer [Thomas V. Fischer, executive vice president in charge of the Industrial Products Group] was in charge of getting things moving. All along he had done a lot of leadership things to get us into '42 percent fructose' and now he swung hard into getting us a sweeter product. At the same time, in cooperation with R&D, he took the lead in planning for our new super-plant at Lafayette, Indiana. Tom Fischer knew we'd have to come up —and come up pronto—with '55 percent fructose,' a product that would be essentially as sweet as sugar."

And that's what went on at Staley during the "lull" when the Decatur starchmakers regrouped for a new assault against the ramparts of the soft drink industry. Because the "second generation" sweetener syrup would require an extra step—fractionation—during processing it would inevitably cost more than the "42 percent fructose," but it was plainly the breakthrough product that was called for by the soft drink industry.

"That pause period saw very few pauses," Bob Smith explained. "During our earlier experiences with the '42 percent fructose' product we had made contacts at the soft drink companies and we had been thoroughly briefed as to what those companies needed with respect to economics, quality control, sanitation, and manufacturing systems. All of a sudden we were on the 'inside' and we knew exactly what we'd have to do back at Decatur in order to score."

And "score" was the right word.

Here's the way the scoring went:

In 1978, Coca-Cola's allied flavors started using the new sweet-as-sugar "55 percent fructose" syrup on the basis of a 75 percent sugar replacement. Nehi went to 100 percent replacement. PepsiCo's Mountain Dew then came in on the total replacement basis. In 1979, Coca-Cola's allied flavors went total, as did Pepsi's Patio and Teem, as did products from Shasta, Welch, and Schweppes.

Then came the biggest news of all. The Coca-Cola people at Atlanta authorized the use of "55 percent fructose" as a 50 percent sugar replacement in Coke early in 1980 to be followed by Pepsi fountain syrup. Late in 1980, the Seven-Up company became the first major organization to authorize 100 percent use of Staley's "55 percent fructose"—in its Seven-Up brand, of course—after which the Dr Pepper brand followed suit to 100 percent replacement.

"Praise be to Allah!" chorused the Staley pilgrims whose journeys to the many front and back doors of the soft drink industry were finally rewarded.

While all those advances were being achieved, chairman Don Nordlund had the courtesy and courage to deliver a white paper entitled "High Fructose Syrups: The Competition to Sugar" before the International Society of Sugar Cane Technologists' 12th Congress in Manila, the Philippines.

He opened his remarks by saying, "Each day we work with two of the world's greatest agricultural resources, sugar cane and corn—two renewable resources with untapped potential."

Nordlund explained that "in 1972, two companies (Clinton and Staley) with a combined annual capacity of 425 million pounds comprised the entire high fructose corn syrup industry. Since 1972, some 4.6 billion pounds have been added. In 1979, the U.S. beverage industry used high fructose corn syrup for 24 percent of its sweetener needs or 1.7 billion pounds. High fructose syrup could achieve 90 percent of the total if Coca-Cola and PepsiCo eventually approve its use as a total sugar replacement in their colas."

Such a prospect, as cited by Nordlund, was a far cry from what a few Staley insiders called "a wild goose chase" in 1965 when one of their research directors, Dr. Hans Wolff, went to Japan to "sniff out" the opportunities of high fructose corn syrup. More than a decade and a half later, Dr. Wolff—since retired—can point to his alma mater being "Number One in the world" in high fructose corn syrups and can also point out that "IsoSweet is Staley's most profitable possession."

The episodes in this chapter seem to provide sufficient support for the proposition that an "also-ran" company in Decatur, Illinois, knew how to win the race for world leadership in the emergence of a new corn-based wonder from the laboratories of science, culminating in the scheduled late-1982 start-up of a plant at Loudon, Tennessee, which will take the company's total annual capacity up to 3.5 billion pounds of the liquid sweetener.

Vice President G. David Satterfield, who has guided the company's internal and external communications programs in the recent era, said, "The past 10 years have been loaded with excitement. Don Nordlund has set a fast pace. Projects have come in waves—one after another. Often they have overlapped. We haven't paused to congratulate ourselves after each accomplishment. We've been too busy for that. There is no interlude for relaxation in the Nordlund management style.

"After Morrisville came the emergence of IsoSweet at Decatur and then came Lafayette and then came plans for Loudon, Tennessee. Engineering and construction have been on a fast track all along. Increasing capacity has become a way of life. Technology has been an up-tempo specialty all along. When we went from '42 percent fructose' to '55 percent fructose,' the adrenaline seemed to speed up in everyone's veins. As the pace increased, so did the enthusiasm. The spirit has been contagious.

"The secret—if, indeed, there is a secret—is a sense of involvement at all levels of the organization. Our people are not observers. They are participants."

Ward Sinclair, staff writer for the *Washington Post,* subjected himself to a sample of Staley synergism in April of 1981. After visiting the Lafayette plant, he wrote: "Staley is pioneering management techniques that are as compelling as the automation processes making the plant one of the most modern in the sweetener industry.

"The plant has expanded twice since 1977, in part because workers keep exceeding production goals. All 240 employees, management or not, are on salary. There are no time clocks. Plant workers, set up as teams, decide who is hired, who is fired; who gets a raise, who doesn't; who works when; who needs disciplining for not doing his or her share.

"Involvement of workers in some of the decisions that rule their lives is not that revolutionary in American industry. Such

220

household names as DuPont, Alcoa, Procter & Gamble and Texas Instruments, among others, have moved in that direction. But in Lafayette, it is being taken farther and faster than elsewhere, and the results—steadily increasing production, notable efficiency, pride in work and team spirit—are laden with implications for the troubled U.S. industrial machine.

"When Staley told workers [at Lafayette] to figure out a schedule, they came up with another twist. They voted to work 12-hour shifts on three consecutive days, then take off three days and return to work three consecutive nights at 12 hours each. Everybody gets day work. Everybody gets night work. One of the obvious advantages is that on every other cycle, each employee has nine straight daylight periods at home—a benefit of incalculable dimension."

No offense to the objectivity of insider Dave Satterfield's commentary regarding spirit, but Ward Sinclair, an independent journalist and respected outside observer, seems to have arrived at the same conclusion.

New worlds to conquer on the sweetener front?

"There'll always be new worlds to conquer in any business based on technology," Don Nordlund commented late in 1981.

"How about a 'for instance?' " Nordlund was asked.

He replied, "For instance, some company is going to come up with a dry, granular, high fructose sweetener one of these days and I want that company to be Staley. Today, dry fructose is too hygroscopic. It attracts and holds too much moisture. We hope to develop a nonhygroscopic '100 percent fructose' corn sweetener which we can make and market and ship cost-effectively. I'd like to see such a product wind up in the old sugar bowl in the kitchen."

CHAPTER FOURTEEN

A LITTLE THING CALLED
FERMENTATION

This author remembers the twenties when he was a young and innocent schoolboy. He distinctly recalls an episode in the basement of his home where his father ordered, "Stand back; let the beer ferment!"

This was the first time the schoolboy had heard the word "ferment." The occasion was his father's initial experiment with "home brew"—during the Prohibition Era.

Memory also suggests that the schoolboy's father added too much granulated sugar and that a week or so later something went wrong, namely, many of the bottles exploded. And, alas, that part of the basement brew which remained mysteriously intact tasted like yeast.

Back to that word "ferment."

Fermentation has been a highly important art and science at the Staley company, a far from capricious benefit. Indeed, some of the company's most interesting adventures over the years have involved fermentation.

Thomas C. Garren, who recently retired following a 28-year career, explained, "Fermentation is a chemical reaction induced by a living microorganism—such as a yeast, bacterium, or mold—or by an enzyme. An example is yeast fermentation of starches to produce sugars. Going one step further, sugars may be fermented into alcohol."

Some of the experiences in Staley's annals have involved in-house developments in fermentation. Other experiences have involved Staley supplying the corn products for fermentation by others.

The date: January 19, 1981
The place: The Elks' Hall, Decatur, Illinois, still decorated with Christmastime's silvery tinsel trappings.
The time: Dinner time—featuring fried chicken, biscuits, mashed potatoes and country gravy. Plus apple pie.
The occasion: Meeting of the Staley Foremen's Club.

At the edge of the predinner "happy hour" hubbub, three old-timers huddled at a small table, having a conversational reunion. The old-timers were Lynn S. "Doc" Hettinger (who started in the Staley plant in 1922 and retired in 1969), Anthony B. "Byron" May (1922–1964), and Ira J. Cox (1923–1969). Buddies who formerly saw each other daily, they've been getting a chance to swap nostalgic stories only when the Foremen's Club has had its monthly meetings.

When this visitor asked permission to pull up a chair, "Doc" Hettinger said, "You should have been at Staley in the good old days." No nudge such as "What happened in the good old days?" was needed. The three old-timers literally took turns initiating reminiscences of past glories. One of their most interesting topics concerned the Prohibition Era in the twenties and early thirties, and involved a Staley product called corn chip sugar, also known as crude sugar.

Their comments included: "You should have seen the fancy, well-dressed hoodlums come into our plant. Gangsters and bootleggers. You could spot 'em from the start. Most of them wore diamond rings bigger than any you've ever seen in all your life.

"Bootleggers were our best customers for corn chip sugar for making moonshine. It always made us nervous when they came because they weren't supposed to be in the plant. They couldn't have bought the corn chip sugar directly from us, anyhow. But they liked to come in and see it made, knowing they'd find a way, somehow, to get their hands on it for their bootleg whiskey and gin.

"Our gunk was a product that came over from the syrup refinery. It was a milky-looking liquid which was poured onto the sheet-metal floors in five bays. Each bay was 100 feet by 20 feet. The gunk crystallized and got hard in about 12 hours. Then workers would go in and break it into chunks. Then the chunks went off to the bootleggers for remelting."

No offense to the old-timers but that's almost what happened —but not precisely what happened. In fact, the Staley company (and Corn Products and Clinton Refining and Union Starch) sold 40–50 million pounds of corn chip sugar a year to brokers' warehouses in New England, Pennsylvania, and West Virginia. In turn, the brokers supplied leather tanneries in the days prior to the advent of plastics when leather represented one of the major industries in the nation, and when the Staley product was essential in tanning animal hides.

Which means: Bootleggers—by whatever nefarious means they found most convenient—had to get their sugar supply from Staley's brokers. Once they had been furnished with truckloads of corn chip sugar, the adroit artisans of illicit fermentation were off and running, constantly playing cat-and-mouse games with federal revenuers who were trying to enforce an unpopular law.

In any event, that era marked the Staley company's first experience in providing an ingredient for alcohol. Corn chip sugar was half the price of cane sugar. Further, it was a readily fermentable carbohydrate. It was, in fact, the answer to a bootlegger's prayer and remained so until 1933, when the Eighteenth Amendment (ratified in 1919) was repealed, after which corn chip sugar settled down to the respectable, ho-hum role of serving the leather industry until the Staley product's discontinuance in 1939.

The company's next affiliation with the intriguing subject of alcohol came in the fifties when the Hiram Walker distillery in Peoria, Illinois, asked the Staley corporation to assume the responsibility of procuring high-quality "Number One Yellow Dent" corn (versus "Number Two Yellow Dent" generally used in corn refining) for Hiram Walker's use in the manufacture of distilled spirits. The Peoria company was well aware of Staley's longtime expertise in buying corn and wanted to capitalize on Staley's purchasing power.

In the early sixties, the company began selling a corn syrup called Sta-Bru to some of the nation's leading brewers and within a few years the product was leaving the Decatur plant, in tank cars, at the rate of several million pounds a year. Permitting greater capacity in beer manufacturing without the need for changing equipment in a brew house, Sta-Bru became a formidable and profitable addition to the Staley line and has remained prominently in the catalog ever since, serving as another relationship to fermentation processes elsewhere.

In the seventies, when a calorie-conscious nation opted enthusiastically for the so-called light beer, Staley became affiliated with alcoholic beverages for the fourth time. As recently explained by Tom V. Fischer, executive vice president who manages the Industrial Products Group, "Our dextrose proved to be ideal in the manufacture of the new generation of beer. It is almost one hundred percent fermentable, thus avoiding residual carbohydrates—which means avoiding the addition of calories. Those breweries which simply don't want to water down their beer, and which are concerned about the finest possible finished product, have found Staley's liquid dextrose a boon to their brewing processes."

As detailed in the previous chapter, fermentation took on heroic proportions in the late sixties and through the seventies when the Staley company went all out in the direction of a new sophisticated enzymatic reaction, commonly called isomerization, for producing high fructose corn syrup. This was a revolutionary liquid sweetener comparable in historic importance to the first enzyme-converted syrups of the late thirties.

Then in the early eighties the Staley company's new affiliation with the subject of alcohol began to materialize. In deciding to go into the business of making ethanol (the same alcohol that whiskey-makers have been obtaining from corn for centuries) the Staley company signaled its fermentation intentions on August 27, 1980, in a news release, as follows:

"The A. E. Staley Manufacturing Company announced today that it will construct a 70,000-bushels-per-day corn refining plant at Loudon, Tennessee. The $200 million facility will produce high fructose corn syrup (HFCS) for the food and beverage industries and power alcohol for use in motor fuel blends (gasohol). The plant will be located on a 190-acre site on the Tennessee River at Loudon, which is 15 miles southwest of Knoxville. Completion is scheduled for early 1983.

"Plans call for the plant to produce 600 million pounds of high fructose corn syrup and 40 million gallons of alcohol annually, with flexibility to accommodate seasonal trends for the products."

In perspective, the emergence of American gasohol was not exactly a shot across the bow of the Middle Eastern petroleum cartel known as OPEC, but it was a symbol of a U.S. determination to find a way to stretch its supplies of motor fuel. Many American companies, large and small, indicated their intention to get into "alcohol for gasohol," the latter being a 90 percent gasoline–10 percent alcohol (ethanol) blend. The sudden interest was brought about by an act of Congress during the Carter administration, a piece of legislation granting a 4-cents-per-gallon (at the pump) exemption from federal tax on 90–10 motor fuel—as long as the supplemental material comes from a nonpetroleum source.

In fact, the decree from the U.S. Congress specified that the government subsidy would apply to alcohol produced from any agricultural product that is fermentable—corn, wheat, potatoes, and whey—assuming the alcohol would be used as an extender in motor fuel.

From the outset, however, Staley management was apprehensive about the long-range potential for gasohol and had decided to produce ethanol at the Loudon, Tennessee, plant only because of a unique set of parameters. These parameters included: (1) the use of a renewable resource (Staley's favorite exercise) for making an extender for motor fuel under conditions involving a government subsidy, and (2) the very real advantage, in terms of economies of scale, in making both high fructose corn syrup and ethanol in a new, highly automated plant, in the Sun Belt hills of Tennessee.

Even though the August, 1980, news release said the Tennessee plant would begin operations early in 1983, a newer target date, "late in 1982," was announced early in 1981. Also, the capacity estimate was upped from 70,000 bushels of corn a day to 80,000 bushels.

As Don Nordlund explained early in 1981, "We view power alcohol as an adjunct or complement to corn refining. Initially, it will give us flexibility and improved economics in Tennessee, balancing some of the seasonality of high fructose syrup. Because of political and emotional pressures, we believe the merits of gasohol were initially overemphasized. Now that supplies of petroleum have become at least temporarily plentiful, there seems to be an overreaction in the other direction."

W. R. Schwandt, a vice president in the company's Industrial Products Group, added, "Petroleum companies have shown that the use of alcohol permits a substantial increase in refinery yields. Alcohol enables a given barrel of crude to produce more total motor fuel. Also, when alcohol is added to gasoline on a 10 percent/90 percent basis, the octane rating of the blend increases two or three points beyond the octane level of conventional unleaded gasoline."

Executive vice president Tom Fischer further added, "In planning for our Tennessee plant, all of us have viewed the alcohol output as the tail, not the dog. Alcohol will be more of a means to an end than an end in itself—a residual product

227

made in the same plant where we'll be 'going for the bundle' in high fructose syrup.

"At the start we'll probably use about 75,000 bushels of corn a day, with 40,000 for high fructose syrup and 35,000 for alcohol. But don't forget we are building in some flexibility in Tennessee. We'll be able to change that ratio as market conditions require."

President Bob Powers contributed his perspective by declaring, "Power alcohol is an opportunistic vehicle which allows us to do some things we want to do in Tennessee—and it demonstrates corn's versatility. However it does not, in itself, demonstrate the direction the company is heading in the development of sophisticated, proprietary technology."

In retrospect, the company's many adventures in fermentation have come a long way since the colorful period of the twenties, when Staley's corn chip sugar gave life to bootleggers' illicit stills in the sanctuary of the hill country where federal revenuers seemed to lurk behind every bush.

CHAPTER FIFTEEN

THE SOARING SEVENTIES

"I'm not sure if my father ever really recovered from my mother's death in 1969," said young Bob Staley (born in 1952) as he recently looked back on the period when he and father Gus and mother Eva lived at 5 Montgomery Place.

Don Nordlund recalled, "It became apparent in 1970 that Gus was walking slower."

Gus was 67 at the time—surely not old. But he seemed to be aging at a rate faster than heretofore. Gus, the chairman and CEO, began to turn over more responsibilities to Nordlund, the president.

When Gus suffered a minor stroke in 1970, the incident provided the first strong indication of the serious deterioration of his health. Earlier, he had a pacemaker implanted during a two-week hospital stay in Houston. The prognosis for prompt recovery was favorable. Yet shortly after he returned home, doctors determined that his body chemistry was rejecting the implant. So the original pacemaker was removed and a different one was installed at the Staley Pavilion of Decatur Memorial Hospital.

In 1971, Gus felt less able to cope with all of his responsibilities at company headquarters, the result being that Nordlund became somewhat of an acting CEO in day-to-day affairs. Gus tried a few vacations, hoping that relaxation would be effective medicine. Yet, slowly and steadily, his health continued to decline. By 1973, the corporation's outside board members, who felt directly charged with the responsibility of assuring continuity of fiduciary and administrative management, met with Gus and suggested he should relinquish his CEO role, but should continue to hold the title of chairman. This was not an easy matter for the outside board members to deal with. Indeed, they were all close friends of Gus. Most of them had been persuaded by him to stand for board election. As patriarch of the Staley clan, he was more than a corporate chieftain; he was a family symbol. Yet, despite the inevitable discomfort of "stepping down," Gus was understanding. According to one intimate observer, "Gus was downright gracious" and was proud that board members had the courage to "bite the bullet" and to face the situation head-on.

Since 1906 when the organization was incorporated, there had been only two people in top command—both Staleys. The principal gratification that Gus felt, as health problems of the seventies seemed to multiply, was his knowledge that a man of his selection, Don Nordlund, was ready to assume the larger burden. In retrospect it can be noted that picking his successor was perhaps the most important decision Gus ever made.

The year 1975 was to be Gus Staley's last year on earth.

Henry M. Staley, Gus's Number Two son, who initially was treasurer, and then vice president as well as a member of the Staley board, recently recalled how late 1974 and early 1975 brought increasing health complications to his father. Henry said, "My dad fell victim to many ailments. He had a worrisome bout with influenza. Then came pneumonia. But it was his heart condition that worried us the most. 'Deterioration of the arteries,' the doctors said. And he became forgetful. One time I saw him come to the office and I noticed he had forgotten to shave.

"He tried to be his own doctor, too, even though we all talked

230

E. K. Scheiter, left, and A. E. Staley, Jr., right, with New York Stock Exchange president Keith Funston at the start of trading in Staley common stock on floor of the Exchange, May 29, 1963.

The $4.2 million Research Center takes shape on the east end of the Staley property in Decatur. It was completed and dedicated in 1960.

Robert M. Powers, at left, was important in the company's research efforts during the 1960s and early '70s. He would become Staley's president and chief operating officer in 1981. Nathan Kessler, at right, also spearheaded the company's technical efforts during this period.

Roy L. Rollins, a company veteran, held a variety of management positions, including director of personnel, director of manufacturing, group vice president, and membership on the Board of Directors. Rollins retired in 1970.

James W. Moore was actively involved in the company's commodity operations during much of his career. He was vice president, commodities, and later group vice president, AgriProducts, before retiring in 1974.

From left, William Barnes III, Thomas W. Samuels, and E. K. Scheiter look on as A. E. Staley, Jr., announces plans for the construction of a Staley Pavilion at Decatur Memorial Hospital. Both the Staley Company and the Staley family have provided several million dollars to the hospital over the years.

A. E. Staley, Jr., officiated at the dedication of the Staley Pavilion of Decatur Memorial Hospital in 1968. Also present, in front row from left, are Monsignor George Powell of St. Patrick Catholic Church; Ellis Arnold, Decatur's mayor; and Thomas Samuels, long-time community leader and Staley legal counsel.

The Staley company entered a transitional period in 1965 when Donald E. Nordlund, left, was elected president. He assumed the duties of chief executive officer in 1973. At right is the chairman of the board, A. E. Staley, Jr.

Customer demand for 55 percent high fructose corn syrup has increased because of approval by major soft drink companies, such as Coca-Cola, which use it in a variety of soft drinks.

Lou G. Doxsie, a Staley vice president for many years, was instrumental in the company's early entry into high fructose corn syrup.

The decade of the 1970s marked the Staley company's greatest period of growth. In 1972, Staley commenced commercial-scale production of high fructose corn syrup, en route to achieving world leadership in high fructose technology.

The Morrisville, Pennsylvania, plant, completed in 1972, became the company's first corn wet milling facility outside Decatur. Corn is shipped year-round from the Midwest by rail, as well as purchased from farmers in Pennsylvania and New Jersey.

Automated processes and computer technology enhance productivity at the Morrisville plant, where high fructose corn syrups and dextrose are made.

In addition to its use in domestic markets, soybean meal is transported from Staley facilities by rail, then barge, to New Orleans for export.

A Staley affiliate processes soybeans at this plant in northern Spain.

The company's initial entry into sunflower seed processing takes place at this plant near Velva, North Dakota.

Recent expansions include the addition of this unit, to produce dextrose and 55 percent high fructose corn syrup, at Staley's Morrisville, Pennsylvania, corn refining facility.

In 1978, a 100 million-pounds-per-year hydrogenated oil unit was added to the company's Decatur vegetable oil refinery.

In 1976, Staley purchased four soybean mills from Swift & Company, including the one above, in Des Moines, Iowa, which was undergoing a plant expansion at the time. The mill began operations the following year.

The Champaign, Illinois, plant has been modified to increase its role in soybean processing.

The Frankfort, Indiana, plant produces soybean meal for the important Indiana and Ohio agricultural region as well as for the Southeastern poultry market.

The Des Moines plant is one of the company's five soybean milling facilities.

The Fostoria soybean plant, located in the northwest corner of Ohio, serves poultry and livestock markets in Canada and along the eastern seaboard.

Ione Staley, eldest daughter of A. E. Staley, Sr., participated in dedication ceremonies at Millikin University for the Staley Library at the school. Behind her, at left, is company chairman Donald Nordlund.

Henry Staley, the second of Gus Staley's four sons, is one of two Staleys currently employed by the company. Henry joined the firm in 1956 and currently is a vice president and a member of the board of directors.

Robert Staley, youngest of Gus Staley's four sons, joined the company in 1977 as a management trainee. He currently is manager of legislative affairs in the firm's Government Relations organization.

The Staley Library at Millikin University was dedicated in 1976.

Livergood Grain Company participates in grain merchandising at the country elevator level. Principal activities of elevators are the storing, conditioning and merchandising of crops from surrounding farms.

Ging, Inc., a Staley subsidiary, operates country elevators in Central Illinois.

Staley Commodities International, Inc. is well known as a leading commodity futures trading firm. It is headquartered at the Chicago Board of Trade.

This corn sweetener plant at Lafayette, Indiana, is a symbol of Staley's growth in high fructose corn syrup. It was the most highly computerized corn wet milling plant in the world when it started operations in 1977.

Corn sweetener production at Staley's Lafayette plant is highly automated. The "brain" of the Lafayette plant is this centrally located, computerized control room.

The first non–Staley-family management team in the company's history includes Donald E. Nordlund, seated, chairman, and Robert M. Powers, president.

The Loudon plant, under construction, became operational in 1982.

The 1981 Staley Board of Directors

Donald E. Nordlund
Chairman and
Director

Robert M. Powers
President and
Director

William Barnes III
Director

Joseph B. Lanterman
Director

Donald C. Miller
Director

Gilbert L. Bieger
Executive Vice
President
and Director

Henry M. Staley
Vice President
and Director

Boyd F. Schenk
Director

Robert K. Schell
Director

Thomas V. Fischer
Executive Vice
President
and Director

Pierre Callebaut
Director

John W. Joanis
Director

Nathan Kessler
Vice President
and Director

Frank H. Wagner
Vice President
and Director

against it. He tried sedatives and other assorted medications which were stashed in his own private pharmacy.

"In February of 1975 he went to Florida to visit his sister, Ione. While sunning in Miami Beach, he learned from Ione that his first wife, Lenore, who divorced him in 1949, was vacationing nearby.

"My father phoned my mother and promptly made a date for a reunion. And what a reunion it must have been, after all those years apart. He and my mother dined together and had a wonderful time. At evening's end, they agreed they would see each other occasionally. But the next day he was due back in Decatur. He flew in on one of the company planes. He looked great. He said he felt great. There was even an alertness of manner and a spark of his old-time self.

"No one felt any unusual measure of concern when my father went to his home to retire for the evening. But early the following morning, March 19, we got the bad news. My father had died of a massive heart attack some time during the night. His death was discovered by a houseman, Andrew James, a third-shift employee at the plant who had worked at my father's home for 23 years."

Having been advised the previous day that her boss was back in town and ready to return to work, his secretary, Estella Launtz, arrived at her desk a little earlier than usual March 19, anticipating a heavy workload in light of all the letters and memos on Gus Staley's desk. She recently recalled, "I was waiting for him to come in. I waited. And I waited some more. Then the phone rang. It was Mr. Barnes [William Barnes III, chairman and president of The Citizens National Bank], one of Mr. Staley's lifelong friends. All Mr. Barnes said was, 'Gus died during his sleep.' I don't think I said a word. I was numb. I had been with Mr. Staley for more than twenty years."

At funeral services March 21, Thomas W. Samuels, an attorney who had been affiliated with the Staley company since prior to World War I, volunteered to give the eulogy. After citing Gus Staley's many business and civic achievements, Tom Samuels said, "He was, by nature, shy and not given to small talk. He was completely indifferent to trivia. He moved the world more by what he was than by what he did."

That was a perceptive sum-up of Augustus Eugene Staley, Jr.,—the founder's favorite son who became president in 1932 more out of duty than desire. Those who knew him best expressed agreement that, above all, he had been steadfast in his determination to provide meticulous stewardship in behalf of the corporate legacy left in his care by "my father, the founder."

But there was a new world outside in 1975—new roads to try, new risks to take, new ideas to test, new capital to raise, new plants to buy or build. The "old guard" leadership was gone. New leadership forces would inescapably bring a compelling new look to a venerable processing company, which had often valued the status quo more than strategies for accelerating growth.

From 1975 onward, the word "Staley" would mean primarily "a company" not "a family." Hard-nosed analysts on Wall Street and elsewhere would be poised to ask "What have you done for your investors lately?" and to express the hope that a new spirit of aggressiveness might serve as a thrust to help nudge along the momentum of the "staid old Staley" cause.

The third era had arrived.

Just as A. E. Staley, Sr., needed a special burst of courage to start the nation's first soybean plant in 1922, the new management team at Decatur needed an equal amount of intestinal fortitude in its all-out drive to be dominant in the high fructose corn syrup business in the seventies.

A timid company, frightened by the multitudinous imponderables, would have opted for a more risk-free position safely on the sidelines, content to be a spectator rather than a participant in a new line of business that would inevitably be super-competitive.

Those imponderables were discussed and rediscussed at Decatur. The various alternatives were examined so often that the deliberations began to seem redundant. Yet, in the final analysis, the board had to be convinced "let's go." And Don Nordlund, eager to put his company out in front, became the high priest of persuasion throughout the seventies, convinced that appropriate rewards would accrue as the result of the highest expenditures of dollars and effort in the corporation's history.

Could the company spring into a dominant position through the "back door," by entering the high fructose field as a sublicensee of an American company which had earlier become a licensee of Japanese technology? Would such an early third-tier entry into the market be that much of an advantage?

Could the Staley company develop its own production expertise and also zero in on an independent outside source for supplying enzymes?

Given the imperative that unit manufacturing costs could be minimized only through the economies of scale at locations involving massive rates of production, could the company develop a sufficient market for a massive volume of high fructose corn syrup?

After all, the company had prospered, to a degree, despite its dependence on rather uncontrollable elements of the commodities market. Would it now want to subject itself to another uncontrollable, namely, the price of sugar that would, in turn, directly affect Staley's profit margins on high fructose syrup? While luxuriating in profitability during periods of peak prices for sugar, would the company have a sufficient cushion during periods when sugar prices plummeted?

Such were the considerations as far back as 1972 when the $35 million Morrisville, Pennsylvania, plant came on stream. By that time the Staley company had actually passed the point of no return. The Starch Era was fading away; the Sweeteners Era was arriving.

Increased facilities for high fructose corn syrup at Decatur; laying in an automated plant at Lafayette, Indiana; increasing and diversifying output at Morrisville; planning a "Sun Belt plant" at Loudon, Tennessee—these became acts of faith.

Thanks in large part to high sugar prices, the company's

profitability was at an all-time high in 1974 and 1975. The roller-coaster ride is best depicted by the following numbers: In 1971, net earnings were $5.4 million, jumping modestly to $6.4 million and $7.9 million for the next two years. Then came the heroic high jump—to $15 million in 1974 when sugar prices climbed and when the company's entire high fructose capacity was sold out.

Then came 1975. With sugar prices soaring out of sight and with additional high fructose capacity available—and with brisk sales of other sweeteners such as conventional corn syrups and dextrose, as well as strong sales of nonsweetener products—net earnings catapulted to the stratospheric figure of $50 million. Beyond doubt, this was the biggest news in the company's history.

In 1976, earnings fell to $38 million. Then down came sugar prices—and down came the 1977, 1978, and 1979 Staley numbers to $24 million, $15 million, and $23 million, respectively.

And such was the up-and-down cycle of the seventies.

It would be simplistic to look at the decade of the seventies solely in terms of net earnings and in terms of the relationship of high fructose corn syrup prices to sugar prices—allowing that the former prices averaged 15 percent below sugar prices during the period. The seventies, in fact, had a deeper meaning. They signaled the advent of a new management style. Exciting as the short-term headlines seemed, the company was actually engaged in developing strategies, technology, and people—especially people—for the onrushing new world of the eighties.

Not as gregarious as first-generation Gene nor as reclusive as second-generation Gus, Don Nordlund has set a fast pace since moving into the chairman's "catbird seat" on the eighth floor in 1975. In his quiet way, he has been, to quote a subordinate, "much more dominant and overpowering than his calm presence would suggest."

As the company's chief motivator, planner, and organizer, he has been unruffled, insistent and, at times, very demanding. "He keeps his cool" was a comment used by several colleagues who have been regularly involved in the pressures of behind-the-scenes activities. Blond and Nordic, he undoubtedly inherited the gift of a calm nature from Scandinavian ancestors—or at least there are some coworkers who believe this to be the case. A point could be made that a steady hand at the helm was needed during the high-adrenaline years of the mid and late seventies when big decisions were almost constantly on the agenda and when Don Nordlund remained unflappable.

Unemotional? Perhaps—on the surface. But unemotional regarding the sensitivities and aspirations of people? No. Consistent? Yes. Persevering? Yes. Exacting? Yes. Temperamental? Never. Easygoing? Hardly. Diplomatic? Always.

His voice is seldom raised. He talks softly, but firmly. Friendly? Yes, in a reserved way—without being a backslapper. Patient and tolerant? Not always. The undisputed boss? Very much so.

When he became president (the Number Two slot) in 1965, it was obvious that he was ticketed for one more upward step. The delicacy of his position seems to have been appreciated most by Nordlund himself. As "Gus's candidate," he had Gus's trust and support. Feeling a strong sense of respect for, and loyalty to, chairman Gus, Nordlund was often torn between his impulse to "go fast" and Gus's traditional "go slow."

Particularly in the late sixties, Nordlund was impatient. On the one hand, he sensed an opportunity (starting with the high fructose sublicense) to put the Staley company in orbit at an altitude few had even dared to dream about. On the other hand, he was not about to preempt authority and not about to be disrespectful of Gus Staley's longtime position of chief executive officer and principal stockholder.

"During this period, Gus and I actually became closer than ever," Nordlund recently commented. "I understood his conservative and responsible philosophy and he understood my anxiety to discard some of the old shackles and to aim—realistically—for the stars. Many of my colleagues and I felt the timing was right for the company to be more aggressive and growth-oriented. We felt we had the tools for building an enterprise

with almost unlimited opportunity. In his position as chairman, Gus could have demolished our dreams—but he didn't."
Nordlund's attitude and personality are revealed in the following recent exchange:

Author: Wasn't it true that the company was going nowhere under Gus Staley's style of management?

Nordlund: Gus had his own distinct style but it's wrong to say the company was going nowhere. He didn't like to take chances, but he was devoted to the cause of maintaining a healthy balance sheet. He made people do their homework. He disliked frivolous things. He disliked superficiality. Actually, there was a strong sense of partnership between Gus and myself in 1968 when we signed a contract to become a sublicensee for Japanese high fructose technology. Lou Doxsie, Ed Scheiter, and Jim Beaumont helped me assemble the fundamental data on why we should move ahead in high fructose and it was my job to convince Gus.

Author: There surely wasn't much risk in a bonanza like that, was there?

Nordlund: I don't see how anyone can ignore the risk factor when a company decides to take on a revolutionary new product. High fructose corn syrup was as much of a technological breakthrough as the transistor and videotape and various other innovations. The soft drink industry had never let a corn sweetener darken its door. Some segments of the food industry had used sugar so long that no one could be sure of the potential inroads for high fructose. One doesn't go all-out, head to head, against the global sugar industry without a great deal of thought. High fructose was no shoo-in. That much we knew back in 1968. The world was not sitting around waiting for a new corn sweetener.

Author: When did the company make its really big gamble?

Nordlund: I'm not sure gamble is the right word, but I'd say the time of our major move was late in 1969 when we decided to go for the bundle by committing a large capital expenditure—which turned out to be $35 million—for making high fructose at Morrisville, Pennsylvania. Actually, all along Clinton had wanted another company to help introduce high fructose to the market. We knew that with Morrisville in place we'd have access to the great eastern market, while Clinton was taking care of the west.

Author: And then what happened?

Nordlund: Using Clinton enzymes, we brought Morrisville on stream in 1972, making the 42 percent high fructose product, which was then the only game in town. Our technical people and our manufacturing people were the real heroes in bringing Morrisville into production. Two years later they helped us put in a high fructose unit at Decatur, too.

Author: How about Lafayette, Indiana?

Nordlund: The decision to build an automated, computerized plant at Lafayette took all the courage we could muster. Even though our studies suggested we should not go beyond processing 35,000 bushels of corn a day, our judgment told us to go for broke by committing to 70,000 bushels a day. That was a bold decision, but I'm surely glad we had the moxie to make it. We began with the 42 percent product at Lafayette in 1977. Less than two years later we began making the 55 percent version there. That plant is our pride and joy—as Loudon, Tennessee, will be when we crank up production late in 1982, adjacent to the great southern soft drink and food industries.

Author: How many total dollars have you sunk into high fructose?

Nordlund: Including the Tennessee plant, we've allocated more than $600 million to high fructose production since deciding to get into the business. Keep in mind there are some "old dollars" in that $600 million. We'd need almost a billion dollars to build all those units today.

Author: Didn't you have periods of uneasiness while pressing for all that expansion in a single product line?

Nordlund: Of course. But we had several very large advantages in our favor. To begin with, we had entered the business early. And we had fantastic support from all our own departments—including marketing, which had a lot of spadework to do.

Author: Was the board supportive in allocating such unprecedented sums of money?

Nordlund: The board's support was my greatest comfort and assurance. The little foot-dragging that occurred—and it wasn't much—came from the internal staff which kept asking "what if?" And "what if?" was the right question during our deliberations on all possible eventualities. We looked at everything upwards, downwards, sidewards. At those intervals when we had to decide "go or no go," once we agreed to move ahead, we had total and spirited support beyond anything I have ever seen. Fortified by all the homework we had done, we had a spirit of confidence and momentum you'd not believe. Plus pride. Plus enthusiasm.

Scholarly observers who write and lecture on business subjects frequently point out that a company develops a strong sense of purpose when a rallying mood is mustered in the launching of an all-out effort in some spirited new campaign. Such was the situation at Staley where a sense of purpose inspired people at all echelons into feelings of high morale and greater accomplishment.

Even those employees not directly involved in high fructose —in such other products as dextrose and regular corn syrup and soybeans and starch—found the new spirit contagious.

They felt like participants in a company on the move. As Nordlund recently commented, "We knew we were on the glory road."

But if the company had needed any endorsement for its renaissance-via-high-fructose, such validation came in May of 1975 when the H. J. Heinz Company of Pittsburgh proposed to acquire the Staley company for Heinz stock valued at $260 million, the offer obviously having resulted from the eastern company's awareness of Staley's stake in high fructose corn syrup. Quite plainly, the "pickle company," noted for its 57 varieties, was on the lookout for a fifty-eighth.

Don Nordlund remembers the incident well. He recently recalled, "I was sitting in my office when an unexpected phone call came in from an officer of the Heinz company—a man I had met on several occasions and a highly respected executive in the food industry.

"The caller said he'd like to come to Decatur to talk to me and he indicated I'd be interested in hearing what he had to say. So we made a date for him to come out to Decatur several days later. I should add that it didn't take much imagination to figure out what he had on his mind. Nevertheless, I respected the confidential nature of his call and decided not to worry about the situation until I had the chance to hear him out, face to face.

"The morning when he arrived in a private jet at the Decatur airport I was there to meet him. The first thing I noticed was that he was not alone. He was accompanied by an investment banker. As I suspected all the way back to that phone call, this was not a social visit.

"When we got to my office we exchanged a few brief and friendly comments, but we didn't waste too much time in ceremonial cordialities. Quite directly and, I thought, abruptly, he laid an offer on my desk—with sort of a take-it-or-leave-it attitude. Very suddenly our friendly discussion became a confrontation.

"Naturally, I realized that as Staley board chairman I had a very important obligation to our shareowners to consider any offer which would involve their interests. So I told the Heinz visitors that I'd take their offer to my board of directors for due deliberation and decision. After a few restrained pleasantries, the meeting adjourned and the visitors were driven back to the airport.

"Knowing that the Heinz takeover attempt would promptly hit the papers and seriously skeptical that such an offer could ever be beneficial to our stockholders, I felt like I was in a squeeze play. I remember saying to myself, 'Thank God for our board.' "

It should be mentioned that of Staley's then 5.3 million shares of common stock outstanding, approximately 40 percent of the total shares was in trust for members of the Staley family and approximately 12 percent of the total shares was held by Staley company directors. This added up to a formidable obstacle for a takeover.

When the Staley board met on June 2 to consider the Heinz proposal, the board voted unanimously in the negative.

Speculation in the financial press suggested that the Heinz planners had done an insufficient amount of plotting and planning in arranging for, or hoping realistically for, support from Staley family interests—support that could swing sufficient weight in Heinz's direction. However, Staley's majority owners were not about to be budged, not about to "sell out."

But the spurned suitors from Heinz, obviously sensing the prospects of success in the field of high fructose corn syrup, were not to be dissuaded by the icy reception at Decatur, Illinois. So, three months later—in September, 1975—they turned their attention to Keokuk, Iowa, where they wooed and won the Hubinger Company, an old-line corn refiner, for $41.4 million.

Perhaps ironically, the Pittsburgh company that wanted to own Staley is now a competitor.

If the Staley company had sponsored a Decatur-wide guessing contest early in 1976 . . .

If the prizes were to have been awarded to those entrants who guessed the right answer to "What product is Staley going to concentrate on next?" . . .

Nobody would have won.

Even if Staley employees would have been eligible, most of them wouldn't have guessed any better than outsiders.

Why? The correct answer to "What's next?" was—hallelujah—soybeans!

Yes, soybeans, which had been an item of in-house neglect and scorn for so many recent years. Soybeans—the black sheep of the family!

Considering that the company's pioneering effort in soybean processing, dating back to 1922, had given Decatur the singular honor of being regarded as "The Soybean Capital of the World" . . .

Considering Gus Staley would probably have stomped out the lowly product, bean by bean, if he had not been respectful of his father's pioneering role as the American "discoverer" of soybeans . . .

Considering that by the mid seventies the Staley company had slipped to the ignominious position of producing only 2 percent of the national output—in an old Decatur plant . . .

Considering that an upstart company named Cargill (in Minneapolis) had headed hell-for-breakfast into a leadership position as a soybean "crusher"—in a positive and profitable manner . . .

And further considering that a Staley competitor named Archer Daniels Midland had moved into Number Two position and was aggressively processing and promoting soybeans in, of all cities, Decatur, Illinois . . .

And additionally considering that this bold, local competitor was legitimizing Decatur's claim for soybean preeminence, thus saving the city's sloganized honor in light of the pioneering Staley corporation's soybean slippage . . .

And, finally, considering the Staley company had taken an heroic posture as the champion of corn sweeteners, seemingly to the exclusion of mundane merchandise . . .

A person would have had to be a bit balmy—intent on winning a booby prize, at best—in entering the guessing contest by hazarding, "The new product Staley will concentrate on is soybeans."

It was both a surprising shock and a shocking surprise when

241

the Staley company announced in March, 1976, that it had purchased four soybean processing plants from Swift & Co., a subsidiary of Esmark, Inc., for $45 million.

Don Nordlund recently reminisced, "We had become a weak sister in a product line which could be the backbone of our agribusiness—and a product line in which our technology was no less than superior. I'll never forget how it all happened.

"One day late in 1975, I was in an airplane, chatting with Jack Harris of Chicago Corporation. Jack mentioned that Swift had decided to reduce its stake in commodities. He said he thought the Swift soybean processing plants, which were well located in the Midwest, could be purchased for a reasonable figure.

"I explained to Jack that as far back as the previous year we had decided, as a matter of policy, that soybeans represented a business we wanted to be in—on a substantial basis. I also explained that we had decided to modernize the east end of our Decatur plant—the soybean processing area. In other words, I told Jack Harris, 'The time is right.' And when he reiterated that the Swift plants might merit our consideration, I told him —actually, I almost blurted out—'We're interested!'

"Without much delay, I found myself opening the discussions with Swift and then turning over the details to Bob [Robert M. Powers, vice president, AgriProducts Group], to Jim [James W. Moore, then vice president], and to Gil [Gilbert L. Bieger, vice president, finance]. I was particularly anxious to get Bob Powers involved because I knew that once the deal would be wrapped up, it would be up to Bob and his people to capitalize on the new investment. If anyone could make soybeans 'fly,' Powers could.

"We had suffered a few disadvantages in being a processor at Decatur—and Decatur only. For our export business we always had to send our soybean meal overland to some Midwest port on the Mississippi.

"It was obvious the Swift plants would give us the opportunity to get back in the big league. So we took over the Swift operations at Des Moines, Iowa; Champaign, Illinois; Frank-

242

fort, Indiana, and Fostoria, Ohio. Considering our company's overall profits had been mighty healthy in 1974 and astonishingly healthy in 1975, we were in a strong position to sign the contract with Swift.

"The purchase of those soybean plants had a beneficial side-effect. The purchase demonstrated the funding capability of our high fructose operation. It showed we could parlay the fruits of corn technology into reinvestment in another business. But mainly it wound up showing we knew our way around in soybeans, to the extent that in three years we cranked up enough soybean earnings to pay for the cost of the four Swift plants.

"Apart from economic advantages of the serious reentry into soybeans, the move served to give credibility to our assertion that anything worth doing is worth doing well. And for those who wondered, 'Why doesn't Staley diversify?' my answer was 'We *are* diversifying in areas of our greatest competence—corn and soybeans.' We felt comfortably at home in these businesses —and we were confident new profits would proliferate."

Was the glory road to spectacular success in corn and soybeans an easy road? Far from it. Were there wrangles and tangles and tussles and endless deliberations in the halls of management? Of course. Were there traumatic periods of stress when the company was hastily positioning itself in fresh endeavors? Naturally. Did the work and worry and planning work out well? Indeed. Were the hassles constructive in their end result? Definitely.

Significantly, if a Staley-watcher uses 1971 as a base year— 1971 being the last year BF (before fructose)—the third era of corporate management, spearheaded by Nordlund, tells its own story in a rather dramatic way, as follows: Over a 10-year period, starting with fiscal 1971, sales skyrocketed from $300 million to $2 billion. Net earnings went from $5.5 million to $105 million. Plus, there were two-for-one stock splits in 1975 and 1976 and a three-for-two split in 1980. In addition, there were six dividend increases since 1971.

Importantly, during the same period the company went from one corn refining plant to four, allowing for the inclusion of the Loudon, Tennessee, plant under construction, and it went from one soybean plant to five.

"Those simple facts tell the story of the most exciting expansion period in Staley history," observed Gilbert L. Bieger, who was the finance vice president during the unprecedented growth period and who subsequently was elected executive vice president. "We've concentrated all along on maintaining a healthy balance sheet. We've been particularly attentive to cash flow, which has been growing at a healthy rate. But the big thing to remember is that we have been able to fund the various waves of expansion while maintaining the integrity of our basic financial foundation."

Bob Powers wasn't exactly an unknown when the seventies started but he was far from center stage. He had joined the company in 1958 and subsequently held positions as a research group leader and as director of R&D for chemicals. He was named vice president, research, in 1971.

Don Nordlund recently explained, "We didn't exactly have Bob Powers locked in a lab but for a while it seemed like he was facing a limited future. Even though Gus Staley had some real appreciation for the importance of research, he had the idea that research people should stay in research and not graduate to broader positions in corporate management. He used to say, 'Chemists normally make poor businessmen.' Under such a cloud, the advancement of Bob Powers moved slowly."

Even though Powers had gained substantial recognition in his various supervisory positions in the research center, he recently said, "I never really knew Gus Staley, even though we were both part of the same enterprise for many years. I never had a one-on-one conversation with him. I never had the opportunity to shake his hand and say 'hello.' "

Considering that Bob Powers would someday be president of the company, it may seem strange that his path and Gus Staley's path never crossed. The explanation is simple: Powers spent most of his time in the research center. Staley spent most of his time in the administration building, a stone's throw to the west. Also, it should be mentioned that by the time Powers began to be well known in the high halls of top management, Gus Staley was incapacitated by failing health and he was unable to devote full time and attention to the job.

Anyway, it was Don Nordlund who became convinced that Bob Powers had an exciting potential. In April, 1975, Powers became group vice president of AgriProducts. He was elected to the board in August, 1975. He became an executive vice president in February, 1979—en route to the presidency.

So, despite his stigma as a research chemist, Bob Powers was able to escape from the lab, discard his white coat, and move upstairs to the tall tower of "The Castle in the Cornfields."

CHAPTER SIXTEEN

THE NEW STALEY COMPANY

When Robert M. Powers was elected president of the corporation November 11, 1980, he was 49 years of age, nine years younger than Donald E. Nordlund, who relinquished the presidential title while retaining the chairmanship and the CEO position. Powers thus became the fifth president in the company's history, following two Staleys and E. K. Scheiter and Nordlund.

As is commonplace in such matters, the board of directors chose Powers with both short- and long-term objectives in mind. Quite apparent to all serious Staley-watchers, Powers was elected because the board, responding to its primary duty of assuring management succession in an orderly manner, felt that Powers had the potential to succeed Nordlund in the top slot—somewhere down the line. Indeed, Nordlund himself had championed this viewpoint.

By the time the 1980 Christmas holidays arrived, the new president was made to feel "at home, and accepted, and just one of the boys" when he was hailed and hazed during an irreverent bit of church basement-type theatrics as staged by the highly amateur group known as the Staley Players.

"The 'thespians' gave me the needle," Powers remarked at the time.

And when the year 1981 arrived, Powers was ready for the new regimen, promptly accepting speech assignments for the Staley Foremen's Club, the Decatur Rotary Club, and the New York Consumer Analysts Group, not to forget the company's Annual Meeting of shareholders February 9, 1981, where he shared speech-making honors with the chairman.

Whereas there was adequate recognition of the new president's role, there was however virtually no recognition of the special significance of the year 1981, per se.

No one baked a cake.

The year 1981 was, in fact, the company's seventy-fifth birthday considering that papers of incorporation had been filed in 1906, when the company was located in Baltimore.

Perhaps the closest thing to a birthday cake was the wedding cake–shaped headquarters building where red and white floodlights were turned on for one night only—January 21, 1981—after many years of darkness. Yet the hastily planned illumination of the upper reaches of the Staley tower had no birthday connotation. The celebration, instead, was appropriately in honor of the 52 newly freed U.S. hostages who had been held for 444 days in Iran.

The corporation had come a long way since the days when the fearless founder peddled Cream starch to retailers in the eastern states. In the 1980 Fortune 500 listings, Staley ranked 303rd in assets, 268th in sales, 48th in average rate of return to investors in 10 years, and 67th in growth in earnings per share over 10 years. With sales of $2 billion, with 4,200 employees, with almost 10,000 shareholders, and with many of the nation's blue chip corporations in its customer ranks, the Decatur company in its diamond jubilee year had become a formidable force on the American business scene.

And the icing on the nonexistent birthday cake was Don Nordlund's 1981 Annual Meeting report that sales and earnings were at the highest level in the company's history.

Yet high fructose corn sweeteners provided a sweet-sour flavor. By far the largest flag on the Staley pole, the high fructose product line had become so dominant that financial analysts tended to judge the company's fate almost exclusively in high fructose terms—a good news/bad news situation.

The good news was that Staley's ever-increasing high fructose capacity was sold out and profits were high—and the further good news was that additional capacity in 1982 was assured. Better stated, Staley had become no less than a world champion in a substantial and revolutionary new business. The bad news was that the Staley stock price slumped through much of fiscal 1981, due largely to the depressed price of sugar. The old sugar syndrome had returned to haunt those in the Decatur hierarchy.

When Don Nordlund was asked, "Why does the stock stay down while profits are substantial?," he responded, "It's the old sugar scenario, with which we've learned to live, but in fairness we should be judged by many factors and not just one. We're actively telling our story to security analyst groups and stockholders all over the country. By degrees the experts are beginning to realize the long-term strength of our total position. They're beginning to see the larger picture."

The "larger picture" recently drew comments from Thomas V. Fischer, executive vice president, who quietly, smoothly, and competently oversees the Industrial Products Group, which represents 65 percent of the company's assets; from Phillip M. St. Clair, vice president, who is spiritedly in command of the AgriProducts Group, including soybean processing, and from president Bob Powers, whose heart will always be—to some extent—in R&D.

Fischer said, "In the early seventies we processed less than 200,000 bushels of corn daily. By the start of the eighties we were processing more than 300,000 bushels a day. And don't forget that high fructose corn syrup is not our only strength in sweeteners. We're a major producer of conventional corn syrups, making more than 30 types, and we are one of three dextrose manufacturers, marketing the product in both crystal and liquid forms. Our sweeteners move out in all directions—

confections, baked goods, jams and jellies, canned fruits, dairy products, beer, and soft drinks.

"And also don't forget the food and industrial starches, not only from corn but also from potatoes and tapioca. We have more than 30 varieties of modified starches for use in convenience foods. Our industrial starches are used by manufacturers of paper, textiles, paints, adhesives, and other industrial and consumer products.

"Naturally, the big excitement is high fructose corn syrup. By the time the Loudon, Tennessee, plant comes on stream we'll have the capacity for producing a total of 3.5 billion pounds a year."

Phil St. Clair was still in the newcomer category in 1981, having joined Staley in mid-1977 after a distinguished career at Cargill, the leading processor of soybeans. The plain fact of the matter is that Don Nordlund never would have been able to woo and win St. Clair if those four Swift & Co. soybean plants had not been purchased by Staley in 1976.

St. Clair recently said, "I think I earned my spurs at Cargill. I was general manager of edible proteins there when the Staley company knocked on my door. I viewed an affiliation with Staley as a great opportunity. Moving into responsibilities at Decatur struck me as offering the kind of job I had been preparing myself for for a long time. I knew that soybeans could be a Cinderella story for Staley and I knew I could help in making such a story happen."

As one of the nation's largest soybean processors, the Staley corporation has not only found profitability but has, in addition, recaptured some prestige as the "know how" company in a field in which it pioneered in the twenties.

"With five mills throughout the Midwest, we have a combined crushing capacity of more than 360,000 bushels of soybeans per day," St. Clair said. "Soybean meal is a vital protein source in poultry and livestock feeds. Soy oil is used primarily as an ingredient in margarine and salad dressings and as a cooking oil, and in a variety of nonfood applications.

"Our soy protein concentrate is increasingly popular as a

fortifier and extender in processed meats and baked goods. The U.S. Army has become a major customer.

"We're in sunflower seed processing, too—something new. Together with two partners, we are constructing a plant at Velva, North Dakota, which will be capable of processing 1,000 tons of sunflower seed per day. This is a promising new business and we intend to be a part of it—in a significant way.

"As part of the AgriProducts Group we operate eight country elevators in south central Illinois and, believe me, this is a business that suits us very nicely. Keep in mind that the elevator is the marketing connection between the farmer and the processor. Whether the farmer has grain directly for sale or simply wants to rent space for storage, it's a service in which we can make friends and make money simultaneously. Our export elevator at Coles Station, Illinois, is an item of pride. It regularly handles 125-car trains which convey grain shipments to the Gulf.

"Also operating under the wing of AgriProducts is the commodity futures trading subsidiary known as Staley Commodities, Inc. It services clients throughout the nation from its headquarters office at the Chicago Board of Trade, its principal customers being grain merchandisers and country elevator operators. This group has been performing well—and it provides an excellent market insight for our own company's commodity activities."

President Bob Powers observed, "We'll go only as far as our technology will take us. There was a time when our company simply didn't have the courage to back up its technology with enough dollars. We were too little or too late—or both. We used to miss the boat every now and then. But we're not about to miss the boat anymore.

"From the mid-fifties to the early sixties we did a lot of basic research," Powers explained. "Then we shifted much of our emphasis into application research and product development. We are now rekindling the whole area of basic research while not neglecting product development. We're strong in biochemistry and we're undertaking some important projects in enzyme technology. We're as serious as any company in the nation in the matter of utilizing renewable resources. Actually, more than 99 percent of our total production today stems from the use of renewable resources. No Arabs are about to cut off our sources of raw material supply.

"Chemicals from carbohydrates—this is an important new direction. There are significant cost advantages in using corn derivatives instead of petroleum derivatives. It is inevitable that we'll be seeing petrochemical replacements from carbohydrates, proteins, and vegetable oil.

"Several companies are keenly interested in our new starch-based product called methyl glucoside, which has an excellent potential in insulation foams, in packaging films, and in alkyd resins used for paints. Other new products using similar technology are showing promise as surfactants in detergents.

"Actually, we are building a pilot plant—which we call a semiworks—in Decatur, to produce several million pounds of methyl glucoside. That shows we're serious in following through when we've got the technology to lead the way. Who knows? Chemicals from corn may become the new high fructose wonder for Staley.

"Our annual research budget was $3 million 20 years ago and almost $4 million 10 years ago. Today we're spending $9 million on R&D and we've got some of the nation's top chemists, chemical engineers, microbiologists, food technologists, and other specialists helping us move ahead.

"The day is not far off when we'll be developing new products, made of renewable resources, to serve as replacements for foodstuffs which are in short supply or in erratic supply or in unreasonable price ranges. Starch-based or protein-based materials could replace cocoa or coffee. Gum arabic, which is used in printing inks, could also find itself being replaced by a new functional product born in a lab.

"The day is also not far off when technology will carry our company into the development of additional products for the export market, where there's really room for growth. We have

251

just scratched the surface in our determination to tap the fruits of renewable resources. This is the excitement of our challenge. This is where you'll see our ingenuity in full force. We're not only a 'today' company, but we're also a 'tomorrow' company."

As in all corporations, the most all-embracing panorama is the view from the top, from that special crow's nest known as the office of the CEO. Donald E. Nordlund has had an opportunity to gain a special perspective during almost 10 years in high command. He recently shared some of his insights in response to a series of spontaneous questions.

Author: Mr. Chairman, what is your perception of the company in its seventy-fifth anniversary year?

Nordlund: Staley is, above all, a contemporary, aggressive organization motivated by the need to be out front in technology—in order to maintain leadership and profitability. Projects we are undertaking in 1981 will have a bearing on our performance in 1991. We are never really standing still. We're fine-tuning and adjusting all the time, staying lean and mobile so that we can adapt to changing circumstances. We strive to strike a balance between being strong today and strong tomorrow. We don't want to mortgage the future by over-concentration on today's results and we don't want to weaken our performance of today by over-concentration on tomorrow.

Author: What's your pet hate?

Nordlund: I dislike surprises. This doesn't mean we don't have occasional surprises—some good, some bad—but we try very earnestly to keep them at an infrequent level. Obviously, we are affected by a wide range of variables over which we have no control or little control, such as inflation, interest rates, tax policies, government regulations, weather—and sugar prices. Naturally, our competitors are impacted by all or most of the same variables. In my judgment it is the Staley company's job to anticipate changes, to capitalize on changes whenever we can, and in some instances to cause changes. We've done some revolutionary things in modified starches and in proteins and, more recently, in corn sweeteners. And we've been very much aware of our environmental responsibilities in our communities—as attested by a recent award from the Izaak Walton League. We've invented systems for pollution control. It's one thing to get out front as a responsible industrial citizen and as an innovator but it's another thing to stay out front. Even the shock of unfavorable surprises is easier to endure when a company is fundamentally strong in its balance sheet, in its manufacturing, marketing, and technology, in its customer good-will and in its employee relations.

Author: What role do your 4,200 employees play in such an endeavor?

Nordlund: Without slighting the crucial importance of our stockholders, customers, and suppliers, I'd say our employees are the most important constituency of all. We're strong because they make us strong.

Author: Is it your job as CEO to set a course, to establish objectives, to allocate the funds to support corporate planning?

Nordlund: No. I wouldn't put it that way. It is my responsibility to be a rallying point, to provide a focus and to help develop policies which will enable the company to provide a fair return on our stockholders' investment. Of equal importance, it is my job to foster the spirit and enthusiasm that permeates the organization. It is my job to provide a climate which will encourage employees to contribute their ideas, their skills, their energies. And it is my job to set a progressive and aggressive pace.

Author: Some of your colleagues have pointed out that you specialize in "stirring the pot." Is this true?

253

Nordlund: This may be true, but I'm not the only one at Staley "stirring the pot." My colleagues are as eager to push ahead as I am. They realize, as well as I do, that there is no room for complacency. If "stirring the pot" means being energetic and enterprising, then I guess you could put that down as a Staley characteristic and as a part of our corporate style and personality.

Author: Who sets priorities?

Nordlund: My associates help set priorities.

Author: Who makes the big decisions in high-pressure situations?

Nordlund: My coworkers help make the big decisions.

Author: Aren't mistakes made in a high-pressure process?

Nordlund: Mistakes are made in any process involving human fallibility. We simply try to keep mistakes few and far between and we're pretty cranky about having any given mistake made twice.

Author: How about your personal fallibility? Your personal batting average is perceived to be pretty high.

Nordlund: I'm as human as anyone in the shop. If my mistakes seem few in number—and I'm not sure that's a valid premise—the fact of the matter is that I'm backed up by some remarkable people whose experience, vigilance, judgment, and intuitive perception are valuable assets. Yet on occasion I have managed to make my own fallibility prevail.

Author: Such as . . .

Nordlund: Such as when in the mid seventies we should have disposed of our Consumer Products Group. In hindsight I can say this segment of our enterprise was quite salable at the time. But I had a reluctance to sacrifice our franchise in the retail marketplace. After all, the company's first product,

Cream starch, was a convenience item for grocery stores. In the mid seventies, several of our outside board members had lost their patience with our consumer products line. They suggested to me that perhaps I was dragging my feet in coming up with a disposal plan. They were right. I was stubborn. Chalk it up to sentimentality and to an unwillingness to raise the white flag. Even though I try not to use 20-20 hindsight on others I surely don't mind using it on myself. Consequently, I simply say "mea culpa" regarding consumer products.

Author: But in the overall . . .

Nordlund: In the overall I've been fortunate—or perhaps I should say the company has been fortunate. In major projects requiring the investment of many millions of dollars, we've had remarkable success. Some people thought our entry into high fructose corn syrup was a touch-and-go gamble. I didn't see it that way. A risk? Of course. But not a frivolous gamble. Our deliberations on high fructose went day and night. And some people raised their eyebrows in 1976 when we bought the Swift soybean plants. They had seen Staley downgrade soybeans and they were understandably puzzled when they saw us embrace a spurned product. Happily, this investment has already paid for itself. And now we are getting into new fields. With starch from renewable resources cheaper as a raw material than petroleum from finite resources, we're on the threshold of inventing substitutes for petrochemicals. There is already evidence that we're innovating successfully and laying the groundwork for expanded technology of the future.

Author: Are research, development, and marketing going to be the dominant functions on the company's road to a new era?

Nordlund: Yes, but don't forget about the manu-

255

facturing function. Too often the glamour of R&D and marketing tends to out-dazzle our formidable processing capability. Without efficient production processes we'd never achieve a leadership role. Without cost control and improved productivity, we'd be seriously disadvantaged. Without superior engineering of our plant facilities, we'd be hard-pressed. Too often the manufacturing function is taken for granted. Without the tremendous accomplishments of the men and women in our plants, we'd be back in the Dark Ages. In many ways, they are the unsung heroes and heroines of our company. Our manufacturing program is predicated on the efficiency and loyalty of our people across the nation.

Author: Loyalty? Didn't your workers, here at Decatur, at your largest and most important plant, go out on strike for 82 days in 1970?

Nordlund: Yes. There was a strike in 1970, but don't confuse that with loyalty. I'm afraid my feathers still get ruffled when I hear people refer to that strike as a bitter period of labor-management hostility.

Author: What happened?

Nordlund: Unlike most of our competitors, we didn't have compulsory arbitration at our Decatur plant prior to 1970. We were always under the gun of a strike threat. The issue of compulsory arbitration was, in our view, a matter of fair play. So we took a strike in order to stand for a principle. From July 22 to October 12, approximately 2,000 hourly rated workers of Local 837, Allied Industrial Workers, were off the job. Yet, in perspective, it is obvious that a lot of good grew out of that strike. Both sides later recognized that a breakdown in communications was at the root of the problem and both sides resolved never to let such a critical situation occur again. It's too bad that sometimes it takes a disagreement to lead to a firmer accord.

Author: Was anything learned?

Nordlund: It was a learning lesson for everyone. We have since capitalized on that learning lesson by forging a stronger bond between the company and the union. By and large, we've eliminated the old "them and us" syndrome. The last two labor contracts were signed expeditiously. There's a lot of loyalty among the workers in the Decatur plant. They contribute heavily to our progress. And the union has brought along some remarkable leadership people. The workers appreciate what we have to accomplish in productivity and cost-control. They know we're in a fiercely competitive industry. And they also know —or, at least, I hope they know—that we in management do not take their production skills for granted. The plain fact of the matter is that people who make the company's products make the company. It is just as simple as that.

What, one might wonder, does Local 837, Allied Industrial Workers, think about working relationships and management attitudes at the Decatur plant? How do Staley's hourly rated union employees feel about the situation?

The answers to these questions were recently provided by William W. Strohl, Sr., past president of Local 837, a pipefitter who joined Staley 20 years ago and who was the union's chief steward in the Decatur pipe shop at the time of the 1970 walkout.

Strohl observed that "management and the union have learned that it's possible to disagree without being disagreeable. We try to head off little problems before they become big problems. The important thing is that the company has respect for the union's rights to function properly and the union has respect for management's rights. The key element is trust.

"Attitudes on both sides are positive. We're in this thing together. We treat each other as equals. The recognition of human dignity prevails. I think it is fair to say that in recent

257

years we have reached new levels of understanding—all the way up to the office of the chairman, Don Nordlund. We're lucky to have an executive of that stature who understands the need for harmonious relationships in the plant.

"An ideal example is the East End Committee—a cross-section of hourly and salaried people who have regular meetings in the 'crush side' and the 'protein side' of the soybean area in the plant. This committee was formed in 1977 to deal with such matters as efficiency, safety, learning how to do things together, and protection of jobs. Nationwide there had been several hexane explosions in soybean processing operations in 1976. Everyone was convinced that 'safety first' should be the order of the day. To reach that goal we all knew that we'd need cooperation up and down the line. And it has all worked out that way.

"The East End Committee sorts out safety requirements and other matters and deals with them promptly. It meets monthly and invites participation by those who can best contribute. We keep looking for better ways to do things. A few years back we had as many as 41 grievances filed in a 6-month period. Thanks largely to the East End Committee, we went to 11 grievances in a recent 12-month period.

"When there are different viewpoints, we try to get to the root of problems promptly. In most cases, we reach common ground without too much delay and we avoid a big fuss. I believe it is important to get hourly and salaried people talking to each other and listening to each other. If there is any secret to the harmony we've had in the plant, that's it."

Somehow, Bill Strohl seems to downplay his personal role. But others don't.

"The listening process."

Virtually all corporations seem to talk about "the listening process"—listening to internal and external comments—because listening involves learning.

Downward communications are relatively simple within most companies—but how about upward communications? To what degree do superiors listen to, and not just talk to, their subordinates? To what degree is reliable feedback achieved? How earnestly does a company tap the ideas and ideals of its middle-echelon and lower-echelon people?

Don Nordlund's reaction to such questions is summed up in a single sentence: "The cross-flow of communications in any corporation is never any better than the climate which encourages employees at all levels to become informed and, importantly, to speak up and to initiate their comments and convictions."

By "speak up" Nordlund means "to contribute constructive ideas for better ways to do the job. Any job." He adds, "We never want to stifle or smother or inhibit. We even encourage offbeat, half-baked ideas when the intent is constructive."

Nordlund recently illustrated his point by suggesting, "Go talk to Nat Kessler, who knows as much about the wet-milling industry as any man alive and who knows the Staley company pretty well considering he has been here since 1944. Nat's a 'free spirit' who specializes in speaking up. Ask him if we encourage or discourage a free flow of ideas. Ask him if offbeat and half-baked ideas are tolerated."

Nat Kessler, vice president, technology, said he wasn't too sure about the appropriateness of "half-baked" ideas, but he nonetheless endorsed the notion that "offbeat ideas often deserve exposure and they're surely not rejected or ridiculed here at Staley. Company policy doesn't fence us in.

"The big trick," Kessler said, "is avoiding the kind of climate which inhibits people, which discourages someone from sticking his or her neck out with a new idea. There are no taboo subjects at Staley."

Kessler explained that in the technology area, "We have ad hoc groups which we call new opportunity teams, made up of chemists and other technical personnel along with engineers and marketing people. These teams attempt to come up with answers for the never-ending question, 'What areas should we be exploring for new products?' Ideas from these teams undergo a lot of screening. Then the best of the ideas are polished off for presentation to the Research Policy Committee composed of Don Nordlund, Bob Powers, Tom Fischer, and our rather new vice president of R&D, Richard R. Hahn—and myself. Quite often lately, Edward J. Koval, vice president of corporate development, also sits in on the Research Policy Committee meetings. I should add that Koval also has certain international responsibilities in his portfolio.

"Some of the proposals presented for consideration get pretty far out. But no one gets scolded. The Research Policy Committee examines each proposal and flashes a green, red, or amber light. Some proposals are given the go-ahead right away. Others are shot down. Wham! Others are put on hold and are sent back for more economics homework or for additional marketing research or whatever.

"Consider our product methyl glucoside, which we are preparing to manufacture. It is extremely promising. Don Nordlund will tell you he never said, 'Go invent a better process for methyl glucoside.' The idea actually came from a group leader in the lab.

"When the climate for experimentation is right, creativity flourishes. Not long ago we had a four-day meeting at Palo Alto, California, on the subject of idea stimulation. We included some new people, feeling that they'd be too green to figure out what's permissible and what's not. We wound up with a list of 450 ideas, a list which was distilled down to 15 meriting investigation. Anyone at the meeting who got up and proclaimed that 'that won't work!' was told to sit down. Anyone who proclaimed that 'that's too long range!' got the same treatment. Granted, not too many long shots are winners, but all it takes is a few to make the attempt worthwhile.

"Sometimes top management gets a gleam in its eye when a new project is proposed. Sometimes top management gets too impatient. It then becomes a research leader's job to say something like 'Cool it' and something like 'It may take me ten years to pull this thing through.' "

To which chairman Nordlund responds, "I've learned to

count to ten." And then he adds, "As long as we continue to make headway in commercially practical inventions based on the use of renewable resources, we'll continue to give our technical folks all the time they want—or at least almost all the time they want."

Renewable resources have been at center stage ever since the Staley firm was founded. Over the years the company's name has become synonymous not only with the word "food" but also with the word "agriculture."

Vernon R. McMinimy, Staley's director of commodity research, has observed that the wide and wonderful world of agriculture supplies more than 99 percent of Staley's incoming raw materials and, in addition, agriculture is the recipient of, or customer for, a large part of the company's processed end products. "From the farm and back to the farm" would be an appropriate slogan for a substantial portion of the company's product line.

A few McMinimy statistics tell the current story:

CORN: Starch and oil are the primary components needed to produce industrial and food products (including sweeteners), accounting for approximately 70 percent of corn used. The remaining 30 percent is processed into animal feeds and, thus, returned to the farm—or to agriculture.

SOYBEANS: Of the total volume of soybeans the industry processes, approximately 23 percent goes into oil, soy grits, and soy flour for food and industrial uses. The other 77 percent is processed into animal feeds and, thus, returned to the farm—or to agriculture.

McMinimy added: "Excluding water and energy, the raw materials which we obtain, other than corn and soybeans, represent a figure between two tenths of one percent and three tenths of one percent."

Towering tall in the middle of one of the world's most celebrated agricultural regions, where central Illinois farmland is valued above $3,000 an acre, the Staley company, in Nord-

261

lund's words, "is proud to be in partnership with agriculture."

Agriculture is, far and away, the premier industry of the nation, with assets approaching $1 trillion—equal to almost 90 percent of the total assets of all domestic manufacturing corporations. Also, agriculture is by far the nation's Number One employer, providing income for 15 million people in growing, storing, transporting, processing, and marketing of all farm commodities.

American farmers do a heroic job in feeding their own country, of course, but that is only part of the story. As an exporter in an increasingly populous world where famine and malnutrition hover in widely scattered regions, the American farmer sends $41 billion worth of crops per year to foreign lands. Thus, the agricultural community brings important revenues into the United States to help offset what America pays for OPEC oil, Volkswagens, Toyotas, Nikons—and sugar.

ITEM: Dr. Walter Ebeling, professor emeritus at the University of California, recently commented that "productivity has grown five times faster in agriculture than in industry over the past five years."

ITEM: Much of agriculture's phenomenal progress has occurred within recent decades. Not until 1954 did the number of tractors on all farms in America exceed the number of mules and horses.

ITEM: The current generation of U.S. farmers produces 75 percent more crops per acre than the previous generation.

ITEM: "Free enterprising" on the farm is as uniquely American as the Fourth of July. Most U.S. farmers stir themselves into action early in the morning. A 12-hour day is not uncommon. But in most Communist countries, farmers' spirit and initiative are in no way the same. At 5 P.M., farmers in the collectivized sector bring their activity abruptly to a stop. Their lack of drive and enthusiasm is perhaps understandable in view of the minimum respect they receive from state leaders. Lester R. Brown of Worldwatch Institute, who has described Soviet farming practices in *Science* magazine, pointed out that "Marx was a city boy." In the USSR, one farm worker feeds seven people, a far cry from the American farmer who feeds 57 people.

ITEM: Even though the United States has only 3,618,467 square miles of surface land compared with the world's 57,509,692 square miles, it accounts for 55 percent of all world trade in grain.

Don Nordlund recently said, "Americans have so many blessings that we are inclined to take them for granted. It's unfortunate that our nation had to learn under stress that dependence on foreign petroleum is an economic and political malady of frightening proportions, leading to world unrest and triggering immense economic and social problems throughout the land. Yet the OPEC countries have perhaps inadvertently done us a favor by challenging our heritage of independence, initiative, and invention. They have helped firm up our country's resolve to show what it can do under duress.

"There is no doubt in my mind that American agriculture will not only increase its food supply at home and abroad, but also it will emerge as the raw material supplier for an array of new, man-made chemicals, plastics, detergents, fibers, pharmaceuticals, and other essentials. Scientists and engineers in the labs of processing industries are digging deeper into nature's secrets in order to make this happen. And it will happen. By the year 2000, a new era of scientific accomplishment will be responding to an unprecedented wave of human needs.

"Soybean oil is being used to extend diesel fuel in Brazil. A small matter, one might say. It may be small in the global scheme of things today, but it is a symbolic and significant sample of agriculture's new role in man's affairs. Brazil is not the only country deficient in petroleum resources. Innumerable big and little nations of the world are looking for solutions to their problems; they are wondering, they are pleading, they are asking if viable, renewable, and theoretically infinite bounties of agriculture cannot move in and assume some of the continuing and increasing burden, beyond food.

"Many solutions will be found, I believe, in the laboratories of processing industries which 'know the territory'—and by 'territory' I mean the agricultural community. Particularly in America, the farmers will find a way to provide the raw materials we'll be needing. And uniquely in America, we will continue to be blessed by those four magnificent gifts: land, climate, technology, and economic freedoms."

Don Nordlund, Bob Powers, and their colleagues believe that such an idealistic scenario is in fact quite pragmatic and is "tomorrow's bottom line" at Staley. And they say don't forget those two little agricultural treasures that will continue to be the source and spark of Staley's progress—the kernel and the bean.

Directors and Corporate Officers

The following brief biographical notations include recent and/or current responsibilities of the persons listed.

ATWOOD, PAUL W. was president of the company's UBS Chemical Division and served on the Staley board of directors during 1959 and 1960.

BARNES, WILLIAM, III chairman of The Citizens National Bank of Decatur, Illinois, has served as a member of the Staley board of directors since 1977.

BASS, RAY S., SR. former executive vice president, secretary and treasurer of the company, was elected a director in 1942. Mr. Bass joined Staley in 1919 and died in 1955.

BEAUMONT, JAMES H. was director of public relations and later vice president in charge of industrial sales. He was elected a vice president in 1967 and served in that capacity until his retirement in 1976.

BIEGER, GILBERT L. joined Staley in 1970. He served as the company's chief financial officer and as an executive vice president and a director from 1971 until his retirement.

BISHOP, WILLIAM B., SR. retired from Staley in 1969 after 41 years of service to the company. He was elected to the board of directors in 1959 and retired in 1968.

BOYER, W. ROBERT joined Staley in 1934 and served the company as controller, treasurer, and vice president, finance. He was elected to the company board of directors in 1955 and retired in 1968.

BRALLEY, JAMES A. joined the company in 1956 as director of research. He was elected a vice president in 1961 and resigned in 1969.

BROOKS, R. WILLIAM joined the company in 1973 as vice president of the company's consumer products group. He retired in 1980.

BURWELL, THORNTON C. joined the company in 1917. He served for many years as a director and as vice president in charge of transportation. He retired in 1957 and died in 1981.

BUTLER, THOMAS B. former president and chairman of the Mercantile Safe Deposit and Trust Company, Baltimore, Maryland, was elected the company's first outside director in 1941. Mr. Butler died in 1968.

CALLEBAUT, PIERRE chairman of Glucoseries Reunies, S.A. in Aalst, Belgium, was elected a director in 1973.

DAILY, ROBERT F. joined the company in 1960 and was elected secretary in 1961.

DAVIDSON, ROBERT H. was elected a vice president and director of the company in 1963 and expanded his role to vice president, marketing, in 1966. He left the company in 1967.

DOXSIE, LOUIE E. retired in 1975 as executive vice president after more than 40 years with the company. He served as a director of the company from 1969 to 1975. Mr. Doxsie died in 1981.

EAKIN, F. A. joined Staley in 1932. A company vice president and director for many years, Mr. Eakin died in 1978.

EVANS, WILLIAM F. a vice president since 1976, is president of Staley Commodities International, Inc.

FISCHER, THOMAS V. executive vice president in charge of the industrial products group, he was elected to the board of directors in 1970.

GREENFIELD, ROBERT E. was first employed by the company in 1926. He served as general superintendent and was elected a vice president in 1947. He retired in 1959 and died in 1977.

GRESHAM, THOMAS L. was vice president and technical director from 1956 to 1960.

JENSCH, CHARLES C. was vice president in charge of international operations from 1966 to 1969. He resigned from the company in 1969.

JOANIS, JOHN W. chairman of Sentry Insurance Company, Stevens Point, Wisconsin, was elected to the Staley board of directors in 1972.

KAPP, HORACE J. joined Staley in 1930 as head of the grain department. He was elected to the board of directors in 1935 and was made a vice president of the company in 1942. Mr. Kapp died in 1980.

KESSLER, NATHAN was elected to the board of directors in 1963. He currently is vice president, technical.

KOVAL, EDWARD J. vice president in charge of international operations, he was elected a corporate vice president in 1979.

LANTERMAN, JOSEPH B. chairman of Amsted Industries, Chicago, was elected to the Staley board of directors in 1975.

McGUIRK, WILLIAM E. former chairman of Mercantile Safe Deposit and Trust Company, Baltimore, Maryland, was elected to the Staley board in 1968. He resigned from the board in 1975.

MARTIN, WAYNE S. vice president in charge of industrial sales and marketing, was elected a corporate vice president in 1978.

MILLER, DONALD C. vice chairman of Continental Illinois Corporation and Continental Bank of Chicago, was elected to the Staley board of directors in 1977.

MILLER, LELAND B. vice president and treasurer since 1981, he was elected a corporate officer in 1973.

MOORE, JAMES W. was associated with Staley for 34 years. He was elected vice president, commodities, in 1965 and became group vice president, agriproducts, in 1970. He retired in 1976.

MURPHEY, ROBERT J. a senior partner in the accounting firm of Murphey, Jenne and Jones, he was elected to the Staley board of directors in 1954 and resigned in 1969. Mr. Murphey died in 1970.

NORDLUND, DONALD E. chairman of the board and chief executive officer of the company, joined Staley in 1956. He was elected to the board of directors in 1958.

PETERSON, ARTHUR Q. was a member of the Staley board of directors from 1950 to 1964. A New Orleans industrialist, he was chairman of Wesson Oil and Snowdrift Company, Inc. Mr. Peterson died in 1976.

PEVLER, HERMAN H. former chairman of the Norfolk and Western Railway Company, Roanoke, Virginia, served on the Staley board of directors for 14 years, from 1963 to 1977. Mr. Pevler died in 1978.

POWERS, ROBERT M. president and chief operating officer of the company, was elected a vice president in 1971 and to the board of directors in 1975.

REDSHAW, LINCOLN L. former president of the UBS Chemical Division. He joined UBS in 1937 and was elected a vice president of that company in 1946. He was appointed president of UBS in 1961 and also at that time was named a corporate officer of the Staley company.

ROEHM, L. S. joined Staley in 1950 as corn division manager and was elected an officer of the company in that year. Mr. Roehm left the company in 1961.

ROLLINS, ROY L. retired in 1970 after 37 years with the company. A vice president in charge of manufacturing, facilities planning, purchasing, industrial relations and public relations, he was elected to the board of directors in 1954.

St. Clair, Phillip M. vice president of the company's agri-products group, joined the company in 1977 as vice president, commodity operations.

Schaeffer, Bruce Z. was vice president of corporate relations. He served as a corporate officer from 1973 to 75.

Scheiter, Edwin K. was past president of the company and a director for 53 years. He joined Staley in 1919 and was first elected a director in 1925. Mr. Scheiter retired as a board member in 1976. He died in 1978.

Schell, Robert K. financial consultant and past executive vice president of the Chase Manhattan Bank, New York, was elected a director in 1962.

Schenk, Boyd F. a Staley director since 1978, he has served as president and chief executive officer of Pet, Inc. since 1969.

Scherer, Raymond C. former director, corporate secretary and comptroller. He joined Staley in 1912 and retired in 1960. Mr. Scherer died in 1976.

Schuerman, Robert L. joined Staley in 1946 and was elected a vice president in 1967. He is currently vice president, government relations.

Schwanke, Robert L. a vice president and controller, he was elected a corporate officer in 1978.

Stanhope, Raymond E. vice president of administration and government relations. He was elected a corporate officer in 1971.

Staley, A. E., Jr. served as president from 1932 to 1958 and as chairman of the board for 34 years. His career with the company founded by his father spanned five decades. Mr. Staley died in 1975.

269

STALEY, A. ROLLIN elected to the company board of directors in 1942, was elected a vice president in 1954. He continued to serve on the board until his death in 1968.

STALEY, HENRY M. a vice president and former treasurer of the company, has served on the board of directors since 1969.

TRASK, WARREN T. joined Staley in 1977 as vice president, industrial manufacturing, and was elected a corporate officer in 1981.

WAGNER, FRANK H. a vice president, he was elected to the board of directors in 1969.

WRIGHT, HAROLD D. a director of the company from 1950 to 1960, he was chairman of Republic Coal and Coke Company, Chicago. Mr. Wright died in 1976.

HONOR ROLL OF SERVICE

Every effort has been made to ensure the accuracy of the following list of past and present employees. In cases where an employee retired in the middle of the year, that person is credited with an additional year of service. All service dates were determined as of December 31, 1981.

50-Year Employees
Active
None

Retired or Deceased
Edward W. Lashinski
John M. Shyer

49-Year Employees
Active
None

Retired or Deceased
Adolph A. Leipski
K. Paul Simroth
A. E. Staley, Jr.
Glenn F. Trent

48-Year Employees
Active
Robert G. Slaw

Retired or Deceased
Eric Augustine
James Lee Carter
James H. Galloway

Glennis A. Moran
Edwin K. Scheiter
Ray C. Scherer
Otto D. Sutter

47-Year Employees
Active
William H. Miller

Retired or Deceased
Sylvester C. Bowman
Louis H. Brand
Claude V. Cox
Irvin G. Cox
Harry W. Gabriel
A. Helen Harder
Arthur F. Heideman
Lynn S. Hettinger
Martha A. Huffman
Dwight J. James
Harold E. Lents
Margaret M. Lupton
Noble C. Owens
Leo R. Riedlinger

46-Year Employees
Active
None

Retired or Deceased
Cecil Beel
Earl L. Bray
Perry Conley
Ira J. Cox
Jack D. Franklin
Walter O. Hansen
Harold W. Kibler
Edmond D. Moore
William Oak
Paul J. Peters
Henry A. Scherer, Sr.
Herbert W. Scholes
William W. Stewart
Carl L. Waltens

45-Year Employees
Active
Charles G. Ellis, Jr.
Harry W. Robinson

Retired or Deceased
Eric Bahlow
Fred Bahlow
Arch N. Beals, Sr.
Elvin F. Betzger
John L. Carmean
Ralph F. Clifton
H. Russell Dash
Alfred J. Donnell
Michael Duggan
John M. Durchholz
James T. Franklin
Frank J. Grossman
Joseph N. Grossman
Raymond R. Grunert
Gertrude F. Hebert
Sylvester Ivens

Elmer J. Lashenski
Claude Luster
Doris H. Murphy
William H. Nickel, Jr.
Henry Parker
George Sheumaker
Robert G. Siweck
Joseph J. Slaw
Norval A. Smith
W. Harry Walmsley
Hansel V. Wetherholt
Ornan A. Williams

44-Year Employees
Active
Albert W. Kopetz
A. Sam Robinson
Frank W. Waller
Harold O. Williams

Retired or Deceased
Ross Alverson
Phil Bateman
Harry D. Bell
Harry J. Brandenburg
Kenneth M. Brobst
Herman R. Crawley
William R. Damery
Searcy Garrison
Robert E. Heffington
Hollis H. Hise
Walter R. Hughes
Paulus E. Jones
Charles F. Lavery
Charles E. Lewis
Frank E. Lewis
Joseph A. McGlade, Sr.
Vernelle R. March

Thomas E. Moran
Dale L. O'Bryan
Lawrence E. Ooton
Eldo C. Riedlinger
Norman Schultz
Kenneth D. Sherman
William K. Snelson
James W. Todd
Vernon U. Van Hook
Frank Watkins
Harold Williams

43-Year Employees
Active
None

Retired or Deceased
Marion H. Bergandine
Gilbert C. Boren
Makies Boyd
Donald C. Carroll
Henry Colbert
Boyd Cornthwaite
Clyde Crawley
William Damery
Mary H. Doherty
Maurice E. Eagan
Fred Emert
Harold D. Gentry
Edward W. Grant, Jr.
Kenith Hagen
Herbert W. Harless
Earl O. Hettinger
Kenneth J. Higdon
W. Dale Himes
Clyde W. Hoyt
Frank J. Kekelsen
Raymond K. Lenover

Thomas Longbons
John W. McDonald
Clifton F. Martin
George W. Owens
Scott B. Page
Donald E. Rogers
Norman Schultz
Kermit Shively
Nathaniel Smith
Troy A. Stratton
Paul G. Stroyeck
Cecil W. Taylor
Russell B. Trowbridge
Evelyn M. Tueth
F. Frank Wagner
Robert S. Walker
Arthur W. Watkins
Marjorie K. White
Joseph D. Yarborough

42-Year Employees
Active
Jace W. Davidson
Chase A. Fitch
Fred L. Martina
Lee J. Owens
Lyle F. Wiegand
Adam V. Wilkie, Jr.

Retired or Deceased
Albert H. Artze
William Artze
Thomas Barbee
Sylvester Boos
Ned Bowers
Glenn R. Bowman
Kenneth E. Buechler
Continued

273

George L. Carnahan
John Cole
Harvey A. Crose
Francis C. Diveley
William E. Duncan
Esther Elder
Morris L. Fisher
Charles H. Fitch
Lowell O. Gill
Glen Grant
Carl F. Grunert
Emery L. Grunert
Henry L. Hack, Sr.
Donald Hall
Homer H. Hanson
Iver G. Hazenfield
Arthur L. Isaacs
Richard A. Jackson, Sr.
Ned Johnson, Jr.
Melvin S. Jones
LeRoy C. Kalb
Roy F. Larson
James C. Layton
Gerald G. Leaser, Sr.
Albert S. Lukey
Mathew McDaniel
Chester B. McGlade
O. Leo McIntyre
Clifford F. Mast
Chester A. May
John T. Mintun
Pete B. Nolan
Michael Paczak
Leroy Parker
Leo L. Provin
Ernest P. Reich
Leo E. Richards
Eugene R. Roberts
Mylo G. Roberts
Charles W. Schmitt, Sr.

Albert D. Smith
Ervin A. Snook
Paul G. Stroyeck
Homer E. Stuart
Levy D. Taylor
John M. Tokarz
Pauline M. Turner
Alonzo D. Wall
R. A. West
Albert G. Welker
Earl C. Wheeler
William B. Yetter
Lawrence C. Yunker

41-Year Employees
Active
Ivan G. Boren
Melvin H. Brandon
Lloyd E. Fisher
Juanita W. Kopetz
Walter R. Moore
Dorothy Ray

Retired or Deceased
Frank R. Allen
Homer Allen
Lawrence Alverson
John F. Anderson
Earl Bailey
Walter C. Batson
Paul Baum
William B. Bishop, Sr.
Lloyd J. Blankenship
Vorris R. Blankenship
Raymond E. Bomball
William H. Bourne
Howard C. Brumley
Everett D. Bush

274

Cager C. Carter
Claro E. Carter
William W. Caudill
James E. Coffey
Everett D. Conder
David Dryden
Albert P. Edwards
James A. Emert, Sr.
Lyden W. Etcheson
Wibb O. Falk
James E. Fuson
Walter F. Gerk
Virgil L. Grady
William E. Grant
Cleo E. Hanson
Julius A. Heisler
Louis T. Heisler
Murray A. Hiltabrand
Gilmore H. Hoft
Jack Hutson
Willard E. Kearns
Bertha R. Keithley
Clarence A. Koshinski
Carl W. Leek
Meredith J. Luster
Clarence W. McGeehon
Raymond R. McGlade
John C. Martin
A. Byron May
Francis L. Morrow
George L. Newberry
Jerry L. O'Riley
Fred C. Orkowski
Ollis E. Owens
Donald D. Pygman
Cletis A. Quillen
Jesse B. Ray
Lincoln L. Redshaw
Harold L. Reeve
William E. Robinson

Emil P. Schimanski
Leo I. Schimanski
Carl E. Sheets
Harold F. Sigmon
Ralph H. Smith
Arthur R. Thompson
Thomas J. Walsh
Ralph V. Whitsitt
Charles R. Wilber
Howard L. Winings
Richard B. Yocum
Isaac York
Charles E. Younger, Jr.

40-Year Employees
Active
Raymond L. Blaase
Otis Chenoweth
Roscoe L. Cook
Joseph Creamer
Dale E. Durnil
Edward F. Ecklund
Ernest E. Force
Harold E. Garner
E. Leroy Gass
Barton N. Gharrett
Elvin M. Hanson
Ada L. Highley
David F. Hite
Leon W. Jess
Robert L. Karloski
Clark J. Kikolla
Arnold G. Kubow
Emerson E. Lawhorn
Joseph A. McGlade, Jr.
James F. McLaughlin
Edward C. Neuendorf
Arthur E. Peterson

Continued

275

Wayne H. Roberts
Robert T. Rogers
Charles Silkwood
Edward E. Skelley
Kenneth M. Stubblefield
Ernest C. Williams

Retired or Deceased
Lawson Albritton
John A. Anderson
Otto Artze
J. Kenneth Ball
William Barter
Willie L. Barnes
Lyle Bauman
James Earl Beals
Estol L. Beasley
Herbert L. Beilsmith
Louis J. Borchert
Maurice H. Brumaster
William P. Brumaster
Robert E. Burchard
Thornton C. Burwell
Thomas C. Carter
Sam B. Chappel
Robert R. Clark, Sr.
Arvle D. Colter
Harry Cooley
Francis L. Coulson
E. Delmar Cox
Louie E. Doxsie
Clarence W. Durbin
Lawrence E. Durbin
Ralph E. Ellison
Earl W. Eschbaugh, Jr.
William R. Fenton
Raymond H. Franklin
Anthony Fratini

Dewey French
James H. Galloway, Jr.
E. H. Clark Gidel
Theodore G. Grabowski
Lucile C. Greenfield
Norman R. Harlin
Charles Harris, Jr.
Ray E. Harroun
Robert M. Hedden
Delmar C. Hazenfield
Thomas W. Henson
Howard P. Hill
Luther H. Hiser
Harold C. Hoyt
John C. Hudak
Gordon E. Jackson
Neta Kilburn
Walter E. Knackmus
Robert E. Koshinski
Charles W. Lawrence, Sr.
William Leek
William H. Lewis
Robert L. Lighthall
William H. Lowen
Patrick H. McHood
Otto S. McKee
William S. Martin
Lowell L. Moore
Clarence E. Moutray
Bessie Neyhard
Delbert J. Owen
Jesse Parker
Judge A. Parker
Lynn W. Quick
Roger M. Randol
J. Ralph Rentfro
Kathryn M. Rhodes
Robert N. Roderick
Franz Saloga
Charles W. Sampson

Gladys V. Schahrer
Kathryn M. Sheehy
Claude L. Smith
Ed Smith
Harvey Smith
Maurice A. Smith
Darrell M. Spicer
Ross O. Stone
William M. Stork
John L. Swarthout
M. Estol Thompson
Erastus R. Tipsword
Virgil D. Tish
Earl E. Traughber
Tom J. Vigneri
Robert E. Willis
Wendell F. Wimmer
Luke Winston
Carl D. Young

39-Year Employees
Active
Jesse W. Angel
Harry R. Atkins
Richard J. Bame
William E. Burchard
Koran Capshaw
R. Harold Doddek
Ralph R. Dombroski
Huston F. Dorsey
Melvin J. Funk, Jr.
Melvin R. Grolla
Paul A. Imel
Homer E. Jacoby
George L. Jones, Jr.
Raymond A. Kaler
R. R. Knepper
Charles H. Lefringhouse
Cecil H. Lewis

Jack E. McAdamis
Herbert E. Milligan
Junior E. Nihiser
Frederick J. Quintenz
Elmer E. Randall
Helen L. Rigsby
Charles W. Schmitt, Jr.
Kenneth R. Schuman
Raymond Wells
Donald C. White
Henry J. White
George N. Williams

Retired or Deceased
Millard B. Bean
William E. Bloemaker
Arthur M. Buckley
Glenn L. Clark
Clyde R. Crawford
Harold R. Crawley
John T. Creamer
Clifford Creekmur
John F. Davidson
Robert E. Deardorff
Arthur W. Deibert
Henry R. Doore
Charles G. Ellis, Sr.
John A. Ewing
William R. Fields
Glenn R. Finley
Dale H. Fisher
Ernie W. Gentry
Harvey W. Gollahon
Homer L. Grider
Robert Hall
John Milton Hanson
Fred C. Harless
Ira T. Hayes

Continued

Floyd E. Hazenfield
Shelley E. Heiland
John M. Howley
Beecham R. Jackson
J. L. Johnson, Sr.
Kenneth M. Johnson
Wilbur K. Johnson
Paul H. Kalem
Charles A. Keck
Floyd R. Klinghammer
Norman O. Lents
C. Lee Lyons
Forrest S. Marmor
Walter H. Meinert
Joseph A. Miller
Thomas J. Murray
John Nickey
Fred Oak
Henry A. Owens
Charles E. Parrill
Laurence C. Paul
George N. Quillen
Hallie W. Poe
Ernest H. Rade
Clarence Rader
J. Bluford Rexroat
Calvin S. Richards
Maybelle B. Rickey
Fred C. Ridlen
Charles E. Roberts
Antonio Romano
Arnold R. Rosenbury
John Rozanski, Jr.
John R. Sanders
Fred O. Schwesig
John Semelka
Lewis M. Smith
W. Irving Smith
Marshall L. Spain
Vernon J. Spaulding

Lloyd T. Stubblefield
Edward Alfred Trent
Henry M. Utterback
Raymond M. Van Gundy
Andrew C. White
Mathias A. White
Robert E. Willis
Adolph Witt
John H. Wyant
Charles J. Yonikus

38-Year Employees
Active
Oren O. Campbell
George D. Crisman
Donald R. Dye
Robert L. Kelly
Everett F. Leisner
Charles W. Murray, Jr.
Marion L. Schubert
Wayne A. Stanley
Lyndell D. White

Retired or Deceased
Floyd Adcock
Ted Appenzeller
Harry Augustine
Hiram Ballance
Velma Barnett
Walter G. Barr
Wendell Bauman
Harold J. Beard
Wells M. Beck
Leown Irl Beel
Hilbert O. Bell
Wilburn D. Boren
Walter C. Bradshaw
Lum Brandon

Carl K. Bronson
Wilber E. Buis
Walter Carr
Herschel A. Coffman
Wilbur Coon
Walter Cooper
Harold J. Cozad
Kenneth H. Cozad
Harold T. Craig
Arthur Cummings
Stanley F. DeJanes
Ira L. Dunham
William E. Dunham
Ernest J. Eckart
James J. Eckhert
Kenneth M. Evans
Jack A. Galloway
Floyd D. Gasaway
Marjorie B. Gillon
Gus D. Grotjan
Prentis L. Harlin
Roy Heffington
Cleotis N. Helm
Kidwell P. Hinton
Conard J. Hiser
James W. Hurley
Carson C. Jackson
Charles O. Jones
Leo M. Kelly
John R. King
Gilbert H. Kratzner
George W. Leonard
Elmer D. Lind
Howard W. Logsdon
Melvin Longbons
Patrick J. McGarry
Morris McKown
Clarence O. Martin
Henry F. Meyer
Charles E. Miller

Charles E. Monical
Adrian A. Morris
Fred Myer
Carl J. Napierski
Luke J. Owens
Emmett L. Page
Arthur E. Patton
Lawrence C. Paul
George N. Quillen
Clarence Rader
Helen Rader
Jesse E. Robinson
James B. Roderick
August H. Rost
Henry Sanders
Harold E. Schable
Martin Schnitzmeyer
Howard D. Sheets
Paul R. Shildneck
Earl E. Shobe
Osea O. Shobe
Earl Sigmon
Merle W. Simmons
John A. Slover
Francis L. Staleton
Frank M. Starbody
Edward Stratton
George Truebe
Hugh W. York

37-Year Employees
Active
Thomas L. Belcher
Charles A. Bradley
Carl K. Bronson
Roosevelt Cheatham
Dean W. Christman
Donald L. Falk

Continued

Nathan Kessler
Wayne C. Mussulman
Roberta A. Noonan
Charles A. Phegley
Alice M. Towne
John E. Travis

Retired or Deceased
L. C. Ambrose
Merwyn N. Armentrout
Harold K. Behrns
Clyde Billings
Lester D. Borden
John K. Bork
Albert M. Boulware
Harry J. Burgener
Lester P. Carter
Nicholas Chervinko
Thomas E. Clanton
G. Murral Compton
Russell Crum
Carl L. Dongowski
Leverett C. Early
John H. Fruchtl
Cecil Kyder Fundy
William Gillispie
Otto Grolla
Anne L. Hague
Richard E. Hehl
Herman C. Jagusch
John P. Jenkins
Dewey L. Johnson
Norville Johnson
Eugene F. Kaler
Kenneth Kennedy
F. Floyd Lenover
Fred D. Lesley
Neva Long
Frank Loughead

Elmer R. McCoy
Clarence E. Marmor
Jack Mathews
William B. Minton
Horance A. Mitchell
William D. Moorehead
Ivan W. Mulvey
Raymond Nihiser
Sylvester J. Nugent
Sylvester T. Peters
Theral R. Pritts
George Raney
Roger O. Read
Virgil L. Reed, Sr.
Herman M. Rice
James B. Rickey
Garland Roberts
Roy L. Rollins
Jerry D. Royce
Frederick Schwalbe
Glenn A. Scott
Claude W. Smith
Leonard B. Smith
Vern E. Smith
Philip J. Spent
Harley E. Strohl
Harry Tomkinson
Donald E. Tueth
Thomas Welch
Russell Wilber
Charles R. Willard
Samuel S. Wood
Ralph Wright

36-Year Employees
Active
Charles M. Adams
Eldon E. Allison
Charles W. Baker

Harvey H. Baker
William J. Ball, Jr.
Wallace D. Bean
Clyde J. Beck
James L. Beckmeier
Lloyd W. Beckmeier
Morris L. Birkhead
Donald E. Bledsoe
Donald L. Camp
Harry Chambers
Herbert W. Cochran
Eugene P. Collins
Robert E. Cooley
Elwood L. Crutcher
Leo W. Edwards
John W. Gideon
Sylvester Graves
Simon J. Harris
Howard M. Hawthorne
Elza Henderson
Howard L. Henson
Clyde G. Hobbs
Harold D. Hutson
Paul Jelks
Bonnie B. Jess
Hubert Johnson
Robert E. Kampf
Charles Lake, Jr.
O. Harold Lewis
Melvin O. Losier
Elzie F. Lourash
Glenn E. Niles
James E. Ooton
Vern W. Ooton
Charles Orr
Charles J. Paine
Clarence D. Parks
Harold L. Pieper
Gerald O. Reece
Pleasant A. Ross

George R. Scharein
L. Jean Schneider
W. Robert Schwandt
Ralph L. Shinneman
Clyde W. Sims
Marvin L. Sorrel
Samuel M. Stout
Roscoe A. Streight
Bill C. Sumpter
H. Jane Sumpter
Willie W. Swindle
John H. Tipsword
William G. Van Fossan
John W. Waller

Retired or Deceased
Coy J. Allen
Paul Atchason
John Austin
James Balderson
R. S. Bass
Harry V. Becker
William O. Bruner
Harold E. Buckner
Carrol L. Burrow
Samuel Carlson
Basil Carter
Thomas B. Cheyne
Raymond M. Clements
Walter H. Connard
Clyde Crawford
Verne S. Crone
Fred Deckard
Dale A. Deibert
Edgar P. Ecklund
Harold Fuson
John H. Galambach
Frank Gaskill

Continued

281

Gilmore C. Gillon, Sr.
Carl E. Grant
Clyde W. Greenwood
John A. Guysinger
Robert C. Hackert, Sr.
Donald W. Hanson
William J. Heer
Kenneth W. Heffington
Otto W. Hertrich
John Higgins
Joseph M. Hilberling
Robert E. Hinton
Emil R. Hoffman
Hylia Hoyt
Roy Ives
William B. Jackson
Andrew S. James
George L. Jones, Sr.
Martin J. Jones
M. Pete Kelley
Paul Kelly
Walter A. Koshinski
Harry A. Lichtenberger
Harrison McArty
Edward Marshall
Herman Miller
Albert Mixell
Franklin P. Moore
James W. Moore
Louis M. Murphy
Charles R. Nuehs
Emmett L. Page
O. Euell Perkins
Raymond Pittman
Henry Ploski
S. Merle Powell
Alonzo R. Ragel
Will H. Roberson
W. Keith Roberts
Percy I. Robinson

R. Wayne Rodgers
Eldin E. Scroggins
Sherman R. Stockwell
Hurschel Taylor
Ralph A. Toll
Harry Tomkinson
Paul G. Troxell, Sr.
B. H. Walker
William Wilson
William Whitmore
Matthew E. Wolfe
Ray Woodworth
Carl Yarnell
Nick York

35-Year Employees
Active
Lyle D. Adams
William Allen
Donald L. Amiotte
Everett S. Austin
Clyde A. Aydt
Forrest B. Bailey, Jr.
Cecil R. Barr
James G. Bean
Lawrence E. Bean
Ray Best, Jr.
Emery W. Blaylock
Paul E. Bork
Edward R. Boyle
Roy D. Bradshaw
Arthur E. Bramhall
John S. Brewner
Joseph B. Brown
Lewis E. Brown
Bill D. Buckley
John H. Carroll
Denver W. Carter
Maurice M. Carter

Walter L. Carter
William L. Carter
Robert S. Collier
Kermit L. Conley
Charles R. Cook
Dean E. Cox
Charles K. Crowell
Willie Dale, Jr.
Donald E. Disney
William D. Doyle
Allan H. Eaton
I. Dwight Engle
Harold K. Entrikin
John Fields
William C. Foran, Jr.
Leonard E. Force
Thomas Foster, Jr.
Marlin P. Fourman
Dewey French, Jr.
William F. Fryman
Herbert G. Gates
James E. Gentry
Calvin B. Gillespey
Edgar S. Ginder
Lyle K. Gray
Jesse A. Grunden
Edgar B. Hale
Ivan L. Harland
Dale E. Harless
Glen Hartman
Robert E. Hawthorne
Richard E. Hector
Wilber W. Hector
George L. Henson, Jr.
Claire W. Herron
William H. Hill
Robert E. Hoots
Freddie A. Howerton
Herbert F. Hurley, Jr.
Alonzo A. Karcher

Horace F. Kepler
Melvin Kinert
Charles J. Kmety
Clifford E. Kretsinger, Jr.
Robert E. Kretzer
Edward Kuizinas
Thurman A. Lambirth
Rex W. Lee
D. Ann Lippincott
Carroll D. Lourash
Floyd G. McElroy
George L. McFarland
Noward G. Malone
Luther J. Mayberry
Warren Metcalf
Arnold J. Metzger
Edward J. Michener
Raymond C. Miller
Harold W. Nichols
Roberta J. Nugent
Roy V. Oathout
Marion J. Page
Alvie L. Paine
Verne A. Parks
George Peacock, Jr.
Joseph L. Pettus
Oral T. Proffitt
DeWayne E. Prosser
Luther L. Quick
William R. Richards
Melvin F. Riddle
Clifford Rigsby
Guy Rigsby
William C. Roarick
Betty L. Roderick
David P. Rosenthal
Robert F. Sanders
Robert L. Schuerman
Ralph T. Sherden

Continued

Harold E. Smith
Harold F. Smith
Jordan L. Smith
Russell N. Smith
James J. Spaulding
Edward J. Stevens
William Sutherland
Percy H. Tolliver
Louis H. Von Hatten
Laurence F. Voyles
Dean D. Wadkins
James W. Walker
Lawrence U. Walker
Clarence E. Wangrow
Raymond O. Warnhoff
James D. Warnick
Charles W. White
Gerald L. White
Rolland A. White
Frank Whiteside
Theodore Wiseley
Howard B. Wood
Charles L. Worlds
Kenneth N. Wright
Lawrence A. Wyatt
William R. York

Retired or Deceased
Arthur E. Adams
Albert H. Adcock
Benjamin Adkins
Boyd Allen
Albert R. Auton
Harold R. Baker
Richard Barfield
Ralph O. Bates
Delton O. Baugh
Harry W. Becker
Omar M. Best

Elmer E. Betzer
C. Merle Blair
Willard J. Blaase
Edward L. Bland
Robert L. Bohn
Chester Boyle
Bud Brandon
Lisle R. Brown
Virginia Brumaster
Adrian E. Bush
Pauline N. Cable
Mike Casper
William D. Cherry
Clinton Childress
Robert W. Cline
John F. Collins
Floyd E. Compton
Arthur W. Conway
John W. Crabtree
David M. Crawley
Willard J. Crittendon
Jesse D. Cummings
Oscar V. Eckhardt
Robert I. Fain
Roy E. Finney
Peter J. Friendt
Theodore Fruth
Cecil K. Fundy
Gerald W. Gersmehl
James E. Gharst
William H. Gipson
William E. Glover
Charles R. Hagen
Dewey Henderson
Mae Hinderliter
Carl Horney
Raymond H. Huffer
John D. Hughes
William B. Jackson
Andrew S. James

Charles Johnson, Sr.
Alva Jordan
Herman Kaltenbach
Paul F. Kelly
John E. Kipp
Henry W. Kleinschmidt
Frank August Koshinski
Edward D. Lahniers
Charles W. Lupton
David D. McCulley
John A. Malchow
Ken J. Maltas
Edward E. Marshall
Earl Mathews
Robert W. Mills
Elizabeth M. Mizeur
Everett F. Moore
Orvan F. Mullis
James Nance
Charles Nesler
George C. Nickell
Eldred K. Olson
Glenn R. Phillips
George C. Pinney
Joseph P. Polluck
Ruth G. Powell
Frank M. Quickel
Harvey N. Rice
William Rich
Walter S. Rinehart
Francis J. Rogier
Roy A. Roller
Agnes N. Rommel
John W. Rutherford, Sr.
Marion Savage
John H. Scribner
William Sharlock
James L. Simpson
Joseph D. Spittler
Robert E. Stroyeck

E. E. Taylor
Guy G. Thompson
Lloyd E. Thompson
Claude W. Thornborough
Fred Tilinski, Jr.
Frank C. Wakefield
Delbert W. Walker
Woodrow W. Waller
Charles R. Walton
Charles V. Welch, Sr.
John L. Welch
Clyde T. White
Laurence P. White
James Milton Williams
William M. Willis
Phillip E. Wills
William F. Wilson
Sam Wood
John H. Wrightsman

34-Year Employees
Active
Theodore E. Born
C. Dean Burdick
Browder F. Butler
Robert A. Carney
David E. Clements
Marvin Cook, Jr.
James T. Couch
Philip B. Crist
J. E. Daniels
Dean H. Durbin
Donald F. Emert
James R. Everman
Harold L. Force
Elmer L. Ford
David L. Freeman
Leo G. Frey

Continued

285

Roland L. Goodman
Thomas R. Hall
Billy Hardy
Raymond R. Harper
Robert D. Harrison
Robert E. Justice
Virgil L. Kahler
Royal J. Kester
Norma B. Knop
Jack W. Kunzeman
Clark A. Lewis
William Lindsten
Vernon L. McCall
Hugh S. McMullen
Robert F. McNulty
Clifton F. Martin, Jr.
Raymond C. Miller
Marion J. Page
Leon H. Peters
Donald L. Petre
John L. Pryczynski

Retired or Deceased
Louis John Appelt
Pearl Frank Bailey
Orval Banton
James A. Bean
Robert H. Beard
Everett L. Becker
Walton Belton
Pat Bowles
W. Robert Boyer
Russell Louis Bridgewater
Robert F. Brix
Henry B. Burge
William J. Burke
G. M. "Pete" Carlson
Lester W. Chaney
Joseph R. Childress

Evelyn O. Clesson
Arthur W. Conway
Lloyd G. Cox
Emmett K. Cunningham
James E. Dennis
G. James Dustin
Ivan E. Force
Norris Ford
Royal Foster
Floyd Gosnell
Linn V. Greenwood
Edwin L. Hale
George E. Hale
Lewis C. Harpstrite
Harlan H. Harroun
Charles Harvey, Jr.
Lawrence E. Hebenstreit
John D. Hughes
William M. Jackson
Eldrid A. Jacobs
Clarence G. Jones
Benjamin D. Kelly
David P. Langlois
Carl F. Leming
Louis Little
Joseph W. Lucas
Harry S. Lynch
Frank Meyers
Gladys R. Mier
Russell D. Myers
George C. Nickell
Michael O'Donnell
Wesley Olson
George L. Peters
John F. Querry
Bernard L. Quigley
Wilbur R. Reed
Ralph Rehfelt
John J. Renfro
Edwin E. Robazek

286

Vito A. Rublesky
Bernard R. Runyen
George A. Russell
Frank Schikowski
Homer D. Shaw
Howard W. Shepherd
Edna M. Sims
Clifford Smith
George H. Smith
William M. Smith
James C. Snelson
Henry W. Sowa
Jack S. Thornell
Carl J. Tomlinson
Martin P. Trolia
Vernice V. Voyles
Harry J. Waite
Lee D. Weddle
John R. Weger
Kenneth B. Wood
Maurice Workman
Kermit F. Wright

33-Year Employees
Active
Floyd D. Adcock
Chester C. Boggs
Robert B. Boyd
Jack W. Burcham
Melvin L. Chapple
Dorothy E. Collins
Leroy A. Dean
William E. Dodd
Raymond A. Eichman
Delmar D. Foster
James A. Hayes
Leonard B. Hoadley
E. Wallace Holden
John H. Huddleston

Wayne H. Hull
Orval E. Hunley
Richard L. Karl
Donald N. Klingler
Norman A. Kocher
Carl J. Koslofski
Dorothy L. Loeb
Dale E. Matthews
Roger J. Mauterer
James B. Mullinix
Clifford E. Newlin
Robert E. Nihiser
Charles A. O'Dell
William I. Oldweiler
William M. Osborn
James D. Peterson
Merrill E. Pound
Richard D. Radasch
Jesse C. Scheibly
Derald W. Schoneman
Gilbert A. Seward
Margaret A. Shepherd
Carl A. Simroth
George E. Spates
Fred E. Starbody
Donald A. Sullivan
Ted M. Taylor, Jr.
Larry M. Trempel
Dean E. Webb
James D. Wetherholt
Clarence S. Williams, Jr.
John K. Yokley

Retired or Deceased
Leslie Adams
Theodore Belenski
William W. Berg
Wallace W. Binkley
Continued

Frances C. Bretz
Charles K. Brittenham
Chester P. Boyle
Edward J. Buechler
Mildred I. Burton
Charles Butler
John Byers
John A. Carroll, Jr.
John Charnetski
Harley S. Chittick
Roy A. Collie
Robert S. Collier
Lester Cummings
Daniel E. Dayton
Harold H. DeJanes
William L. Ewing
Byron L. Fast, Sr.
Robert D. Finley
Daniel J. Fitzgerald
Arnold French
Vern N. Giles
Michael N. Griffin
Louis Hall
Fontus L. Harlin
Jesse S. Harlin
Carl W. Henson
George Hewitt
Arlie V. Hines
Orville C. Hinton
John A. Hirsch
Francis Peter Holyschuh
William G. Hughes
Leonard M. Huss
Ralph B. Johnson
Charles H. Jones
Chester P. Jones
Phillip Jordan
Wendell Kerr
Eugene P. Kerven
Paul L. Kinney

Paul Kirkpatrick
Karl H. Klaus
Wendell Kurr
Willis H. Liston
Charles Long
Richard Lyhne
Charles P. Lynch
James A. McAnelly
John T. McCollum
Roy G. McGlade
William J. Maginn
Phillip C. Meyers
B. Alvin Morgan
William Mossman
Richard E. Nagle
Herbert I. Poteet
Kenneth H. Reed
Homer T. Reidelberger
Todd C. Riley
Robert L. Ruthrauff
John W. Salter
Paul E. Schahrer
Mildred E. Schroat
Howard W. Shepherd
Theodore Shondel
Benjamin H. Smyers
Rudolph Sowa
William R. Spicer
Glenn Sternes
William E. Stimmel
Arch C. Taylor
Clyde E. Thompson
Donald Thompson
John F. Traughber
Henry E. Vaughn
Forrest E. Vogel
Karl E. Webb
Joseph E. White
William E. White
Sidney Williams, Jr.

Kenneth D. Wittig
Henry J. Woermann
Lyle York

32-Year Employees
Active
Joseph L. Adams
Kenneth W. Alexander
Arthur Alfred
Archie N. Beals, Jr.
Richard L. Blaylock
John E. Boyer
George S. Bray
Donovan G. Brewner, Sr.
Vera F. Bryan
Dwight J. Butterfield
Marcus W. Clark
John Coleman
George L. Collins
Robert D. Craig
Cecil R. Davis
Fountain L. Dixon
Woodie J. Dumas, Sr.
Thomas D. Duncan
Dennis L. Durbin
Vincent W. Durbin
Alvin D. Fennig
George A. Finch, Jr.
Dale W. Fleischauer
William E. Gibbons
Paul W. Gollan
Dewey Gosnell
Laurence W. Haver
Frederick N. Henemeyer
Floyd A. Horn
Wayne M. Houser
Theodore W. Jackson
T. Leon Jones
Samuel B. Jump

Maurice E. Kapper
Darrell R. King
Donald R. Kush
Darrell L. Larson
L. Leon Lawrence
Waymond Ledbetter
James W. Lowery
Ralph F. McLaughlin, Jr.
Floyd Maddox
Arthur L. Mense
Robert M. Metzger
Louis H. Miller, Jr.
Lewis J. Mitchell
Wilbur F. Morrison
Robert L. Owens
Robert E. Poe
Robert L. Quick
William H. Reimer
Norman H. Rodgers
Herbert L. Roszell, Jr.
Gerald R. St. Pierre, Jr.
Ronald V. Saunders
Paul O. Short
William D. Sloan
M. Dale Smith
Woodrow W. Smith
Lester L. Snyder
Roger H. Sommer
Claude L. Stine
Delbert F. Stout
Robert A. Swift
Oliver M. Sy
Morris Tatum, Jr.
Glenn A. Vance
Raymond L. Van Scyoc
Bobby L. Walker
Victor F. Walters
Robert G. Wittig
Warren L. Wollrab
Ivan N. York

Retired or Deceased
William F. Allen
Forrest W. Apperson
Jay A. Ball
Jesse Barker
Harry Bateman
George Batorson
Charles R. Beal
Alfred Belue
Wayne Blick
Joseph A. Boggs
Paul L. Breyfogle
Russell Bridgewater
Forrest G. Britton
John Byers
Robert Byrum
Clifford L. Carroll
James Cheshier
Oliver D. Compton
William C. Cook
Hoyt O. Coverstone
Robert Cowgill, Jr.
Lowell A. Davis
Dewey Deckard
Melvin Eagleton
Howard File
Ora Fisher
William O. Frydenger
Lewis A. Fuqua
Fred H. Gentry
Alvy J. Gosney
George E. Grabe
R. E. Greenfield
Orval W. Hale
Roy V. Hanley
Horace D. Hanselman
Ralph E. Henderson
Emil R. Hoffman
Roy S. Hornback, Jr.
Herman E. Houser

Sherwood C. Howard
Donald H. Huffman
Bernard J. Incarnato
Willis Johnson
C. Dean Keithley
Chester E. Kester
R. E. Kilty
Gerald Kite
Ruth E. Kolb
Walter F. Kwasny
Willis Johnson
Edward Leuthauser
Elmer Luallen
Russell D. McCoy
Joseph C. Medley
David T. Mitchell
John W. Morey
Willis H. Mosby
William H. Murphy
Carl Oakes
Harry R. O'Riley
Russell B. Overly
Frank H. Penney
Maurice W. Price
Earl E. Riddle
Clarence E. Roderick
Richard W. Rozanski
Robert L. Ruthrauff
John J. Saloga
James Sams
Robert A. Sawyer
Virgil A. Schniederjan
Harry J. Schultz
Charles E. Seibert
Donald Siloski
James W. Smith
Maurice F. Smith
Gustav S. Sowa
Arch Spears
John C. Springer

William Story
Ernest M. Strahle
John W. Talley, Sr.
Gehl Tucker
Charles W. Vaughn
Forrest L. Wilmot
O'Dell Woodcock

31-Year Employees
Active
Charles A. Austin
Robert F. Bean
Joseph R. Beckler
Robert E. Bilyeu
Floyd E. Blair
Stanley R. Blair
Cecil L. Blancett
Dale C. Born
Robert M. Brinkley
James B. Brown
Thomas A. Burcham
Lyle W. Burgess
Robert D. Buxton
George E. Canaday
William W. Carr
John F. Carter
Richard D. Clow
Charles L. Cox
Ralph C. Davis
Clyde O. Doran
Robert W. Doty
Robert M. Ellegood
Robert W. Etherton
Ivan L. Finfrock, Jr.
Walter B. Fisher
George F. Fort
Walter J. Funk
Theodore L. Garrett
Hershel E. Gawthorp

Joe W. Grayned, Jr.
Chris G. Greanias
Leroy L. Haas
Henry L. Hack, Jr.
Clarence W. Harvey
Bobby G. Heiserman
William R. Hooper
Donald E. Hoots
Richard D. Hoyt
Harry W. Jackson
James H. Jackson
Jay L. Johnson, Jr.
Walter J. Kuizinas
H. Eugene Law
Arthur M. Leach
Darrell G. Livesay
Gary L. Loeb
Dale L. McClure
George J. Martina
Wilbur J. Maus
James B. May
Reeder C. Miller
Rolland W. Miller
Carl B. Minton
Richard C. Moore
Thomas J. Nolan
Billy Paslay
Wendell D. Ray
Levander Robinson
Robert E. Rodgers
William L. Salefski
Donald W. Sapp
Richard A. Sloan
Burton E. Smith
Glenn E. Smith
Robert E. Stine
Archie G. Sturgill
Richard A. Warner
D. Lee Wendel

Continued

Randall J. Whicker
John T. Williams

Walter W. Rade
W. H. Randol, Jr.
Kathryn M. Rhodes
Arthur W. Salogga
John J. Saloga
Donald J. Schneider
Rufus A. Scott
Norman A. Scranton
Oma E. Scribner
L. Chester Sharp
Robert E. Smith
Walter H. Smith
Medford M. Tate
William J. Thornborough
Glen Waddell
J. A. Wagner
Lawrence L. Ward
Harold Whitacre
Ivan R. Williams
Sam B. Williams
Perry L. Withrow

30-Year Employees
Active
Charles R. Alsbury, Jr.
Leslie G. Anderson
M. Joan Blaylock
Joe Belluchi
Irwin D. Blickenstaff
Solomon Briggs
Alfred W. Brunlieb
Wendell G. Bryant
Raymond E. Bundy
Leslie E. Carr
Ellis Carter
Luther E. Childress
Robert W. Christerson
Charles Conaway
Russell E. Cook

Floyd E. Dickerson, Jr.
George M. Donelan
Herschel C. Dowdell
Paul E. Durchholz
Everett W. Eaton
Robert E. Eaton
Henry W. English
Louis J. Feriozzi
William G. Fleming
R. Gene Ford
Lloyd G. Grace
Richard L. Hackl
Robert E. Hatch
Ronald H. James
Harold T. Johnson
Richard H. Kitchens
Darrell W. Law
Ted W. LeHew
N. Richard Lockmiller
James A. McGee
Glenn L. McMahan
Eugene A. Madia
Merle H. Mathias
Richard D. Mayberry
James O. Melton
Donald J. Miller
William J. Mundwiler
Albert C. Nixon
C. Everett Patrick
Robert D. Potts
James A. Rethinger
Samuel Risby
Raymond D. Rozanski
George J. Rubenacker
James E. Ryan
Harold G. Sayrs
Richard E. Schuman, Jr.
Robert G. Short
Donald M. Shuey

Continued

293

Wendell G. Smart
Paul F. Smith
Richard H. Spain
Harold E. Stine
Judson E. Strong, Jr.
Fred A. Tapscott, Jr.
Charles W. Walker
Harry A. White
Robert G. Woodcock
Wilbur D. Workman
Charles L. Yarborough
Helen A. Zindel

Retired or Deceased
James A. Allen
William Atwood
Donald C. Baldwin
Dwight Ball
Donald J. Ballard
George Baughman
Robert F. Beadleston
Walter C. Bledsaw
Carl H. Bomball
Guy S. Bowers
Claude Bowles
Everett W. Brown, Sr.
John Leonard Brown
Charles L. Bruner
Kenneth J. Bundy
Lewis E. Carr
Eugene Chapple
John P. Cordray
William H. Cross
Floyd K. Cuttill
Donald C. Dance
Frank Dant
Ernest W. David
George A. Dean
Oscar Earl Dinger

Donald O. Donovan
Bert E. Doore
Robert W. Ethridge
Howard F. Flacke
Kenneth L. Foulks
Homer E. Gardner
Ernest W. Gerk
Clifford M. Grant
Margaret W. Grant
Adolph Green
Samuel Woodrow Green
David H. Hardcastle
Clint Hargis
George R. Harlin
Eldrid E. Hassinger
Lester P. Hayes
William H. Hinderliter
Sylvester Hines
Clarence E. Hornaday
Curtis M. Hughes
Montelle R. Huxtable
Marion F. Jackson
Robert E. Jones
William A. Jordan
Leroy Lamb
James E. Long
Ralph W. McClintock
Edward N. McRobert
William E. Malone
Dewey Mathews, Jr.
Marion S. Mattinson
Clarence L. Middleton
Harley E. Mize
George A. T. Moore
Harry Morthland
Frank Munroe
William Nickel, Sr.
Leo L. O'Daffer
William H. Peterson
Edna T. Powell

Leo D. Pressley
Harry J. Reavis
Edward Redman
Edwin L. Rentfrow'
Delmar Rentshler
J. Clifford Reynolds
Joseph G. Rigby
Henry W. Roarick
George F. Roberts
John L. Robertson
Grover A. Roderick
Frank E. Russell
Anna S. Sablotny
Robert M. Scheibley
Edwin F. Schwalbe
Fermen H. Sharp
Opla B. Shaw
Curtis Simpson
Clyde Smith
Roy B. Stafford
William R. Thompson
Richard H. Tong
Henry H. Trent
Lawrence C. Trolia
James A. Wagner
Ezra H. Welton
David P. Weybright
Harold C. Wilber
Wayne Williams
Samuel F. Wolf
Hans Wolff
George E. Young

29-Year Employees
Active
George L. Albert
John D. Andrews, Jr.
William C. Ashley
Edger L. Baker

Robert A. Baker
Alan L. Bentz
Mary I. Blacet
Bernard J. Bork
Roth R. Brewer
Alvin L. Butler
Nello P. Caluzzi
James T. Collins
James T. Creek
Hubert E. Crum
Oscar R. Curry
William R. Davis
James P. Degand
James R. Dial
Harland A. Drake
Dale R. Elliott
Leslie S. Forbes
Leon M. Fornwalt
William M. Freeman, Jr.
Earl L. Hammer
William K. Harmon
Monroe Hicks
Leslie E. Kraft
Ellis R. Lehman
William L. Morgan
Jackie L. Payne
Herb Phegley
Donald G. Plankenhorn
Marvin W. Porter
Donald G. Redman
Ervin E. Runion
Other H. Summerlott, Jr.
Beecher E. Tracy
C. Eugene Wendel

Retired or Deceased
Dale Alexander
Maxwell Anderson

Continued

Vince P. Askew
Louis D. Bailey
Art Banks
William Bauch
Charles F. Belinski
D. F. Bowman
William H. Bowrey
Fred W. Brandt
Frank Hanly Brock
Alvin E. Buechler
Ben Burton
John R. Cain
Ralph F. Clark
Ivan Conder
Walter Cornell
George A. Dean
Ray E. Driscoll
Howard L. Duncan
Maurice M. Durkee
Gertrude L. Fain
August Fischer
Percy Fry
Francis C. Gilbert
Guy E. Goodwin
Edmund W. Gossett
George W. Hale
Murrell S. Hall
Adolph Hansen
Roy Hartman
William T. Hayes
Clarence C. Hollis
Raymond Hunk
John J. Joynt
Joseph Kanariem
Edward Kushmer
Harley Lientz
Clarence W. Lyons
Tillie McGlade
Clifford A. Moore
Charles E. Owens

John Paczak
Frank L. Prell
Clarence Reed
Edwin L. Rentfrow
Albert C. Rodgers
Lester W. Ruthrauff
Cedric B. Rybolt
Ernest A. Shadrick
Howard G. Sheets, Jr.
Charles Springfield
A. L. Stubblefield
Edward Taylor
Howell Taylor, Sr.
Charles P. Thornborough
Josephine Trusso
Wayne L. Venter
George H. Walker
James R. Wallace
Ernest W. Wilkes
Ernest W. Weller
Gladys I. Whitacre
Francis Wilson, Sr.
William Winter
Arthur W. Witt

28-Year Employees
Active
Vincent E. Albert
Merle D. Alcorn
James T. Babcock
William E. Beals
Charles D. Bitzer
Arnold E. Bork
Alfred E. Born
Floyd M. Brandon
Charlie O. Brown
Jack C. Brown
Robert L. Camac
James M. Cardwell

296

Carroll Colter
Gareth E. Cowgill
Wayne E. Cox
Eleanor P. Dazey
Ronald E. DeVore
Alphondus M. Dobbins
Jerry A. Finch
Lawrence A. Flaugher
Joseph L. Gentry
James C. Glazebrook
Charles A. Hall
Lester A. Havener
Frances J. Herron
Andrew A. Horn
Donald A. Johnson
Dale J. King
Leonard E. Knox
Clyde W. Largent
Billy G. Letner
Ottis L. Livingston
Ronald D. McCoy
Henry C. Massey
Charles R. Michels, Jr.
Warren N. Moore
Alvin C. Morris
Richard S. Nichols
Donald L. Peck
Robert G. Pence
Virgle A. Rambo
August L. Sandvick
Teddy D. Shirar
Wilma Y. Sidwell
John W. Smith
Robert E. Sowers
Edward K. Stratton, Jr.
Earl D. Strohl
Otis R. Theriault
Matthew Thomas
Eugene W. Timmerman, Jr.

Floyd E. Turner
Vivian J. Vander Burgh
Billy J. Walker
John M. Wilcox
Donald D. Williamson
Stuart A. Wolken
Edward E. Wood

Retired or Deceased
Walter Arnold
Russell Bergschneider
Lloyd M. Bourey
Ben H. Boyd
Paul J. Braun
Rufus D. Broadnax
Cecil H. Brown
Bernard S. Burkhardt
Walter R. Compton
Herman Cook
James R. Cox
Maurice S. Dappert
Francis Davidson
Lawrence E. Dial
Opal L. Dillow
Ernest M. Durnil, Sr.
John L. Etcheson
Cleve Flesher
Arthur M. Fox
Pleasant D. Franklin
Thomas C. Garren
Alva J. Gawthorp
Carl C. Gehring
Levi O. Ginger
Wayne Glosser
August K. Grunden
Nelson B. Hammer
Walter C. Hammer
Virgil M. Hector

Continued

297

James A. Henderson
Guy E. Hudgins
William Jaske
John J. Kneuzberg
John Louis Kossieck
John F. Krause
Edward H. Kushmer
Estella Launtz
John H. Lawler
LaMont E. Leaser
Eli O. Lents
John M. Lindsey
Roy M. Logan
Marion A. Maurer
Carl Miller
Lawrence Miller
Herschel Morris
B. H. Muthersbaugh
A. Tom Pratt
Edwin L. Rentfrow
Henry L. Roberson
Patrick Ryan
William F. Schmuck
Frank Shields
Harold R. Smith
Francis T. Somers
Paul S. Strong
Max Taitel
Curtis Thomas
Franklin C. Thompson
Charles P. Thornborough
Jesse M. Tinch
Larry G. Trempel, Sr.
Alfred Trierweiler
C. William Turner
Harry G. Utley
Howard L. Vanderberg
William A. Van Dyke
Henry Volle
Paul D. Watters

Charles D. Weever
David L. White
David W. White
Ernest Whitrock
Adam Wilkie
Racie M. Williams
Andrew I. Willis
Frank S. Withrow
Clarence Wood

27-Year Employees
Active
Donald K. Allison
Homer F. Altevogt
John E. Barber, Jr.
Fred M. Binkley
Clifford L. Blankenship
Albert L. Blazer
John P. Bolas
Charles M. Cecil
Orval L. Clayton
Franklin E. Conroy
Jack England
Max E. Espinosa
Herbert Feezel
Billie L. Fetrow
Robert P. Flannigan
Charles T. Frey
Carl J. Gaitros
Carl G. Gieseking
David A. Gullette
Glen L. Hutton
Frank E. Janes
Harry L. Johnson
Jesse F. Jolly
Rolland B. Little
Samuel A. McClure
Marvin D. McLean
James L. Martin

Gerald L. Miller
Robert R. Miller
Francis E. Mitsdarffer
Robert J. Murphy
Francis J. O'Donnell
Max A. Napierski
James O. Parnell
Malvern G. Poor
George M. Prust
Thomas C. Radley
Maurice F. Rauch
John D. Robinson
Helen P. Schwartz
Norma J. Shafer
Larry L. Shook
Robert L. Sinnard
James L. Smith
Lyle E. Smith
Dwight M. Stockdale
Edwin A. Tilley
John V. Tuschhoff
Donald W. Whiteley
James R. York
John D. Younger

Retired or Deceased
Rex Amon
Jesse N. Armentrout
John I. Bourne
William A. Bruns
Wayne H. Burrow
Herbert C. Bush
Robert C. Cowgill
Howard L. Duncan
William R. Estrop
Jack P. Fletcher
William A. Fogle
William C. Frew

Hiram Guyse
Robert A. Hahn
Arthur H. Harris
William S. Hawk
Elizabeth Henderson
Clyde D. Henley
Roy O. Hopkins
Harley Huffman
Earl Johnson
John M. Jones
Fred W. Karasch
Stephen F. Langsfeld
James A. Lotzgesell
Ira V. McAnelly
Joseph T. McElyea
James B. McEwen
John A. McInery, Jr.
William C. Maple
Thomas A. Mathews
Charles E. Miller, Sr.
John D. Miller
Carl J. Mintler
Eugene L. Morrow
Paul Nave
Myrl E. Norcutt
Charles H. Parks
Jack H. Payton
Bruce Piraino
Wyde C. Pollard
Morris B. Rabenold
Walter C. Rankin
Roscoe V. Ridlen
Solomon Robbins
Henry L. Roberson
Clarence R. Roddy
Walter Ruley
Karl H. Schrader
Edward A. Schultz
Willie I. Scott

Continued

Frank Shaw
Claude W. Smith
George R. Smith
Vernon Steele
James M. Stewart
Richard L. Swearingen
William J. Swindle
Tom Tackleson
C. William Turner
William E. Welch
John W. Wells
Alfred West
Ivan F. Wieland
Karl Williams
Troy E. Williams, Jr.

26-Year Employees
Active
Robert K. Bandy
Rex D. Bauer
Billie D. Bell
Delmar C. Carter
W. Dale Carter
Benjamin D. Cochran
Jerry W. Corwin
Jerry Cory
Don E. Cuttill
William M. Doty
Thomas A. Eggers
Jerry L. Ellis
Charles L. Fisher
Thomas G. Freeman
Charles Gallegos
Bennie L. Hack
Jerry L. Hall
James E. Hammer
Paul C. Hammon
Robert A. Harmeier

Godfrey J. Heger
Russel L. Helton
Beverly L. Hoots
Gary L. Hopkins
John E. Howe
Robert D. Hull
John D. Hunt
James O. Ingold
Paul R. Joynt
Donald L. Lourash
Melvin L. Manecke
James P. Mayberry
Carl W. Merriman
Vernon J. Meyer
Frederick W. Miller
Donald D. Musick
Frances H. Noland
Ilmar Palm-Leis
David L. Pritts
Richard E. Purcell
Donald D. Reynolds
Roy E. Riggs
Clarence E. Runyen
Carl E. Schock
Kenneth L. Schrishuhn
William F. Schwesig
James R. Scott
Gary V. Sheets
Raymond L. Slaw
Daniel R. Spicer
Richard E. Strocher
Robert E. Sutton
Charles L. Swaim
Robert L. Thomasson
Jesse C. Thompson
Theron L. Tinker
Kenneth L. Varley
Ray L. Virden
Robert W. West
John R. Wheeler

300

Sherrel T. White
Charles A. Wilhelm

Retired or Deceased
Ernest E. Allen
William Baker
Marvin I. Barton
Emery E. Blythe
Peter Bogush
Mark L. Bone
Everett W. Brown, Jr.
Joseph T. Casey
Harry J. Casley
Capitola M. Chadwick
Charles Clow
Sam Cutrara
Carroll H. Dant
Joe Davis
L. Lamarr Davis
Clyde Denton
Luther A. Dillon
Manuel C. Duarte
Harris Dudley
Margaret Girl
William C. Frew
C. M. Finson
Calvin L. Frost
William C. Griffin
Verner Gosnell
Edward J. Gottmer
Thomas E. Grinestaff
Francis W. Haskett
David C. Hawkins
Edwin L. Hedburg
Woodrow W. Heffley
Harold R. Hiser
James E. Holman
Gerald L. Horton, Sr.
Edward J. Hueckel

Luther Humiston
Doris H. Jones
Rudolf V. Jungman
Charles Koshinski
Edwin H. Koshinski
Miles Lee
Ford E. Lewis
Jack L. Lewis
Edward S. McKey
Carl Maddy
Charles E. Martin, Sr.
Katherine B. May
Lee Miles
Emery W. Minton
Helen M. Miskell
Herman E. Mize
John J. Murphy
Malcolm C. Osborn
Ozzie Owens
Harold E. Parrish
Jack Payton
Harold C. Payne
Andrew Rethinger
Ethel R. Robb
James S. Robertson
James Rogers
Roy E. Shay
Charles F. Slaughter
Oliver Slaw, Jr.
Marvin J. Sommer
John A. Stigers
Mary Stockdale
Howard U. Stuart
Carroll W. Sutton
William S. Swinford
Clifton F. Taylor
Elmer M. Tomlinson
Theodore C. Uhll
Glenn Vaughan

Continued

John A. Wagoner
Orville L. Watkins
Ida Mamie White
Huey C. Wickiser
Merle W. Williams
William Williams
Shirley Winslow
William F. Witt
Ernie J. Wombacker
Frank Wood
William L. Woodard

25-Year Employees
Active
Margaret R. Albert
David F. Banfield
Ray S. Bass, Jr.
John E. Bird
Ruth E. Buechler
Graydon L. Capps
Edward E. Carney
Elvin W. Carter
Powell W. Clary
Wilma B. Cloney
Donald E. Crawley
Charles W. Cremer
Robert W. Emmons
Russell M. Foster
C. E. Freeman
Darwin B. Gerald
Harold R. Gilman
Kenneth D. Glosser
Darrell L. Goff
Robert E. Gonyer
Melvin W. Hancock
Dale F. Harper
James R. Harvey
Edward F. Helm
Jon F. Hosler

Kenneth M. Howard
Gene A. Hyland
Hunter L. Kickle
Ronald O. Kornewald
John T. Kuizinas
Donald E. Lewis
Larry E. Lewis
William B. Litz
James M. Manuell
Harold L. Martin
Arnold D. Mitchell
Donald E. Nordlund
Thomas F. Protzman
J. William Robinson, Jr.
Ruth A. Schultz
Rolland W. Short
Eddie L. Smith
Leon D. Smith
Marshal L. Spain, Jr.
Willis F. Sprague
Henry M. Staley
James I. Stinson
Larry L. Thomas
Ronald L. Thompson
William M. Traughber
John W. True
Frank Verbanac
Lee R. Vest
Either O. Walters
Thomas A. Wheatley
Norville D. Williams
Lloyd J. Williamson
Lem Wilson
Verna G. Zeigler

Retired or Deceased
Irvin Andrews
Clarence E. Bailey
Rhea Bennett

Henry Berube
Eugene M. Bobby
Thomas H. Boyd
Clark W. Briggs
Howard U. Brown
Edward Buckley
A. C. Burt
Raymond A. Chenoweth
Vern W. Coffman
Kenneth Comp
William Coppenberger
Alma E. Cox
Chester N. Crockett
Mark L. Cummings
Herbert D. Daniels
Jeremiah C. Delaney
Roland Earle
John R. Easterly
Anthony Elcewicz
Oliver Etheridge
Charles A. Farris
Paul F. Fawcett
John Flowers
Vincent P. Fogarty
Caleb W. Galligor
Ben Garner
Bose F. Goad
Jack A. Grant
Robert M. Guynn
Obie L. Harlow
Theodore Hastings
Grady Hemphill
Roy H. Hill

Horace C. Hinkley
Dillard Hitchcock
Charles A. Hood
Harold Hull
Thomas L. Hurst
William P. Johnson
Elmer W. Kuster
Gerald Langrand
Arthur E. Lanham
Michael M. McEvoy
John W. McMillen
Tony Maddox
Donald C. Magie
Lillie S. Meyers
Chesley M. Mitchell
John Monaco
William B. Napier
Green D. Newberry
Robert E. Nisbit
John Picard
Darrell L. Pritts
William H. Randolph, Sr.
Joseph K. Ray
Donald W. Reynolds
John Ricketts
Glen A. Smith
Billie G. Soran
Kelley G. Taylor
Bernard P. Thurber
Karl A. Voss
Leonard Wells
Joel B. Williams
Gordon A. Winchester

INDEX

About the Author

Dan J. Forrestal has been engaged in communications-related activity since his high school days, when he began writing for the sports pages of the *St. Louis Globe-Democrat.* "I was a part-time 'stringer,'" he recalls. "My published items were measured by an old-time accountant who used knots on a string for the measuring exercise, thus determining my paltry compensation."

After college, Forrestal became a regular staff member on the newspaper, moving up to a wide variety of responsibilities in the preparation of news and feature material, with time out for a sabbatical as a syndicated war correspondent in World War II. He was assistant managing editor of the *Globe-Democrat* late in 1946 when he took what he refers to as "a sharp turn" into industrial life, joining Monsanto Company for a 28-year period of overseeing the St. Louis-based chemical corporation's international public relations programs.

He requested early retirement from Monsanto in 1974 in order to embark on a third career—in counseling and in writing. He has written two books on corporate communications (1968 and 1979), each entitled *Public Relations Handbook* (Dartnell, Chicago). Also he has written an anecdotal 75-year history of Monsanto (1977), entitled *Faith, Hope and $5,000* (Simon and Schuster, New York).

Forrestal has authored numerous articles for national magazines, dealing mainly with the hits and misses of corporate communications. In several of his published pieces, he has commented on the role of business histories in the world of nonfiction literature, hazarding the belief that "honest, straightforward corporate profiles can be credible and exciting, especially if the sponsoring companies' cliff-hanging trials and triumphs are properly portrayed."

Forrestal resides in his native city of St. Louis with his wife, Esther, and "a highly communicative basset hound named Maggie Forrestal."